tough love

SUNY series in Queer Politics and Cultures
―――――――――
Cynthia Burack and Jyl J. Josephson, editors

tough love

sexuality, compassion, and the christian right

cynthia burack

Cover image: © Jamie van Buskirk / iStockphoto.com

Published by State University of New York Press, Albany

© 2014 State University of New York

All rights reserved

Printed in the United States of America

No part of this book may be used or reproduced in any manner whatsoever without written permission. No part of this book may be stored in a retrieval system or transmitted in any form or by any means including electronic, electrostatic, magnetic tape, mechanical, photocopying, recording, or otherwise without the prior permission in writing of the publisher.

For information, contact State University of New York Press, Albany, NY
www.sunypress.edu

Production by Diane Ganeles
Marketing by Fran Keneston

Library of Congress Cataloging-in-Publication Data

Burack, Cynthia, 1958–
　Tough love : sexuality, compassion, and the Christian right / Cynthia Burack.
　　　pages cm. — (SUNY series in queer politics and cultures)
　Includes bibliographical references and index.
　ISBN 978-1-4384-4987-6 (alk. paper)
　ISBN 978-1-4384-4986-9 (pbk. : alk. paper)
　1. Christianity and politics—United States.　2. Conservatism—Religious aspects—Christianity.　3. Church and social problems—United States.
4. Christian conservatism—United States.　5. Religious right—United States.
6. Compassion—Religious aspects—Christianity.　7. Abortion—Religious aspects—Christianity.　8. Homophobia—Religious aspects—Christianity.
9. Homosexuality—Religious aspects—Christianity.　I. Title.

BR516.B83 2014
277.3'083—dc23
　　　　　　　　　　　　　　　　　　　　　　　　　　　　　　　2013008687

10 9 8 7 6 5 4 3 2 1

For Aris

Contents

Acknowledgments	ix
Introduction	
The Christian Right's Compassionate Conservatism	1
Left, Right, Left: Forward March	5
The Faces of Compassion	9
Different Rhetorics for Different Folks	12
Fixing Moral Boundaries	17
"The Politics of Yuck"	19
A Word about Words, and So On	24
Chapter 1	
Let's Both Agree That You're Really Sinful:	
Compassion in the Ex-Gay Movement	29
Reparative Therapies	29
The Narrative of Development	34
Out of Bondage	39
The Compassionate Gaze	45
Leaving Homosexuality	47
Taking the Ex-Gay Challenge	50
Chapter 2	
What about the Women? Compassion in Postabortion Ministries	57
From Abomination to Compassion	57
It's about the Women, Stupid	61
Postabortion Syndrome	65
Compassion before Abortion	69
Helping Hurting Women	73
Sorting Out Compassion	79

Chapter 3
Christian Right Compassion: What Would Hannah Arendt Do?   85
    Identity in Politics   85
    Caution: Hazardous Compassion Ahead   87
    The Miserable Ones   93
    Love among the Outcasts   97
    A World of Others   99
    Revisiting Compassion Campaigns   105
    Arendt and Christian Love   109

Chapter 4
Just Deserts: The Compassion of Ayn Rand   115
    Who *Is* John Galt?   115
    Rand, Sex, and Gender   119
    Objectiv(ist) Compassion   126
    Ayn Rand Always with Us   142

Chapter 5
Drawing the Compassionate Line: Love, Guilt, and Melanie Klein   145
    The Psychoanalytic Turn   145
    More Narratives of Development   147
    Making Good   152
    Bad Group!   156
    Being Reparative   161
    Can "Compassion" Harm?   167
    Compassionate Warriors   172

Afterword
Compassion, Where Is Thy Victory?   175
    Whence Compassion?   175
    A Last Word on Theory   177
    Feeling(s) and Knowing   185

Notes   193

Index   235

Acknowledgments

I have been very fortunate to have received interest in and support for my work from friends and colleagues. Mark Blasius, Mark Casey, Judith Grant, Harry Hirsch, Julie Ingersoll, Cricket Keating, Laree Martin, Claire Snyder-Hall, Angie Wilson, and anonymous reviewers contributed to this book by reading all or part of the manuscript and providing feedback. Fred Alford, Marla Brettschneider, Jean Elliott, Judy Garber, Jim Glass, Jyl Josephson, Jeff Mann, Ahron Taub, Stacy VanDeveer, and Diana Zoelle gave me opportunities to talk about my work while I was thinking about and writing this book. My former colleague Rebecca Wanzo was a wonderful source of lively wit and incisive intellectual commentary. Lee Evans provided smart companionship, wine, and chocolate, and Amy Bonomi kept watch for winter storms. My partner, Laree, has tolerated with good humor my biregional lifestyle and my mania for organization. Finally, although we are sworn not to "out" each other, I would be remiss not to acknowledge the intellectual comradeship of the band of wry and thoughtful journalists and researchers who have shared their wise counsel at many Christian right events. Many thanks to all for creating an environment conducive to thinking through the questions that have fascinated me for many years.

It is a great privilege to be able to publish this book, my second, with SUNY Press. I'm grateful to Larin McLaughlin, who saw my last book to publication, and to Beth Bouloukos, the present editor for the Queer Politics and Cultures series. It is also a pleasure to work with Jyl Josephson, my series coeditor, on this enterprise, which has produced several of the kinds of books I love to read.

I am grateful for the research assistance of Min Sook Heo, Katie Linder, and Hyejin Kim in the Department of Women's, Gender, and Sexuality Studies. Thanks to Dan Moshenberg and the Women's Studies

Program at the George Washington University for office space during a 2006–2007 sabbatical. I am also grateful to the Centennial Center of the American Political Science Association for office space as a visiting scholar in 2007 and for short periods thereafter. I received some funding for this project that enabled me to travel to public events at which I gathered data from the College of Humanities at Ohio State through a Research Enhancement Grant. In addition, I benefited enormously from a Hallsworth Fellowship awarded by the Politics Department and the School of Social Sciences at the University of Manchester, UK, during the winter and spring of 2009. Thanks also to Diane Richardson and Monica Moreno Figueroa for inviting me to present my research at the University of Newcastle during the Hallsworth Fellowship period. Publication of this book was funded, in part, by a Subvention Grant awarded by the Ohio State University Division of Arts and Humanities.

An early version of material from chapter 4 is reprinted with permission from University of Toronto Press (www.utpjournals.com): "Just Deserts: Ayn Rand and the Christian Right," *Journal of Religion and Popular Culture* 19 (2008) http://www.usask.ca/relst/jrpc/art19-justdesserts.html. And an early version of chapter 3 was published as "Compassion Campaigns and Antigay Politics: What Would Arendt Do? *Politics and Religion* 2, no. 1 (April 2009): 31–53 Copyright © 2009 Religion and Politics Section of the American Political Science Association. Reprinted with the permission of Cambridge University Press.

I also would like to acknowledge my debt to the writers whose work I concentrate on in this book: Hannah Arendt, Ayn Rand, and Melanie Klein. Why Arendt, Rand, and Klein? Each of these thinkers has something fascinating to say about the subject at hand. As theorists, all three were produced and influenced by notoriously violent social and political events of their time and place: for Arendt and Klein, World War II and the genocidal campaign against European Jews; for Rand, who was also Jewish, the Bolshevik Revolution and the early years of the Soviet state. They were contemporaries and émigrés; all three ended up speaking and writing in English, a language that was not their mother tongue. I imagine them in a dialogue—or more likely a lively debate—with each other over fundamental issues, the "human condition." This book situates them in something like that debate on the intersection of politics, sexuality, and compassion.

I have come to believe that today many have a particularly shortsighted view of gender nonnormativity, one that typically involves same-sex sexuality, transgender identity, or obviously transgressive modes of dress or public deportment. That's a shame because such an understanding misses deeper modes of nonconformity that aren't as accessible to view and that, as a result, don't fall under the scope of the popular concept of gender performativity as it is usually interpreted. Arendt, Rand, and Klein were middle-class heterosexual European women, the kind of women who, in the world that produced them, would not have been expected to engage in work that commanded the attention of thoughtful people, not just in their own time but well beyond it. Not only that: each brazenly defied some, if not all, norms associated with respectable womanhood. It is no insult to contemporary theorists to assert that we can still learn something from these women today.

Introduction

The Christian Right's Compassionate Conservatism

In November 2006, the Reverend Joel Hunter, pastor of a Florida megachurch, announced that he had decided not to serve as the new president of the Christian Coalition after having been designated as the conservative Christian organization's next president only a month earlier. In media coverage of the resignation, Hunter was quoted as saying that he had wanted the Coalition to pursue an agenda of "compassion issues": "I hope we can break out of 'liberal' and 'conservative.' I'm not sure when compassion became fitted under 'liberal.'"[1] In 2008, Hunter was enlisted as one of then-presidential candidate Barack Obama's prayer partners and later delivered the closing prayer at the Democratic National Convention in Denver. Hunter is one of many Christian conservative leaders who is designated as a "new evangelical"; ostensibly moderate, Hunter diverges from many in the Christian right by urging Christian conservatives to expand their agenda to include such issues as poverty and climate change. However, this expansion of the agenda has its limits. Like his more traditional fellow believers, Hunter rejects abortion rights and lesbian, gay, bisexual, and transgender (LGBT) rights and recognition.[2]

A compassionate sociopolitical agenda that is prolife and antigay is increasingly a feature of American political life.[3] Over the last twenty years, the Christian right has matured as a social and political movement, and its compassionate projects and pedagogies on contested moral/cultural issues such as sexual and reproductive rights are one manifestation of that maturation. In some of its ideology and activism on sexuality the

1

Christian right has added softened rhetoric and a variety of compassionate projects to its more familiar repertoire of harsh public rhetoric and punitive policy recommendations.[4]

Critics of the right often dismiss "compassionate conservatism" as an empty slogan intended to mystify the real roots and aspirations of conservative politics. What is Christian right compassion? Or to be more specific, what kind of compassion—if that is what it is—circulates through conservative Christian activities and activism? I argue that close attention to Christian right compassion, its modes of dissemination, and its effects provides important information about Christian conservatism, notions of traditional morality, and contemporary American culture and political life. But to reach that understanding, critics of the Christian right must be willing to take Christian right compassion seriously. That is, we must be willing to forestall reductive readings of compassion as a manipulative political strategy. Some students of the Christian right, including Melani McAlister, Bruce Pilbeam, and Chip Berlet, take this kind of perspective on compassion.[5] Their work, and the work of other scholars I draw upon below, encourages students of ideology not to settle for superficial explanations of either left or right when examining political motivations.

In this book I make a case for why we should give the Christian right's compassionate projects this kind of careful attention. To accomplish this I trace the lineaments of a variety of Christian right projects that are understood explicitly by those who develop them, those who work within them, and those who are served by them to be undergirded and motivated by Christian compassion. Then, to illuminate the operations of compassion and what is at stake in its deployment in sexuality politics, I turn to the work of theorists whose quite different orientations toward democratic politics, love, and compassion enable us to reconceptualize and critique Christian right compassionate interventions into the sexual and reproductive dimensions of intimacy.

Although Reverend Hunter pronounced himself confused about the link drawn by many between liberalism and compassion, the link is well established in popular ideology and in the social and policy aspirations of welfare liberals and progressives. As a mode of political motivation, compassion is usually identified with welfare liberals, whom conservative critics have understood as compassionate in ways that are excessive and misplaced. The bleeding heart of left-wing politics constitutes a well-known stereotype. Not coincidentally, the stereotype licenses ridicule of putative softness, weakness, and, as scholars such as George Lakoff point out, gestures to the effeminacy of a parent who nurtures instead of setting boundaries and dispensing punishment.[6]

The alternative, which Lakoff also describes, represents the other side of a binary cognitive model that those on both the political left and political right use to conceptualize politics in terms of family life. Nor is this distinction merely hypothetical. A study of political behavior finds support for Lakoff's theory that Americans use binary cognitive schemas to conceptualize politics in terms of family life. Using 2000 National Election Study data, James Barker and James D. Tinnick III conclude that "values regarding childrearing predicted political attitudes across a variety of issue domains," including gay rights and abortion rights.[7] When "the family" operates as a metaphor for conceptions of morality, Christian conservatives rally to a "strict father Christianity" that prioritizes authority and order and that entails punishment for violations of the moral order.[8] Christian conservative compassion thus aspires to displace, circumvent, and subvert corrupt liberal compassion and substitute for it something that bears some resemblance but that is both meaningfully different and more biblically virtuous.

The link between liberalism and compassion also finds support from social psychology. For many years psychologists have investigated and confirmed correlations between personality traits and liberal/conservative ideological orientations.[9] In some of these studies personality dimensions highlighted in the so-called "Big Five" model of personality—variations of extraversion, conscientiousness, agreeableness, emotional stability, and intellect—are strongly identified with either liberal or conservative political beliefs. One Big Five dimension that has not been seen by psychologists as identified either with liberal or conservative ideology is "agreeableness," but recent research suggests that the ostensible political neutrality of this personality dimension has been overstated. When "agreeableness" is disarticulated into constitutive subtraits of "compassion" and "politeness," the liberal/conservative neutrality of agreeableness disappears. In its place are consistent correlations between conservative ideology and politeness and between liberal ideology and compassion. Here, compassion is "empirically and conceptually related to the value domain of egalitarianism."[10]

Whatever form conservative compassion takes in the political realm, for its proponents it must compare favorably with a liberal ideology that, under the sign of egalitarian ideals, ignores moral corruption and lets evil off the hook. For Christian conservatives, compassionate campaigns in the areas of sexuality and reproductive rights not only compare favorably with liberal compassion but share other similarities with each other. First, they seem to conflict with other conservative approaches to these cultural issues that are harsher in tone and punitive toward their objects, and second, they include careful instruction about political processes related to the issue area. Besides the general forms of political pedagogy associated with them, there are also important differences of substance that reflect the distinctions between the arenas in which compassionate antigay and antiabortion projects are carried out.

The arena for antigay compassion campaigns in the area of gay rights is the ex-gay movement, which includes instruction for conservative Christians on the origins and treatment of same-sex desire. Ex-gay pedagogy rests on narratives of development that seek to chart etiologies of same-sex desire and to foreclose blame toward those afflicted with such desires.[11] In the area of antiabortion politics, general-purpose groups, single-issue organizations, and megachurches have launched a number of initiatives that distance critics of abortion rights from murder rhetoric and approach abortion from a compassionate perspective.[12] Proponents of this sector of the antiabortion movement refer to it as "postabortion awareness and recovery ministries" or simply "postabortion ministries," for short, and I follow this nomenclature.

One question that might arise in considering the compassion campaigns of the Christian right movement in the areas of sexuality and reproductive rights is whether LGBTQ people and women who have had an abortion need compassion—indeed, whether compassion is an appropriate category of political thinking and motivation when it comes to these citizens. This is a legitimate concern and one addressed by a number of scholars who are concerned either with the condition of the public sphere or with the standing of particular categories of citizens. My goal here is neither to make the case that the Christian right emphasis on compassion represents an appropriate application of political emotion nor to make a case for extirpating compassion from politics altogether. I return to this question of the role of compassion in politics in the afterword, but for now my focus on compassion is explanatory and analytical. In this text, I present evidence that compassionate ministries are not only theological, but also social and political projects. I analyze these projects and make three major arguments about Christian right compassion: first, that it encourages an undemocratic politics of ideological moral meddling; second, that it encourages invidious political distinctions between deserving and undeserving citizens; and third, that it discourages responsibility for harm-doing to those it stigmatizes.

Left, Right, Left: Forward March

Compassion has a long political history, and intellectuals as diverse as Aristotle, Jean Jacques Rousseau, and Susan Sontag have limned its definitions, conditions of possibility, manifestations, and effects.[13] A definition that circulates in many discussions is Aristotle's, which specifies three evaluative judgments as its condition: that what has befallen a person is very serious; that it is not (or not only) the person's fault; and that it exposes the observer's vulnerability to similar possibilities.[14] As Lauren Berlant notes, although there are many versions and definitions of this prolix term, one way to understand compassion is as "an emotion in operation." Compassion is relational, alluding to the action between sufferer(s) and actors who are capable of responding to or alleviating suffering: "Compassion measures one's value (or one's government's value) in terms of the demonstrated capacity not to turn one's head away but to embrace a sense of obligation to remember what one has seen and, in response to that haunting, to become involved in a story of rescue or amelioration."[15] This unavoidable relationality contains within it a potential pitfall of compassion: the conscious willingness to withhold it. As Elizabeth Spelman points out in her consideration of the "political life of compassion," calls for compassion can engender cruel condescension as well as harsh judgments on the moral agency of sufferers.

There is also a pedagogical dimension to compassion: "[I]t is crucial to appreciate the multitude of conventions around the relation of feeling to practice where compassion is concerned. In a given scene of suffering, how do we know what does and what should constitute sympathetic agency?"[16] Spelman examines Harriet Jacobs' 1861 *Incidents in the Life of a Slave Girl, Written by Herself* and finds Jacobs/Linda Brent enunciating the responses she wants her story to evoke from her white Northern readers. Similarly, the pedagogy that infuses right-wing compassion is a key component of compassion campaigns. One way that citizens learn what constitutes appropriate compassionate agency is by having their ideas about compassion informed by instruction within the context of broad sets of collective political impulses—for example, orientations toward "the family" and morality. Like progressive compassion, which is a form of pedagogy as well as an ideology, compassionate conservatism operates as pedagogy for those predisposed toward conservative explanations and situated in conservative social and political contexts. In the case of the Christian right, moral and theological instruction and policy goals are linked together and disseminated by ministries and national organizations, as well as through Christian popular culture.

The conservative alternative to left compassion is compassionate conservatism, a creed with a political, as well an intellectual, genealogy. Popularized by conservative theorist Marvin Olasky, compassionate conservatism repudiates the public policies associated with the welfare state for ignoring the moral and spiritual needs of their recipients.[17] During the 2000 presidential campaign, George W. Bush appealed to bipartisanism and compassionate conservatism, although he softened the edges of the concept by not enunciating fully the critique of liberal compassion found in the work of conservatives like Olasky and Charles Murray.[18]

During the Bush administration, the following passage appeared above Bush's name in a press release on the White House website. The page, entitled "Fact Sheet: Compassionate Conservatism" begins: "I call my philosophy and approach compassionate conservatism. It is compassionate to actively help our fellow citizens in need. It is conservative to insist on responsibility and results. And with this hopeful approach, we will make a real difference in people's lives."[19] What followed was a laundry list of ideas, policies, and action items the president's advisors understood as consistent with compassion as a "governing philosophy." As Bruce Pilbeam points out, Bush's compassionate conservatism was always at odds with the conception of that ideal wrought by its authors because it was insufficiently committed to foreclosing big government programs and devolving assistance to the poor to community organizations.[20] Bush did, however, conceptualize compassionate conservatism as authorizing funding and support of antiabortion Crisis Pregnancy Centers and programs.[21]

Such critiques of the large bureaucratic welfare state set the stage for contemporary compassionate conservatives to decry liberal compassion not only as requiring a large state that flies in the face of libertarian aspirations but as indiscriminate: as failing to distinguish appropriately between those of good and poor character. Indeed, the inculcation of virtue and the eviction of those who fail or refuse to live up to prescribed moral standards are the very point and purpose of close contact between those who deliver social welfare services and those who need them.[22] A conservative spokesperson who illustrates the effectiveness of such arguments is Star Parker, an author, popular speaker on the Christian right circuit, and founder of CURE, the Center for Urban Renewal and Education. Although Parker rarely sounds like a compassionate conservative, the biography she recites in her work and in public addresses, her critique of the devastating consequences of welfare state amorality, and her commitment to "fighting poverty and restoring dignity through faith, freedom and personal responsibility" resonate with the tenets of conservative compassion.[23]

For activists on the political left, skepticism about compassionate conservatism takes two forms: skepticism about motivation and skepticism about content. With regard to motivation, critics read compassionate conservatism against the backdrop of conservative appropriations of liberal ideals and practices. These include the appropriation of civil rights discourse that places conservatives on the side of minorities seeking civil rights; a reconfiguration of equality that rebuffs concern with inequality of wealth and income as "class warfare"; and a redefinition—and even partial embrace—of feminism.[24] Of these, the Christian right appropriation of feminism may be the most surprising development. As Doris Buss and Didi Herman point out, this strategy has an older, less sophisticated version: "marginalizing feminists as raging radicals." But it also has a newer and more sophisticated version, which is, for example, practiced by the Vatican in international politics: representing "radical" feminism as inadequate to serve the world's women. Echoing much internal feminist critique, this narrative situates the feminist movement as simultaneously a regional, "western-dominated movement" that fails to represent the diversity of women in the global south, as a movement that fails to represent even the diversity of Western women, and as a movement that cannot meet the range of women's needs because of its reliance on a narrow rights agenda.[25] Here, conservatives appropriate internal feminist critiques of white, Western, middle-class feminism and deploy them against dimensions of feminism that are inconvenient and antagonistic to traditionalism.

Another kind of appropriation is the migration of sociological explanations of dysfunctional or antisocial behavior from the left to the right. Sociological explanations of criminality that cite poverty or membership in an underclass have usually been rejected by the right as justifications for harm purveyed by ethically challenged left-wing apologists—"defining deviancy down," in Daniel Patrick Moynihan's alliterative phrase.[26] However, the right now acknowledges the usefulness of some sociological characterization by mimicking such explanations for women who choose abortion. Such women may be characterized as "wounded" by early life traumas, thus impaired in their ability to engage in moral thinking and action. In particular cases, Christian conservatives now often consider the effects of trauma in the same ways that progressives often have: not to excuse particular categories of harmful actions, but to explain their genesis and to understand the individual cognitive and emotional—if not the social—circumstances in which individuals make decisions.

Those on the left who are particularly critical of the content of compassionate conservatism target different aspects of the governing philosophy. Some tend to be skeptical that the ideal means anything more than a marriage between neoliberal market ideology and social conservatism: an attempt to mystify business interests and market them to culturally conservative citizens. Linda Kintz shows how it is that the antigovernment populism of "ordinary Americans" is fused and confused with the antitax and antiregulatory interests of corporations in the constitution of a "Transparent American Subject" that represents (Southern) conservatism.[27] Although they do not always call attention to potential conflicts of interest between their own culturally conservative concerns and the interests of business elites, Christian right leaders are aware that they must be attentive to the propensity of the Republican Party to marginalize their policy interests in favor of a business agenda.[28] Some academic critics emphasize other problems with the content of compassionate conservativism. In her critique, Nancy Campbell charges Olasky and William J. Bennett with using a flawed historical narrative of American social policy to undergird a current set of policy initiatives. These initiatives redefine "coercion as a compassionate form of discipline and control," especially over poorer citizens and those who violate traditionalist ideals of character and behavior.

As much as critics and proponents of compassionate conservatism disagree, however, neither would dispute that at the heart of conservative compassion is the necessity to draw distinctions and make boundaries between categories of objects. Conservative compassion splits the objects of political attention into groups, directing compassion toward one group and condemnation toward the other. For Christian conservatives, this means compassion toward people who resist their same-sex desires and condemnation toward people who embrace some kind of queer identity; compassion toward repentant women who have had abortions and condemnation toward those who advocate abortion rights. Although today it is conservatives who are most comfortable with values talk in their politics, clearly there are quite different sets of values at work in left and right perspectives on compassion and in the respective critiques that each side levels at the other.

Conservative critiques of left compassion take many forms, some more direct than others. ConservativeHome, a website that provides "comprehensive coverage of Britain's conservative party," denounces "condom (or Russian roulette) compassion" as the "dangerous belief that people can be protected from sexual promiscuity or drug use." While conservative "advocates of harm avoidance believe that people can be persuaded, cajoled or frightened into changing their behaviours," liberal "harm reducers" "believe that it is better to protect people from the consequences of their behaviours than to try and change those behaviours."[29] Compassionate conservatism, by contrast, is "optimistic about how conservative ideas . . . can advance social justice."[30] While the term "condom compassion" is not part of the general discourse on the threat posed by liberal compassion, the idea that liberals are indifferent to the consequences of personally or socially disastrous behavior—or even perversely encourage them—is common.

It is by no means the case that all American conservatives would identify themselves or their aspirations as "compassionate." At times, conservatives who repudiate the compassionate label scorn the loss of core conservative principles that such a concept may encourage. In addition, conservative public figures such as Ann Coulter base their reputations on a pugilism and punitiveness that is hard to square with compassionate rhetoric and principles. But even in venues where conservative activists meet to network and to hear conservative leaders, compassion is often a theme, the tea party movement's recent repudiation of the ideal notwithstanding. Seeking to recuperate the descriptor long after it was largely abandoned by President G. W. Bush, Bush speechwriter and political commentator Michael Gerson invoked it to account for the appeal of Senator Rick Santorum in the 2012 Iowa Caucuses. Gerson wrote of Santorum's surprising success in the Caucuses as "the return of compassionate conservatism from the margins of the Republican stage to its center."[31] Within the movement, the doctrine of "co-belligerence" that justifies groups such as Protestants and Catholics working together for common ends also describes the way in which compassionate and other conservatives often negotiate different paths to common political ends.[32]

The Faces of Compassion

Many advocates for abortion rights and LGBTQ rights are convinced that the conservative compassion of the Christian right movement is a political strategy rather than an authentic orientation. The justification for this belief is not far to seek. First, the compassion of the Christian right is still antiabortion and antigay; indeed, it would be legitimate to modify the compassion with which I'm concerned and refer to it consistently as "antiabortion compassion" or "antigay compassion" to distinguish it from other forms of compassion that do not share its provenance and pedagogical aspirations. Second, people who are the ideal objects of the antiabortion and antigay political projects of the Christian right often understand themselves as harmed by those projects regardless of the fellow feeling that may motivate their enactment. The gap between harm—fear of identification, loss of rights, social stigma, loss of employment related to discrimination, inability to procure benefits that other citizens take for granted—and the professed love and concern of organized others can engender suspicion and cynicism. This is so both for LGBT people and for women who have had an abortion, who support the right to abortion, and who will avail themselves of the right to have an abortion in the future.

It makes sense that activists in the queer and prochoice movements reject the idea of conservative Christian compassion. From the homophile movement of the post-WWII period to the present day, the path to a political movement of and for people with same-sex sexual orientation or nonnormative gender identity and expression has required repudiating stubborn social attitudes and traditional moral convictions (to say nothing of visceral feelings) about the detestability of same-sex desire and sexuality. People who come out as gay, bisexual, queer, or transgender usually grow up steeped in these traditions and modes of feeling. As a result, we recognize the invitations to shame and renunciation held out by antigay politics and religion. And many of us who do not renounce our sexuality nevertheless recognize the tantalizing prospect of acceptance that our ex-gay compatriots respond to when they renounce their sexual and romantic feelings, appoint "accountability partners" to help them manage their identities, and ask God for forgiveness for their sexual transgressions.

Advocates of abortion rights know the contentious history of reproductive rights in the United States from criminalization in the nineteenth century to the 1973 Supreme Court decision in *Roe v. Wade* and the prolife mobilization of the 1970s to the present. Indeed, since the Court's 1965 decision in *Griswold v. Connecticut*, which gave married couples the right to birth control information and technologies, the idea that Americans enjoy a constitutionally protected right to privacy in intimate decision making has been under attack. The innovation of antiabortion politics since the 1980s is the targeting of individuals—women who seek abortions and abortion providers—for publicity, harassment, and sometimes violence.³³ In this context, compassionate concern for women who are making, or who have made, an abortion decision, can seem either a striking departure from the movement's course or yet another technique of shaming citizens into sexual abstinence and conformity.³⁴

The Christian right's compassion campaigns are undeniably strategic, intended as they are to buttress widespread support for denying LGBT people access to rights and public goods and women their reproductive rights, choices, or justice. However, these campaigns are not strategic without remainder, which is to say that they do not *only* exist to mystify the real aims of conservative Christian morality politics. The assumption that Christian right compassion discourse is merely strategic window dressing for punitive politics is a reasonable one. However, if this were so we might expect to encounter compassion discourse only or virtually only in public settings—contexts in which movement leaders communicate the movement's goals and principles to those outside the ingroup and act to secure political goods such as laws and court decisions. On the contrary, the Christian right movement is rife with compassion discourse directed toward ingroup members at the very same time that leaders produce and direct to those same members of the ingroup quite different narratives of homosexual abomination and child murder. What this suggests is that Christian right movement leaders are not inept at producing political rhetoric on these two core moral and political issues of our time, but neither are they merely manipulating public opinion. Rather, the bifurcation between the narratives of compassion and abomination signals that Christian right ideology is complex and that Christian conservatives are being called upon to internalize and deploy meaningful moral and political distinctions on these issues.

It is also true that at least some aspects of compassion campaigns seem to be generated in response to public criticisms of Christian right politics. For example, for many years, critics of the movement's antiabortion rights politics charged that the Christian right evinces concern with endangered fetuses and not with pregnant women, babies, and their material needs. In response, the movement has reconfigured its antiabortion projects to respond to the needs of women and children as the movement understands them, including some material needs of pregnant women and infants. In addition to the charitable work of church congregations, some of these needs have been addressed through Crisis Pregnancy Centers. Of course, the primary objective of Crisis Pregnancy Centers is to persuade pregnant women not to have an abortion, and these antiabortion nonprofit organizations have been identified as sources of false advertising and inaccurate medical information intended to influence women's pregnancy-related decisions.³⁵

Certainly, the Christian right and its critics do not understand women's and children's needs in the same way, and the gulf between these understandings constitutes a legitimate ground of political activism. Vigorous disagreement between political adversaries about the nature and meaning of compassion does not obviate the possibility that activists on both sides are motivated by some version of compassion whose terms must then be exposed and analyzed.

Different Rhetorics for Different Folks

In *Sin, Sex, and Democracy: Antigay Rhetoric and the Christian Right*, I was interested in the ways in which the Christian conservative movement has become more sophisticated over time at practicing an ideological version of market segmentation, constructing different kinds of rhetoric and politics for different contexts. I argued that the movement crafts and disseminates different kinds of rhetoric about gays and same-sex sexuality for its different audiences and that these different rhetorics are a sign of the maturity of the movement. The narratives about queers/same-sex sexuality I found in my research and that of others who study the Christian right lie along two axes: the first axis is the intended audience of communications from leaders to followers. On this axis, we have messages that are intended for, and addressed to, the ingroup (ideological Christian conservatives and potential converts) and messages that are intended for both the ingroup and the larger public. I include both ingroup and public audiences in the latter category for two reasons: because rhetoric directed at non(conservative) Christians has important pedagogical functions for Christian conservatives who consume it and use this instruction to engage in a variety of different kinds of social and political activism.

The second axis describes the sociopolitical contexts—therapeutic and political—in which Christian right opinion leaders intend the narratives to function. The therapeutic context is concerned with understanding the origins of same-sex desire, healing homosexuality, and "restoring" natural heterosexual functioning. The political context is concerned with legal rights, constitutional interpretation, public policy, electoral politics, and the distribution of public goods as well as mobilizing followers with a vision of what is at stake in the normalization of same-sex sexuality. As this matrix suggests, we can identify four principal narrative combinations, constituted of variations on intended audience and context.³⁶

		Socio-Political Context	
		THERAPEUTIC	POLITICAL
Intended Audience	INGROUP	(Childhood gender) Development/ Compassion for same-sex attracted Christians and Christian families with same-sex attracted members	Abomination (choice)
	INGROUP AND PUBLIC	Healing of Adults from same-sex sexuality/Compassion for same-sex attracted people	Democracy (majoritarianism, choice and rights)

Figure 1. Christian Right Narratives of Same-Sex Sexuality (Reproduced from Burack, *Sin, Sex, and Democracy*, p. 28.)

The Christian right's antiabortion politics and rhetoric also map onto this matrix. The antiabortion movement has political and therapeutic contexts, and the movement increasingly distinguishes between rhetorics that are appropriate for the ingroup and those that are appropriate for both ingroup and public audiences. As with the Christian right's antigay politics and rhetoric, the boundaries between these "cells" are porous, and there are some movement actors whose tactics are atavistic in that they violate the movement's new messaging strategies. One case of this kind of stubborn atavism I identified in *Sin, Sex, and Democracy*: comic-format witnessing tracts known as Chick Tracts, many of which offer vivid denunciations of same-sex sexuality, abortion, Catholicism, and Islam. Nonetheless, it is useful to recognize that the therapeutic wing of the antiabortion movement is where compassionate discourse and action are situated, while the political wing is the principal setting for versions of an antiabortion message that are constructed for different audiences and different venues. As we shall see, the politics of the movement are actually more complicated than this schematic explanation suggests, but that complexity doesn't obviate the value of an initial distinction between the two factions of antigay and antiabortion activism.

In sociopolitical contexts in which antiabortion activism occurs, the rhetoric with which most outsiders are familiar is abomination rhetoric that equates abortion with murder. This narrative still survives in ingroup and many public settings, but it has been supplemented by a more sophisticated version of the message that addresses the value of a culture of life and the "natural family" for the functioning of democracy and that exploits a widespread abhorrence of genocide. In therapeutic contexts, compassion holds sway, though again there are differences between rhetoric directed to the ingroup and rhetoric intended for both ingroup and public audiences. One difference is the differential focus on a born-again salvation experience in ingroup settings and media and a more secular message of caring and assistance directed to the mainstream public. This difference between ingroup and public rhetoric in postabortion ministries is consistent with the difference between rhetorical contexts found in the ex-gay movement. There, a public message of "choice" undergirds the democracy- and rights-oriented public face of the Christian right. Ingroup rhetoric identifies the divine source of compassion as well as the urgency of salvation for all participants in the movement's work.

		Socio-Political Context	
		THERAPEUTIC	POLITICAL
Intended Audience	INGROUP	(Childhood gender) Development/ Compassion for same-sex attracted Christians and Christian families with same-sex attracted members **Compassion for women and men touched by abortion/Importance of compassion as a strategy for abortion reduction and criminalization ("ending abortion")/ Emphasis on salvation and a relationship with Jesus Christ**	Abomination (choice) **Abomination (murder)**
	INGROUP AND PUBLIC	Healing of Adults from same-sex sexuality/Compassion for same-sex attracted people **Compassion for women and men touched by abortion**	Democracy (majoritarianism, choice and rights, **culture of life, natural family**) **Abomination (genocide holocaust)**

Figure 2. Christian Right Narratives of Same-Sex Sexuality and **Abortion.**

One of the virtues of ethnographies of social groups and movements is that they can tease out the wide range of personal motivations, states of mind, and even dissenting ideas that encourage individuals to affiliate with social movements. The abomination perspective that in recent years has characterized the ingroup political rhetoric and pedagogy of both antigay and antiabortion movements no doubt harbors many Christian conservatives who come to their participation by way of a diverse set of motivations, feelings, and ideas. Some of these may be at odds with the reigning ideology of the movement in which they are situated. So, for example, in her ethnographic study of prolife activists, Carol J. C. Maxwell finds prolife activists who explain their direct action on behalf of "babies threatened by imminent death" as inspired by a strong impulse toward "care and protection."[37] In somewhat similar ways, many Christian conservatives who are involved in the punitive political side of the antigay movement have described their own motivations as inspired by love of God and solicitude for the imperiled institution of heterosexual marriage. Maxwell notes that with respect to antiabortion activism, "an unexpected array of private motivations underlay a fairly uniform mode of public expression."[38] Notwithstanding the array of private motivations that may bring people to activisms of various sorts, in this study, I focus on categories of public expression and how these categories work differently, yet work together, to accomplish antigay and antiabortion ends. I focus especially on the categories that designate particular forms of compassion, not for fetuses and heterosexual ways of life but for the persons whose bodies and wellbeing stand at the center of the culture wars.

As critics of the movement argue, a potent vein of political strategy runs through the compassionate enterprise. Nonetheless, compassionate rhetoric in the arena of sexuality politics is not strategic without remainder. Instead, it is complex and oriented toward different audiences for different ends, including gaining a political advantage and encouraging the cultivation of particular spiritual modes of being. Depending upon the context and manner of its deployment, compassion can function as a political tactic oriented toward those who would not identify as Christian conservative, but it is also an attempt to perform other tasks.

The first of these tasks is to resituate conservative Christians as appropriately moral subjects, both to themselves and to others by, for example, recuperating the loving example of Jesus. For one small example of this process, consider this line from conservative provocateur Ann Coulter's address to the Conservative Political Action Conference (CPAC) in Washington, DC, in March 2007: "I was going to have a few comments on the other Democratic presidential candidate John Edwards, but it turns out you have to go into rehab if you use the word 'faggot,' so I—so kind of an impasse, can't really talk about Edwards."[39] Among the conservatives who criticized Coulter was Alan Chambers, ex-gay leader and president of Exodus International. On behalf of a "worldwide network of former homosexuals," Chambers rebuked Coulter for her use of the term "faggot": "[T]his hurtful word is used to demean an individual who is valuable to God. There is nothing to be gained by denigrating others with crude slurs. In doing so, we disgrace ourselves and discredit the truths we seek to elevate."[40] Chambers' criticism of Coulter did get some attention outside the conservative movement, but its context and register suggest that his principal audience was those involved in the ex-gay movement and the wider Christian conservative community.

The second, and related, task of compassion campaigns that may be overlooked by critics of the movement is to confront and balance the disgust that is a common response of heterosexuals to homosexuality and homosexuals and to generate and call forth a different kind of response to this particular kind of subject. Therapeutic literature produced within the ex-gay movement for a Christian conservative audience, such as pamphlets in the *Love Won Out* series, demonstrates this goal. In the pamphlet, "How Should We Respond? An Exhortation to the Church on Loving the Homosexual," ex-gay Joe Dallas writes that "the church must repent of hostility toward homosexuals. . . . and recommit to bold love."[41] With regard to political strategy, it may be that all of the goals of compassion discourse can function as political strategy in their own ways, as methods of recuperating the reputation of the movement and drawing more citizens into its politics, if not its theology. But I shall argue that there is good reason to believe that the constructing and calling out of newly configured Christian responses to what have long been defined in the movement as sites of ungodly abomination—abortion and same-sex sexuality—are independent goals of the movement, albeit ones that functions in ways that reward closer inspection.

A corollary of the view that compassionate rhetoric on the right is merely strategic is the perception that Christian conservatives themselves are not compassionate people—that the harms perpetrated by Christian right sexuality politics expose the malign truth behind the "mask of compassion."[42] Obviously, it's not possible to know which individuals possess a "prosocial value orientation," a disposition toward others that includes a concern with the other's well-being as well as a sense of responsibility for its achievement.[43] As Robert Wuthnow points out in *Acts of Compassion:*

Caring for Others and Helping Ourselves, it is more useful to understand compassion not as "a particular set of behaviors" but in terms of a "cultural framework" that enables the possibility of certain kinds of discourse and action.[44]

In his study, Wuthnow is concerned with questions about how Americans balance or reconcile values of individualism and compassion. This project is about something else: thinking about how compassion functions in the public sphere and, especially, how compassion may be conceptualized and put to work by those who operate within the ambit of a particular political movement. It is not that the personal orientations of followers and activists in that movement are beside the point but, rather, that the focus remains on the movement's goals, strategies, pedagogies, and their political effects.

Fixing Moral Boundaries

Whatever their differences, moral ideology and rhetoric—including rhetoric about compassion—have in common that they are boundary projects of one kind or another. It is appropriate to focus on compassion discourse as a matter of fixing boundaries because making the distinctions essential to good boundaries is key to understanding the very meaning of compassion. In fact, the Christian right fixes boundaries in two senses of that term: fixing in the sense of setting, or determining, and fixing in the sense of repairing moral boundaries from the damages wrought by permissive welfare liberalism.

Seen in this light, the boundary projects of Christian right and left compassion could not be more different. On the one hand, left compassion is a boundary-expanding project that seeks to include ever larger populations in human rights and welfare protections, including the poor and vulnerable, noncitizens, and those who do not share normative conceptions of gender, religious belief, and sexual continence. This is not to suggest that left compassion is immune to criticism. Besides criticisms grounded in traditional forms of morality, progressive compassion is vulnerable to questions about resource scarcity, the ideological positionality of the state, the effectiveness of state actions to alleviate suffering, the unintended consequences of positive rights approaches, and the hubris of social interventionism. These critiques come from a range of positions, including social and market conservatives, neoconservatives, and even feminists.

On the other hand, Christian right compassion, like the compassionate conservatism of the larger conservative movement, is a boundary-maintaining project. Compassion campaigns are constructed not only as good public relations, as many critics suppose, but also—and crucially—to instruct movement followers about where the lines of compassion are to be drawn, as well as in the rhetoric, feeling states, biblical significance, and social implications of compassion. Such pedagogy prepares those who identify with Christian compassion to become competent ambassadors for its projects and, it is hoped, to influence public perspectives on compassion. Writing about American compassionate conservatism under the aegis of the Centre for Social Justice, a conservative British organization, Tim Montgomerie defines the concept as having "two complimentary sides: one seeking to modify conservatism, the other side seeking to modify society's idea of compassion."[45] While Montgomerie's definition is accurate, it obscures a step: the influencing of public attitudes about compassion requires a consistent pedagogy within the ranks of conservative compassion that upholds and transmits the "right" ideas about who deserves compassion and under what circumstances. An example of this transmission of right ideas is found in the evangelical women's organization Christians for Biblical Equality (CBE), which defined the boundaries of compassion with regard to same-sex sexuality when it rejected a resolution of the Evangelical and Ecumenical Women's Caucus that supported civil rights for lesbians and gay men. As Julie Ingersoll points out, the CBE clarified its conservative position on same-sex sexuality to distinguish between "Christian love" and "the practice of homosexuality."[46]

What becomes clear when we look inside the compassion campaigns of the Christian right is that there is much at stake, both politically and theologically, for Christian conservatives as they fashion the rhetorics and institutions of compassionate Christian conservatism. Compassion campaigns advertise to the outside world the boundaries of appropriate concern and love for the same-sex-attracted and women who have had an abortion or may one day have one; they reconcile compassion with the punitive politics of other sectors of Christian conservatism; they direct the labor and spiritual resources of compassion to same-sex-attracted and postabortive Christian conservatives, thus enabling believers to care for their own and "feel sorry for themselves" in a way that reinforces the shared belief system; they guide those to whom they minister toward belief in and adherence to Christian conservative political and theological orthodoxy; and they meet the needs of compassionate Christian conservatives to see themselves as Christ-like in their approach to the urgent needs of hurting people in a fallen world.

The compassionate ex-gay and postabortion projects that result are varied; they reflect local conditions, leaders' convictions, political considerations, theological variations, and the perceived needs of different constituencies. This suggests that there is likely to be much variation across diverse kinds of compassion campaigns. While that is so, I argue that there are also patterns of belief, rhetoric, practice, and feelings that allow us to make fruitful generalizations about Christian right compassion. With regard to feelings, there are many potential candidates for "emotions that matter"[47] to the right, but I argue that disgust is an especially important emotion to study for its relationship to the kind of Christian right compassion we find in ex-gay and postabortion ministries.

"The Politics of Yuck"[48]

In his novel, *Grief*, Andrew Holleran tells the story of a gay man who has come to Washington, DC, shortly after the death of his mother to teach a university class on AIDS literature. Twenty years after the deadly peak of the disease, he finds the students generally "matter-of-fact" about same-sex sexuality and identity, discussing them in terms that reflect "enlightenment" and "tolerance." Even so, as the narrator reflects on the experience of teaching the class, he reveals his belief that "their real thoughts involve disgust."[49] There is no way to know whether the narrator—or Holleran, who instructed such a class at American University—accurately perceived the students' underlying responses to same-sex sexuality. But there is reason to believe that the feeling that has lately traveled under the name of "homophobia" has disgust at its core. Like Holleran, we might well consider carefully the role of disgust in antigay attitudes and perhaps even in the constitution of at least some forms of conservative compassion.[50]

In her psychoanalytic account of disgust, Susan B. Miller argues that this "gatekeeper emotion" is fundamentally about protecting the *self*, and not just the physical body, from threats. Disgust "promotes . . . certain illusions" about the self and provides a "protective fantasy" that we are "pure and good."[51] The need to protect the self, as well as one's own group, from perceived threats and to shore up our sense of goodness are key to the deployment of disgust, which psychologists agree is likely to be experienced as a "particularly visceral feeling" even when compared with the embodied sensations associated with other emotions.[52] Miller notes that among the common catalysts of disgust are "feces, slimy messes that touch the skin . . . disturbing ideas and visions, immoral acts, and repellent people." Disgust denotes "infectious, contagious awfulness." It is an ineluctable reaction to "an encounter with something experienced as outside the self" that is poised "to transfer noxiousness to the self."[53]

Queer people inhabit a world defined in large measure by heterosexuality. The concept of heteronormativity speaks to the "institutions, structures of understanding, and practical orientations that make heterosexuality seem not only coherent . . . but also privileged.[54] Moving to a different level of analysis, scholars of nonnormative sexuality generally have used two terms to denote the motivation behind prejudice against homosexuals: heterosexism and homophobia. The terms do some similar work, but they are also meaningfully different. Heterosexism is social-institutional; it is the parallel to other kinds of isms with which we are familiar: racism, sexism, ableism.[55] Whether conscious or unconscious, it privileges one side in a binary of social categories and works to marginalize those identified with the other side. On the other hand, homophobia is essentially a social-psychological term that takes aim at individual feelings and motivation against homosexuals. Coined by the psychologist George Weinberg, homophobia is an attempt at psycho-social explanation that medicalizes antigay feeling by implying that it is a disorder that can be treated.[56] Such an account of homophobia ironically reverses the more common identification of same-sex sexuality with deviance and with the marking of bodies, either as a cause or a consequence of homosexuality.[57]

Construing antigay sentiment as a "phobia" is an attempt to expose the visceral feelings that homosexuality and homosexuals frequently provoke in heterosexuals or in those who are discomfited or appalled by their own same-sex desires. As we know, phobias are fears of a particularly urgent and persistent kind that may interfere with the phobic person's ability to pursue ordinary daily existence. Is homophobia a "phobia"? In 2002, psychologists at the University of Arkansas released the results of a study that explored this question in the context of broader research of phobias that included fears of blood injection, spiders, and insects. The researchers found that aversion to homosexuals is not a phobia but, rather, is a reaction of disgust for which no psychological diagnosis or treatment is appropriate. Not only is "homophobia" a social issue rather than a treatable psychological order, but the distinction between fear of an object and disgust for an object exposes quite different psychological and social meanings.

How does the distinction between fear and disgust matter to the study of marginalization and stigma of people who are identified with abhorrent acts? In her study of the legal and political implications of shame and disgust, Martha Nussbaum argues that disgust is meaningfully different than fear because, along with shame, disgust is an emotion that is "especially likely to be normatively distorted" and, thus, "unreliable as [a] guide to public practice."[58] What Nussbaum means by this distinction is that, however useful and ubiquitous disgust has been in the social and psychological development of human beings, disgust reveals its roots in magical thinking about purity and contamination—the desire to deny our common human fragility and dependence. The distinction is clear in Ange-Marie Hancock's study of the "politics of disgust." Hancock demonstrates that welfare recipients in the United States became publicly sanctioned objects of disgust through the construction of a defamatory raced and gendered public identity: the welfare queen.[59]

The Arkansas psychologists point out another difference between disgust and fear that is likely to be of more immediate interest to queers and to members of other groups that inspire disgust than any academic discourse: while "fear provokes a 'get me away from that' reaction, disgust manifests as 'get that away from me.'" Hence, disgust is more likely to motivate attack than flight, a distinction that is crucial "when what a person intends to avoid or attack is not an animal or an inanimate object, but another human being."[60]

The political reaction that occurred in response to the inclusion of homophobia in the phobia research is instructive. When the psychologists who were studying phobias advertised their results on "homophobia," Christian conservative spokespersons for organizations like Concerned Women for America (CWA) responded swiftly with the view that the finding constituted vindication for traditional morality. Although the psychologists identified bias against gays as a problem, conservatives were buoyed by the fact that they identified it as a *social* and not as a *psychological* problem. For Christian conservatives, it was easier to ignore a social rebuke—one that can be dismissed on the basis of the presumed social liberalism of academics—than a finding of emotional pathology. The latter would require impugning either the scientific method by which the research was carried out or, in a postpositivist vein, the putative objectivity of scientific research in the secular academy. On the other side of the political continuum, spokespersons for LGBT organizations responded with a shrug. *The Washington Blade* quoted Connie Ress, of the Gay and Lesbian Alliance against Defamation (GLAAD), that it didn't make any sense "debating this word versus that word as a label." She noted that the important issue is that LGBT people are objects of discrimination, not what term is applied to account for the motivations that fuel oppression.

But the difference between disgust and fear does matter if the issue with which we're concerned is how Christian right leaders and followers express and shape the emotional contours of debate about same-sex sexual orientation when they talk among themselves. And more recent psychological studies explain why. A set of studies explore the relationships among disgust, particular contemporary social debates, and political ideology. In "Disgust Sensitivity Predicts Intuitive Disapproval of Gays" Yoel Inbar and his colleagues report that individuals who are sensitive to disgust are more likely to exhibit "negative intuitive moral judgments of gay people." Citing the relevant research on the role of disgust in moral judgments, the authors conclude that "the more disgust sensitive participants were, the more they showed unfavorable automatic associations with gay people as opposed to heterosexuals."[61] Who are the disgust sensitive? In "Conservatives Are More Easily Disgusted Than Liberals," the researchers, using a different set of subjects and instruments, find a consistent positive correlation between conservative ideology and higher sensitivity to disgust, whether the disgust is related to bodily fluids, abortion, or [male] same-sex sexuality: "participants higher in disgust sensitivity were more opposed to gay marriage and abortion."[62] In addition, the researchers confirmed that disgust-sensitive conservatives were more likely than their liberal counterparts to ascribe moral significance to their own reactions of disgust, essentially transforming intuitive emotional reactions toward people connected with abortion procedures and those who engage in same-sex sexuality into moral and policy judgments.

Christian conservative rhetoric on the subject of homosexuality appears to vindicate the findings of the psychologists. If this literature is any indication, conservative Christians have little fear of homosexuals—though they may fear the "homosexual agenda"—but a great deal of disgust. Even Christian right literature on same-sex sexuality that is made with the highest production values and presented as social science reveals disgust in its glossy pages. So, for example, the Family Research Council produces a brochure, entitled "The Slippery Slope of Same-Sex Marriage," that reports the popular survey research on "strong negative reactions" to same-sex sexual behavior. "This 'ick factor,' far from irrational, is rooted in the subconscious realization of what is normal and what is not, and which forms an inescapable part of our being. And it may be that by underestimating the power of this innate understanding, gay activists have made their greatest tactical error."⁶³ What this passage and many examples of Christian right rhetoric confirm is their belief in the moral relevance of disgust and repugnance, an understanding of the relationship between the self and an objective realm of morality and politics that most on the political left do not share.

Similarly, in the context of abortion, one feature of ingroup discourse that might seem puzzling to an outsider is how common it is for antiabortion groups to display pictures of aborted fetuses *to each other*, and not only to those they hope to convert to their cause. I have attended meetings at which the primary focus of discussion is political strategy or communicating an overview of where the successes of, and challenges to, the prolife movement lie. It is not uncommon for such meetings to begin with a viewing of photos of the aftereffects of abortions before participants move on to the specific topic under discussion. These photo displays seem calculated to inspire particular kinds of emotional reactions—especially disgust and outrage. They are the antiabortion movement's version of the kinds of photos that at one time were a staple of the public rhetoric of the antigay movement: photos of men making out with men, women making out with women, men in drag, and queers in various stages of undress. The use of these kinds of images in public expresses the conviction that disgust is, or can be, a universal signifier of moral wickedness. Their use in the private recesses of the movement expresses the understanding that Christian right followers share an epistemology of emotion that can be counted on to inspire and motivate political activism.

Traditionalist disgust is palpable in much of the literature associated with the Christian right, but so is earnest compassion pedagogy that appeals to Christians to examine their own disgust and to try to overcome it in particular ways and for particular purposes. One example of this literature is Brian Keith Willams's *Ministering Graciously to the Gay and Lesbian Community: Pouring in the Oil and the Wine*. Williams uses a variety of emotion words to describe homosexuality as an object, the feelings about same-sex sexuality of other conservative Christians, and those he has confronted in himself: "detest," "repulsed," "repugnant," "repulsive," "disgusting," "disdain," "horror," "infested," and "ghastly." The fluency of these verbs and adjectives suggests the author's position that what inspires disgust and revulsion, is, in fact, objectively repulsive and ghastly. The task at hand is to transform these quite natural responses into a stance that is informed by God's charge to intervene in the lives of, and minister to, people in need of salvation and repentance.⁶⁴ Feelings, their role in confirming judgments about sinfulness, and the alternative explanations that might arise from the application of alternative explanatory systems are so important that I return to the topic of disgust and its relation to compassion in the afterword.

A Word about Words, and So On

Because of the complexity of the variety of different objects I call upon in this book it's necessary to clarify the language that I will use to refer to the movements and the particular sectors of the movements on which I'll concentrate. I understand the Christian right as a movement to be antigay and antiabortion. It is antigay in that it aspires to restigmatize same-sex sexuality; roll back public policies associated with civil and human rights for lesbians, gay men, bisexuals, and transgender people; and prevent new protections of civil and human rights for members of these groups. It is antiabortion because it aspires to end the legal right to abortion, including legal access to contraceptive and abortifacient pharmaceuticals, and in many cases, to restigmatize and limit access to barrier types of contraception. Hence I will, from time to time, refer to the Christian right movement as a whole using these terms.

Within the Christian right the smaller ex-gay and postabortion recovery movements are also antigay and antiabortion to the extent that they share these broad ends and aspirations. When I use the term "antiabortion movement" I will refer to the set of projects, initiatives, and organizations that aspire to put an end to abortion rights and include in that designation both those groups that focus on the death of the fetus and employ abomination rhetoric and/or tactics of harassment, and those groups that are dedicated to postabortion compassion and healing. When my focus is on the compassionate wing of the antiabortion movement I will use the movement term, "postabortion ministries," to indicate the more specific focus. Similarly, when I address the compassionate wing of the antigay movement I will use the movement terms, "ex-gay movement" or "ex-gay ministries" to denote that object. The sexuality- and reproductive rights-related compassion campaigns of the Christian right are complex and, unfortunately, the representations deployed in left-right political discourse often flatten their complexity. One goal of this book is to keep straight important distinctions between ideological and institutional entities within the Christian right so that it's possible to clarify the outlines between different categories of Christian conservative activities and activism.

Finally, occasionally in this book I refer to the movement or ideology that supports women's right and access to reproductive liberty as the reproductive rights movement. By using this term I don't mean to make a hard distinction between the broad set of claims and activisms that have taken place under the signifier "reproductive rights" and more recent critiques of the standing of poor women and women of color under a principle that privileges individual choice or rights rather than justice. Calling for reproductive justice in a context in which many women are deprived of fundamental resources through which to exercise control over their intimate reproductive lives adds a valuable perspective to debates over abortion and reproduction, as well as the consequences of poverty and political marginality.[65] Whatever we call women's demand for control over intimacy and child-bearing—including a right to bear children—the Christian conservative postabortion ministries and ideology that I focus on in the chapters to come don't distinguish between reproductive rights and justice perspectives in their work.

Chapters 1, "Let's Both Agree That You're Really Sinful," and 2, "What about the Women?" provide an empirical examination of the ex-gay movement and postabortion ministries, respectively, as types of Christian right compassion campaigns. In these chapters I address these two manifestations of compassion separately and in relation to each other, offering examples of the many ways in which Christian conservative believers are socialized in compassion that is then deployed to social and political effect. Such a survey involves elucidating to some extent the terms, history, leaders, key texts, and organizations that constitute ex-gay and postabortion ministries.

In chapter 3, "Christian Right Compassion" I begin to examine Christian right compassion theoretically and as it is put to work in campaigns on sexuality and reproductive rights. Among modern thinkers, Hannah Arendt is the most incisive and uncompromising intellectual critic of compassion as a motivation for politics, and this dimension of her thought has attracted a great deal of attention among scholars. Because Arendt did not take compassion at face value as a motivation and guide to politics, and because she gave close attention to what she understood to be the paradoxical and destructive consequences of political compassion, I use her extensive critique of compassionate politics as a way to take up the question of what kind of compassion the Christian right deploys. Arendt did not have conservative compassion in mind when she developed her uncompromising critique of a politics of compassion, and it is in part the misfit between her own critiques of compassionate politics and the

Christian compassion of ex-gay and postabortion ministries that clarifies the political significance of organized moral disapproval. Applying evidence from Christian right compassion campaigns, I conclude that many aspects of Arendt's thought, including her conceptions of political judgment, pariah identity, and plurality as a basis for politics, can be directly and fruitfully applied to compassion campaigns and can illuminate the danger they pose to democratic public life.

In chapter 4, "Just Deserts," I argue that the most pivotal feature of Christian right compassion campaigns is the fixing and defending of boundaries between those who deserve compassion and those who do not. Those who are familiar with Ayn Rand as a novelist and putative philosopher may be surprised to see her read as a kind of theorist of compassion. But Rand was a moralist who was preoccupied with compassion and especially with guidelines and criteria by which it could appropriately be dispensed. There have been many ideological applications of a distinction between deserving and undeserving in US history, but I show that there is strong precedent for the specific contours of Christian conservatism in Rand's work.

Rand has had a tremendous impact on American conservatism, as the recent surge of interest in her work demonstrates. Although she was unapologetically anti-Christian, many of her strongest adherents are now found among Christian conservatives, and this strange intersection deserves close attention from students of the political right. Laying bare and comparing key elements of the ideology of compassion in Rand and the Christian right exposes, in Rand's terms, the "motive force" behind the deployment of Christian conservative compassion.

In chapter 5, "Drawing the Compassionate Line," I turn to psychoanalytic theory to consider a final question: if Christian right compassion works as a group ideology to distinguish deserving from undeserving citizens, what psychosocial effects is such compassion likely to engender?" To answer this question I employ relational psychoanalysis, and especially the prolific thought of Melanie Klein and those who have extended her work, to critique Christian right compassion. Much of Klein's thought revolves around categories that she understood as universal: emotions such as love, hate, envy, and greed and psychic defenses such as splitting, denial, and projection. Her work is marked by an interest in boundaries of self and other, and later relational theorists extend this focus to theorize group dynamics and the vicissitudes of group boundaries. In this chapter I introduce the terms of relational psychoanalytic thought that are most fruitful for analyzing Christian right compassion crusades. I use these concepts to show how Christian conservative compassion works psychologically to encourage group bonding and idealization and to discourage responsibility for harm to stigmatized groups and subjects.

Finally, in the afterword, "Compassion, Where is Thy Victory?" I turn one last time to the implications of Christian right compassion in the area of sexuality. With regard to motives, beliefs, and practices, the landscape of Christian conservatives and conservatism is too complex to be completely captured by any one label. But even so, the phenomenon of compassion campaigns, and their proximity or distance from the abomination politics with which they share some features, raises important moral, psychological, and political questions. In the end, I believe that the worry that ex-gay and postabortion compassion campaigns are fundamentally duplicitous and not really compassionate should be displaced by another set of concerns. These include: if compassion campaigns such as the ex-gay movement and postabortion ministries do harm, what kinds of harm do they do and to whom? What are the consequences for citizens in a democracy, and possibly to democratic politics itself, of attitudes and policies toward fellow citizens shaped by compassionate ideologies grounded in disgust, aversion, distinctions of merit and punishment, and the denial of harm to stigmatized groups?

As is clear from my focus in this book I am interested in both democratic politics and moral psychology, and I'm especially interested in how these two domains intersect and interact. Threaded throughout this analysis of Christian right compassion are theoretical commentaries on love (of other, of self, and of one's group); the ideological tenets of Christian compassion; the function of moral absolutes in politics; the threat posed by organized group denigration; and the public interest in respect and responsibility toward others. One of the themes I'm most engaged by is the difficulty of knowing what we are doing and the many strategies and defenses we are capable of employing to keep that knowledge from ourselves, as well as from others. In the end, I think that's what this book is about.

1

Let's Both Agree That You're Really Sinful

Compassion in the Ex-Gay Movement

Reparative Therapies

In this chapter, I focus on the movement to establish the contexts and details that are essential for understanding the ex-gay movement as a subculture of compassion within antigay Christian conservatism. Even as the more explicitly political segments of the Christian right have become more sophisticated in the construction and execution of punitive projects intended to stigmatize queer people and deprive them of equal rights, the ex-gay movement has developed and refined its compassionate approach to same-sex identity. Analyzing that approach requires understanding a number of facets of the movement: the relationship of the movement to antigay "science," the psychological infrastructure that justifies the extension of compassion, the ideological value of ex-gay testimonies, and the terms of the foundational ideology that inspires same-sex-attracted people to cooperate in the denigration of their sexual desire and intimate relations.

Because the American ex-gay movement is overwhelmingly Christian-identified, researchers legitimately can approach the movement as a religious social and cultural project. However, unlike postabortion ministries, the ex-gay movement boasts a significant arena of secular, scientific experts and expertise. These experts are dedicated to certifying same-sex sexuality as objectively abnormal and, in many cases, to transforming same-sex attracted people into functioning heterosexuals. Derived as it is from psychoanalysis, most of this secular ex-gay discourse is therapeutic, and some, which focuses on children's developmental dynamics, is prophylactic; thus, it expresses an ingroup therapeutic concern, not only with treating homosexuality but with preventing it in minors. On the other hand, no doubt because of the censure and criticism to which its practitioners have been subjected, some of this discourse also expresses outrage at the social and cultural damage these experts believe is committed by queers who assert their nonnormative sexuality and refuse to acknowledge the normality and superiority of heterosexuality.

By beginning this discussion of the ex-gay movement with these experts I do not mean to amplify their role in the movement or to dissociate them and the secular, scientific discourse they have created from the largely Christian ex-gay movement as a whole. To the contrary, I begin by demonstrating overlap and coordination between "secular" and Christian spheres of the movement that calls into question the claims of those on the ostensibly scientific side of the movement to intellectual independence and an objective basis for their antigay efforts. Compassion is a feature of both these arenas of the movement as experts, therapists, pastors, family members, and self-identified ex-gays minister to those members of their community with unwanted same-sex attractions. But given the substantial overlap and interpenetration of scientific expertise with Christian beliefs about sexuality, it is accurate to understand and analyze the compassion of the ex-gay movement as *Christian* compassion.

The stigmatizing of same-sex sexuality by the American mental health establishment and its treatment through reparative therapies dates to the early twentieth century in the United States.[1] A turning point in the politics of same-sex sexuality and its treatment came in 1973 when the governing board of the American Psychiatric Association voted to overturn the classification of homosexuality as a mental illness in the *Diagnostic and Statistical Manual of Mental Disorders* (DSM). The decision was controversial, and was challenged by some members, but it was ratified a year later by a vote of the Association.[2] Dissenters from this decision and other pro-gay statements by professional organizations such as the American Psychiatric Association and the National Association of Social Workers protested the decision by continuing to carry out "reparative" or "conversion therapies" with homosexual clients and by forming an alternative organization of mental health practitioners: the National Association for Research and Therapy of Homosexuality (NARTH).[3]

Reparative therapies are one form of treatment in the ex-gay movement's ensemble of interventions. Reparative therapists aspire to treat people who are unhappy with their same-sex desires, to reroute their sexual desires, and to turn them into functioning heterosexuals. A broad category, reparative therapies have enveloped a range of treatments from aversion therapies to a variety of outpatient and inpatient psychotherapies. And the therapies continue to be contested. The American Psychological Association has recently promulgated its most critical report to date on the practice and therapies designed to change sexual orientation from same-sex to opposite sex.[4] Responding to criticisms of the therapies by major mental health associations, in 2012 the California legislature passed a law banning the use of reparative therapies with minors. The law has been challenged by NARTH, the American Association of Christian Counselors, and the Pacific Justice Institute.

Today, NARTH is the major international secular institutional center and clearinghouse for reparative therapies. NARTH is widely understood to be a secular organization whose objections to same-sex sexuality are scientific rather than religious, but this identity belies the deep links and cooperation that prevail between the conservative Christian ex-gay movement and NARTH and its affiliated mental health practitioners. These points of contact fall into four categories: fundamental beliefs that cannot be established scientifically, the transfer of ideas from psychological researchers to the religious community, shared personnel, and the ideological perspectives that NARTH and the Christian right share.

Jack Drescher, a psychologist who has written extensively on antigay interventions in the mental health professions, notes that as the gap between antigay, "reparative," psychological theory and the mainstream mental health profession has deepened, the organizations that represent these views behave more and more like "fundamentalist religious denomination[s]."[5] What Drescher refers to is the commitment of reparative therapies proponents to beliefs that cannot be sustained merely by scientific evidence. So, for example, central to reparative therapies, and to the broader ex-gay movement, are beliefs about the necessity and naturalness of binary and complementary gender roles.[6] Indeed, the movement is committed to supporting, elaborating, and even self-consciously staging gender role differentiation, a project that is evident in publications, ministries, and even the banter in which ex-gay aspirants engage in venues such as the annual meeting of Exodus International, the world's largest ex-gay ministry.[7]

Just as evident in a movement that advertises itself as "offering help to those who struggle with unwanted homosexuality"[8] are the visceral denunciations of those who transgress normative heterosexuality. The reader can judge the prose style of this scientific writing from, for example, an essay on studies of lesbian parenting by Gerard J. M. van den Aardweg, a member of the NARTH Scientific Advisory Committee: "Of course, all damage by gay parenting will be blamed on malignant homophobia and not on the blind selfishness of . . . lesbian mothers, who may imagine they love their children, but, in fact, do them serious injustice. They sacrifice their children, who are so vulnerable because they naturally love their mothers, on the altar of their 'holy homophilia.' If this is not psychological violence, child abuse, what is?"[9] Adherence to—or, for that matter, defiance of—creeds such as gender role complementarity and the essential depravity of homosexuals is more often associated with political activism than it is with science, and this adherence allies the researchers of NARTH with the Christian right and traditionalist believers.

In addition to fundamental beliefs that resist scientific proof in both movements, there are other connections between the "secular" proponents of reparative therapies and traditionalist religion. Second is the transfer of ideas, in which the Christian ex-gay movement relies on psychologists and psychoanalysts in the ranks of the antigay mental health community for its own theories about how same-sex attraction develops. This intellectual transfer has given the ex-gay movement a reliable source of ostensibly scientific ideas and arguments. These constitute a domain of "suppressed" "stigmatized knowledge" that conflicts with dominant academic and therapeutic knowledge.[10] One example of such an expert is Joseph Nicolosi, a founder of NARTH, a psychologist by training and practice, and one of the principal successors of early antigay psychoanalysts. His writings provide key arguments about how particular gender and family dynamics cause homosexual desire, how it is that all people are heterosexual by nature, and why, although all of the major psychological professional associations disagree with the conclusion, homosexuality *is* an illness. But these ideas did not originate with Nicolosi. After Freud's ambivalent theorizing of same-sex sexuality, which was progressive for his time, a number of psychoanalysts took up the issue in a decidedly negative way. Among those who began in the 1960s to establish the key tenets of antigay psychodynamic theory that Nicolosi now disseminates were Sandor Rado, Lionel Ovesey, Irving Bieber, and Charles Socarides, another founder of NARTH.

Christian conservatives consistently have borrowed the arguments of these figures for over forty years. Major texts of the ex-gay movement demonstrate that as the antigay psychodynamic psychologies of same-sex attraction have changed in subtle ways, the conservative Christian ex-gay literature has changed to reflect the new psychological explanations. Antigay clinicians have produced a narrative of development that the Christian ex-gay movement relies on in its counseling of repentant homosexuals as well as in its literature on Christian parenting and childhood. The major themes of the narrative of development were well developed in midcentury psychoanalytic works. In the 1970s and 1980s antigay psychoanalytic and psychotherapeutic ideas were absorbed into a literature that mixed Christian moralizing and political attunement with developmental psychological theory.[11] By the 1990s, such works almost uniformly offered critiques of mainstream scientific studies on the possible biological origins and immutability of same-sex sexual orientation.[12]

A third connection between the "secular" work of NARTH and its psychodynamic researchers and the antigay work of the Christian right involves the extensive elite personnel intersections between the two groups. Joseph Nicolosi was a frequent expert contributor at Focus on the Family's Love Won Out ex-gay conferences, where he spoke both as a psychologist and as a traditional (in his case, Catholic) believer. Child psychologist and Focus on the Family founder, James Dobson, provided a blurb for Nicolosi's book, *A Parents' Guide to Preventing Homosexuality*, and routinely recommended it to parents concerned with the nonnormative gender behavior of a child. Jeffrey Satinover, one of NARTH's prominent psychiatrists and a member of its Scientific Advisory Committee, once served as medical advisor for Focus on the Family. The website of NARTH's Janelle Hallman notes that "her passion is to share God's word in a way that speaks to some of the deepest needs of broken and hurting people. She has spoken for Focus on the Family, Exodus International, and other Christian organizations."[13]

Finally, viewing NARTH as a text clarifies the deep connections—indeed, coconstruction—of the ostensibly secular and religious arms of the antigay movement. I surveyed the NARTH website as I began to write this chapter, and the NARTH homepage for September 12, 2006, included the following headlines: "UK Christian Faces Court for Handing Out Bible Verse Leaflets at Gay Rally," "Exodus [International] Releases First Book: A Guide to Help Evangelicals Reach the Gay Community," and "Christian Psychologist Suspended by Police over Former Affiliation with Pro-Family Group." Other headlines directed readers to such sources as Christian-NewsWire, LifeSite ("Your Life, Family, and Culture Outpost"), and Focus on the Family's Newsletter, CitizenLink, for articles whose themes were Christian conservative, rather than scientific. In August 2011, NARTH featured a news item, "Presidential Politics Places NARTH Issues on Front Page!" that focused on the presidential candidacy of Republican Michele

Bachmann. As the title suggests, the article highlights NARTH's framing of same-sex sexuality, but the reparative therapy that initiated mainstream news interest in Bachmann's husband, Marcus, was being performed at the Bachmanns' Christian counseling clinic.[14]

The Christian conservative and scientific parts of the antigay movement have been inextricably related to—indeed, dependent on—each other. The Christian ex-gay movement has relied for its intellectual underpinnings on ostensibly secular knowledge about human development and teleology, even though much of that knowledge is repudiated by the contemporary scientific community. Although compassion has not been a prominent part of the rhetoric associated with the antigay psychiatric literature and with "secular" reparative therapies, there is a protocompassionate element to the literature and therapies. These clinicians believe that people who do not experience opposite-sex desire are both profoundly damaged and unable to create and enjoy foundational human relationships. The attempt of reparative therapists to therapeutically repair developmental damage and enable heterosexual love does suggest the kind of compassionate concern that's often associated with the clinical relationship. The Christian conservative ex-gay movement incorporates salient aspects of secular literature and clinical practices and integrates them with a message of God's commandments and Christian compassion for homosexuals. What results from this convergence are narratives of development that hold out hope that damaged gays can become, if not healed former gays, at least people who better understand the environmental dynamics that can predispose them to tenacious same-sex desire.

The Narrative of Development

The Christian ex-gay movement long has been "the right's kinder and gentler anti-gay campaign."[15] This descriptor suggests that other precincts of the Christian right's antigay movement are less kind and gentle, and so they are. When Didi Herman mapped the changes in the orientation of the Christian right over a period of fifty years, she found that in the early years of Christian conservative attention to the problem of homosexuality, pity coexisted with firm resistance to normalization. By the early 1970s, the concern with "gay militancy" was rising among Christian conservatives, and compassion would give way, at least in the explicitly political sectors of the movement, to the conception of same-sex sexuality as "a sin with a movement behind it" that must be fought.[16] Even as the larger

Christian right movement mobilized against homosexuality, however, the ex-gay movement continued to cultivate compassionate dimensions.

The 1970s saw the first Christian ministries to homosexuals seeking to become heterosexual, and the movement was quickly institutionalized, first by the founding of Exodus International in 1976 and, second, by the establishing of the first ex-gay residential ministry, Love in Action, in 1979.[17] In the early years, Christian counselors applied an exclusively spiritual message of change that promised reformation of sexuality without inquiring into the psychological dynamics of same-sex attraction.[18] And as the movement matured into the 1980s the literatures and therapies of the Christian ex-gay movement came to reflect psychodynamic explanations produced by antigay psychiatrists and psychoanalysts, now embedded in a context of Christian conservative spirituality and exhortation.[19]

For believers, compassion follows from the understanding that same-sex desire is usually a matter of unchosen developmental dynamics. The explanation for lesbian desire includes developmental failures but is often more complicated—or incoherent—and in addition to interpersonal family dynamics includes the likelihood of sexual trauma.[20] Because unchosen developmental issues are understood to cause same-sex desire, the narrative of development relieves same-sex-attracted (often shortened to SSA) people of responsibility for their condition.[21] Those who fall victim to these dynamics or traumatic events are not responsible for them except in the sense that they are charged by God to resist their immoral sexual urges.

Most authors of the development literature disarticulate same-sex desire from gay identity. Thus, they fix identity either at the point of behavioral capitulation to desire or at the point of willful entry into a "homosexual lifestyle." One blunt articulation of this distinction is from the website of the ex-gay organization Love in Action, and it is consistent with the basic argument about sexuality found in the writings of NARTH researchers: "There is no such creation as a 'gay' or 'homosexual' person. There is only homosexual attraction and behavior; accordingly, there can be no change from a sexual identity that never existed in the first place."[22] In the ex-gay movement lexicon, "strugglers," also known as "overcoming" women and men, are those who ask God to remove their same-sex feelings and desires to form romantic relationships with people of the same sex. Toward strugglers who actively resist their same-sex desires, the appropriate response is helpfulness and loving compassion, a charge that entails not validating an active lesbian or gay life. Many participants in the movement come to understand themselves as celibate "ex-gays"—not heterosexual, but not, or no longer, actively involved in same-sex relationships and community.[23] In 2007 Alan Chambers, president of Exodus International, disclosed his own skepticism about the term, "ex-gay." Chambers noted that after many years as a husband and father he still struggled with same-sex attraction and that he doubted the transition to heterosexuality could be either "sudden or complete."[24]

Although different authors and thinkers in the ex-gay movement attribute same-sex desire to different influences, the most widely cited of all causes has been some species of dysfunctional family dynamics—the going awry of gender identifications and the homosexual orientation that results. From 1998 until 2009 Love Won Out, the ex-gay brand of Focus on the Family founded by Focus gender specialist John Paulk, disseminated the theme of familial dysfunction as a cause of homosexuality.[25] In 2004 Jyl Josephson and I attended a Focus on the Family Love Won Out meeting at North Heights Lutheran Church in Minneapolis, Minnesota, in which the participants were instructed in this developmental narrative. It was a common feature of Love Won Out meetings that a mental health professional provided the psychological scaffolding that ex-gay speakers would use in their own testimonies and teaching. In Minneapolis, NARTH's Nicolosi presented a broad outline of the kinds of developmental failures that occur in families and precipitate the deficits, arrests, failed identifications, and compensatory defenses that result in homosexuality.[26] In the developmental narrative, the fault of same-sex desire does not lie in those afflicted with it, but in their histories, and particularly in their family relations.

The narrative of development is complicated at its core, and that is probably one reason why it has begun to fall out of fashion in some quarters of the ex-gay movement. It constitutes a powerful indictment of many Christian families that few in the movement follow to its logical conclusion. One who does is Anita Worthen; the mother of a gay son, the wife of an ex-gay man, and the co-author of *Someone I Love Is Gay*, Anita and her husband, Frank Worthen, founded New Hope Ministries in San Rafael, California.[27] Tanya Erzen, who spent eighteen months doing ethnographic research at New Hope for her book, *Straight to Jesus*, cites Anita Worthen's views on family—including her own—responsibility for homosexuality: "Anita believes that parents have to acknowledge their role in causing homosexuality in their children and to try not to alienate them at the same time. . . . 'I don't want the parents to go away feeling that they're horrible people,' Anita explained. 'But I feel the only healing for parents is if they accept their responsibility—of what they've done. I can't tell them what they've done. I can tell them my story because I did everything wrong and nobody can take that away from me.'"[28]

However, most authors and spokespersons in the movement try to minimize the impact of the indictment of families and family relations even while they relate their own personal stories that often include familial abuse, neglect, and estrangement. In an attempt to reconcile the developmental narrative with the imperative to serve families of strugglers, Focus on the Family's former senior gender analyst, Melissa Fryrear, noted in a 2004 Love Won Out session that there is "no such thing as a perfect parent" but later described the characteristics in mothers that might predispose a daughter to lesbianism: "doormat[s]," "manipulative," "domineering," and/or "self-consumed."[29] In offering a master explanation for same-sex desire that's premised on deviance and adaptation to environmental failure, the ex-gay movement has had little choice but to confront parents and family members with evidence of their responsibility for the production of homosexuality *and* for their failure to recognize its signs early enough in the developmental process to try to arrest it.

One way out of this quandary is to suggest, as many have, that the failures that cause same-sex desire may be *perceived* by the prehomosexual child rather than *actual*. In its focus on actual developmental failures, the narrative of development itself does not tend to support this hopeful interpretation, but it is a useful caveat when the movement addresses itself to the Christian conservative family members of strugglers and unreformed lesbians, bisexuals, and gay men. In a session for friends and family members of gays and lesbians I attended at the 2008 Exodus International Freedom Conference, Fryrear emphasized this caveat. So even when the psychological-developmental narratives on which ex-gay ideology rely blame parents for developmental failures, Christian parents may avail themselves of the explanation of a child's misplaced perceptions.

In July 2008, Angelia Wilson and I attended the annual International Freedom Conference of Exodus International at the Ridgecrest Christian Conference Center in Ridgecrest (near Asheville), North Carolina.[30] There, strugglers; self-identified ex-gays; Christian conservatives involved in ex-gay ministries; and relatives and friends of gays and ex-gays gathered to receive and provide information, share testimonies, and worship together. The psychological infrastructure of the event was familiar because it is widely shared across the ex-gay movement and, indeed, continually constructed and disseminated by hegemonic actors such as Exodus. In keeping with extant ideology, most speakers reinforced the narrative of development and offered testimonies that emphasized the malign consequences of a homosexual lifestyle. Many outlined appropriate gender differences and the pleasures of gender complementarity. Following a common script, many attributed a variety of problems in living—chronic loneliness, drug and/or alcohol addiction, compulsive sexual promiscuity, failed relationships, depression, and the urge to commit suicide—to their gay lifestyle and celebrated their freedom from homosexuality, which was simultaneously freedom from these painful life circumstances.[31]

By following the scripts provided by antigay psychological narratives of development, the literature of the ex-gay movement and discourse in ex-gay venues create a Christian popular psychology of emotion. This Christian pop psychology reinterprets academic and psychoanalytic theories of emotion, in some respects turning them on their head, to achieve accounts of emotion that advance ex-gay ideology. So, for example, strugglers learn a distinction between true and false selves that is quite different than the concept that was developed in the context of psychoanalytic theory proper: the true self is the heterosexual woman or man that God wants each of us to be; the false self is the deceptive self we may create under circumstances of homosexuality to hide what we are doing from the world. By contrast, Donald Winnicott's formulation of these concepts emphasized the difference between a sense of self created in response to a profound lack of attunement from caregivers and a more spontaneous self formed in an environment of emotional attunement.[32]

Likewise with shame and guilt: shame is the feeling we may have when acting out same-sex sexuality that our essential being is wrong and bad. Compassionate ex-gay leaders do not endorse this comprehensive sense of shame, and the compassion of the movement is meant to discharge it if the circumstances are appropriate—if, for example, the aspiring ex-gay person is committed to no longer indulging in sexual sin. In contrast to shame, guilt is the certain knowledge that we have done something wrong. Indeed, as these examples, drawn from Christian therapy and ministries websites demonstrate, guilt is the indictment from God that confirms we have transgressed his rules for us.[33]

> Guilt is what takes place when a person realizes their failure. . . . While guilt is seeing what you've done, shame is seeing yourself as a failure because of what you've done.[34]

> Despite what some would have us believe, there is such a thing as true moral guilt. . . . We do people no favor by saying "Don't

feel guilty" when in fact, according to God's Word, they are guilty. Our goal should be a conscience cleansed of sin, not a conscience that denies sin.[35]

Like all things, guilt is a Godly designed emotion. . . . Guilt, as recognition of our wrongs, is a necessary first step in the path to repentance.[36]

So guilt is more than a feeling—you are *actually* guilty because you have broken God's loving and wise standards. Most of the time when you feel guilty, it's because you *are* guilty.[37]

The real purpose of guilt is to help us to admit and learn from our mistakes. God gives each of us a conscious [sic] that helps us to do the right thing and to make the right choices.[38]

For Christian conservatives, the meaning of emotions is transparent. Whether the emotion is guilt, shame, or disgust, the emotions of the righteous reflect the truth of God's divine order just as the emotions of those who struggle with sexual sin reflect their degraded spiritual condition and the distance between their current self and the mature Christian ideal toward which they strive.

Crucial to upholding this philosophy of affective transparency are the testimonies of ex-gays and -lesbians themselves. These testimonies reinscribe the relationship between affective life and divine order. They also serve as vehicles for articulating a particular ideal of love and compassion toward those who struggle to escape the grip of same-sex desire and attachment. The conventions of these ex-gay testimonies are such that a predictable component of the genre is the soliciting of compassion for strugglers. With the standing conferred by sexual brokenness and healing, authors explicate both the nature of true compassion and the form of compassionate relation that should prevail between believers and the same-sex afflicted.

Out of Bondage

Beginning in the 1970s, with Kent Philpott's *The Third Sex? Six Homosexuals Tell Their Stories*, ex-lesbians and ex-gay men have stepped forward to tell the stories of their conversions to heterosexuality.[39] Today, the first-person conversion literature is so vast that it either attests to the success of reparative therapies or vindicates the cynicism of critics that struggling ex-gays sustain their fervor for sexual change by becoming "full-time professional heterosexuals."[40] Most of these works rely in one way or another on collective and/or personal developmental narratives—accounts of the development and progress of homosexual desire before a spiritual awakening that wrenched the author away from sin and into a new life of fidelity to God's will. Ex-gay testimonies are available on the web, including in blogs, on YouTube, and on websites hosted by individual church ministries and national ex-gay organizations such as Parents and Friends of Ex-Gays and Gays (PFOX), Exodus International, and Exodus Student Ministries. Two resources are "Our Stories," found on the PFOX website, and "Ex-Gay Testimonies," posted to YouTube.[41] Whether they appear in individual blogs or on the websites of ex-gay or Christian conservative organizations, these brief testimonies tend to share certain characteristics, including an attempt to explain same-sex attraction as the consequence of harmful childhood experiences or family dynamics and the misery of living life as a homosexual before being "convicted" before God and turning away from life as a gay person.

Some ex-gay testimonies take the form of books that are advertised and sold at ex-gay events. These memoirs tend to include an additional component often not present in the abbreviated versions of ex-gay transformation: a plea for love and compassion toward the same-sex attracted, especially those who are struggling with their sexuality and whose destinies God has laid on the hearts of the writers. A recent contribution to this literature is by Janet Boynes, ex-lesbian and founder of Janet Boynes Ministries, a nondenominational outreach dedicated to providing services to individuals who wish to "leave homosexuality" and churches that want to be informed on issues relating to homosexuality. Boynes is a friend and associate of Representative Michele Bachmann (R-MN) and her husband, and Bachmann is prominently quoted on the Boynes Ministries website: "Janet's life is a powerful testimony of the changes that Christ can bring through His healing power from the bondage of sin. To see Janet is to see the face of joy, freedom, and peace. I wish everyone could meet this dynamic, young, Christ-filled woman who has dedicated her life to spreading the joy that she has found in a deep relationship of forgiveness from the Father. I hope everyone listens closely to Janet's compelling testimony."[42] Providing back cover blurbs for *Called Out: A Former Lesbian's Discovery of Freedom* are Bishop Harry R. Jackson Jr., senior pastor at Hope Christian Church in Beltsville, Maryland, just outside Washington,

DC, and Tony Perkins, president of the Family Research Council. Jackson and Perkins have collaborated on many projects, including the attempt to prevent the City Council of Washington, DC from extending the right to marry to same-sex couples in our nation's capital.[43]

In *Called Out*, Boynes recounts a childhood of poverty, fatherlessness, physical and emotional abuse, and sexual assaults. For several years in her adult life Boynes was exclusively involved in intimate relationships with women. However, on matters of sexual desire and consensual sexual activity Boynes' story appears consistent with a bisexual interest in boys/men as well as girls/women. Boynes describes herself as a child as being "interested in boys, as most little girls are" and having "crushes on boys;" later Boynes has relationships with men, including one she falls in love with and nearly marries. Before Boynes was born again the temptation of sinful same-sex sexuality lurked: "Temptations and desires began creeping up on me and a girl named Leanna began to catch my eye. I still associated with guys and was attracted to them, but I could feel myself changing. Lesbianism was always in the back of my mind, just waiting for me to embrace it."[44] But it was only after being born again that Boynes succumbed to same-sex desire and began to live as a lesbian. Boynes' memoir of this period is consistent with ex-gay narratives that link same-sex sexuality with other forms of dysfunction and addiction. While engaged in relationships with women Boynes suffered from an eating disorder, used and sold cocaine, lied to police, and beat lovers. Finally, she returned to God and quickly abandoned what she calls the "lesbian lifestyle."

Part 2 of *Called Out* is Boynes' "Message," and the key phrase—repeated as the first line of every one of seven chapters and concluding sections—is: "When God calls, He calls in love." In a chapter that offers the message "for the church," Boynes addresses her "brothers and sisters in Christ" with the charge that "as the church, the body of Christ, we have failed to love as we should." She rebukes believers for "hold[ing] up signs with slogans like, 'God hates gays'" and asserts that as "followers of Christ Jesus, our message *cannot* be hate. It *must* be love."[45] Having reinforced the importance of loving compassion, Boynes advocates for the kind of ministry in which this love could find its proper object. "I would like to suggest something that some might consider a radical way of reaching out to the homosexual community, but it is an option I believe could bear incredible fruit: let us open the doors of our churches and homes *to those who wish to leave homosexuality*. . . . We will never be able to make a difference in the lives of gays and lesbians unless we are able to offer a realistic alternative, a way out. It starts by opening our doors."[46] Boynes exhorts the church to "send out a consistent message, one that speaks and acts in love while not compromising values or becoming accepting of sin." This condemnation of homosexuality is "tough love" but also "healing love."[47]

Boynes' *Called Out* is similar to other books by ex-gays but for one feature that gives her text a particular utility to the movement: because Boynes is African American, her commentary on LGBTQ civil rights claims lends personal credibility to the familiar ex-gay movement boundaries within which compassion should operate. The first portion of Boynes' answer to the question "Is homosexuality a civil rights issue?" is worth quoting directly: "Homosexuality is *not* a civil right issue—*absolutely not*. I was born black. I became a lesbian. They are *not* the same. I did not choose the color of my skin. I did choose to enter a lesbian relationship and to live a homosexual lifestyle for fourteen years. I also chose to leave that lifestyle, but I cannot choose to stop being black. There is a difference. The color of my skin is an immutable quality of my being while my lesbianism was a deliberate series of actions resulting in a lifestyle choice."

Boynes continues with an analysis that pairs forms of discrimination against African Americans in U.S. history with the assertion that homosexuals do not suffer these particular forms of harm in the present: "[Homosexuals] have the right to own property and they also have the right not to be property. They have the right to learn to read and to obtain an education. . . . They have the right to cross state lines without fear of being hunted, beaten, and imprisoned. They have the right to let their voices be heard without being lynched. These are all rights blacks had to fight for through hundreds of years of struggle, but homosexuals do not deal with *any* of these civil rights issues."[48] By this standard there is no justification for a contemporary civil rights movement for any group of US citizens, a position that would be consistent with the conservative, including the "multicultural conservative," perspective on the African American civil rights movement. As Angela Dillard suggests, the early phase of the movement—approximately from *Brown* to the Civil Rights Acts of the mid-1960s—is the "heroic" period in which second-class citizenship for African Americans was effectively challenged. This chronology permits black conservatives to salvage a civil rights movement with "moral legitimacy" and distinguish it from all that has transpired under the civil rights banner from the late-1960s to the present.[49]

In foreclosing the possibility that discrimination against sexual minorities violates their civil rights, Boynes makes another move that sets her testimony apart from that of the majority of ex-gays. Only in the

"Questions and Answers" section of the book, a section followed by the epilogue and "Further Resources," does Boynes refer to the Black Church as an institution and to black churches as religious communities, and she does so explicitly in the context of denying claims for LGBT relief from discrimination. Rather than ignoring homosexuality or merely ministering to those "struggling with homosexuality," she charges the Black Church with "stand[ing] against the progression of homosexuality in our society": "I want to encourage every black person reading this book to make it known to your government officials, to your churches, and to society that trying to make homosexuality seem normal is not and never will be the same thing as our long and hard struggle for civil rights."[50]

Such an antigay appeal to Christian conservative African Americans, a staple of the white Christian right movement since the 1990s, gains force for being articulated by someone who is in a position to compare experiences of minority racial and minority sexual identity.[51] But the appeal also has the effect of reinforcing the boundary between loving compassion and strenuous political opposition. God calls in love, but only when the troubled person is already renouncing a sinful identity. When there is no renunciation, God calls his people to mobilize their neighbors and to contact their government officials.

Not all entrants into the ex-gay literature are repentant homosexuals; a small subcategory of this first-person ex-gay literature is produced not by ex-gays and -lesbians themselves but by ministers or family members of those afflicted by same-sex desire. A contributor to this niche of literature is Nancy Heche, therapist, speaker, and mother of actress Anne Heche. In Heche's case the homosexuality was not her own but that of, first, her minister husband, and then later, her daughter, who from 1997 to 2000 was involved in an intimate relationship with actor and comedian Ellen Degeneres. In *The Truth Comes Out* Nancy Heche tells her story but also narrates her own transformation as a Christian. When she first discovered that her daughter was involved with Degeneres her attitude was that "Anne's newfound lesbian love affair [was] like a betrayal of an unspoken vow: *we will never have anything to do with homosexuals.*"[52] However, this antagonism is finally replaced by grace and the necessity of love:

> At the end of the day I must love. I must bless. I must believe. The Apostle Paul's thoughts in 1 Corinthians 13 echo through me:
>
> Nancy, when you speak, people will put their fingers in their ears and go "lalalalala" if you don't have love.

> Nancy, you can get your academic degrees and know a little about a lot of things, but it means nothing without love. . . .
>
> It's not about how much you say or how much you know or how much you do; it's about how much you love.[53]

Heche has been a popular speaker at ex-gay meetings, and she has co-edited a volume that emphasizes the importance of compassion and uncompromising fidelity to scripture in dealing with same-sex desire: *The Complete Christian Guide to Understanding Homosexuality: A Biblical and Compassionate Response to Same-Sex Attraction*.[54]

Although there is some space in the conventions of ex-gay writing to accommodate unique dimensions of authors' lives and experiences, there are common features that owe much to the conventions of ex-gay testimonies as they have developed. Books in the genre offer expansive narratives of fallenness and of the inevitable return to God, but in addition they provide authors the opportunity to expatiate on the role of believers and the church in dealing with same-sex sexuality. Having crossed over from homosexuality, authors can speak to believers of the misery attendant on a homosexual lifestyle. And they can also instruct believers to maintain openness and loving compassion toward the repentant while holding a vigorous line against acceptance of same-sex sexuality. In brief ex-gay testimonies that circulate on the internet authors narrate an abbreviated version of unhappy homosexuality and a final surrender to God's will that propelled them to their present state of commitment to God's will for sexuality. While these narratives often attest to the promise of heterosexuality for their same-sex-attracted readers, they are spare testimonials to the misery of living outside God's grace and the happiness of finally securing it.

In the long and sometimes lonely quest for healing from homosexuality, many strugglers turn to ex-gay ministries and organizations, the testimonies of other ex-gays or strugglers, and other resources. However, because none of these resources is without its own peculiar hazards to the enterprise of coming out of homosexuality: meetings and support groups place strugglers in close proximity with others like themselves; books and materials offer the only ministry-sanctioned accounts of same-sex relations; and in addition to ex-gay testimonies and ministry websites, the internet offers a virtually inexhaustible abundance of sexual material to test the self-restraint of strugglers. As a result of these hazards, strugglers rely on a web of support and correction to help them navigate a world of sexual temptation.

The Compassionate Gaze

In ex-gay residential settings and other meeting places, participants consent to surveillance measures that reinforce the disciplinary rules of the movement. These measures are devised by the communities that embrace same-sex-attracted people, and they function in both real-world and virtual venues. In therapeutic and social settings, prohibitions on "gay" behavior, humor, dress, grooming, and gestures in addition to the prohibition on sexual contact prevail. Tanya Erzen details many of the rules that were in effect during her research at New Hope Ministry, including a prohibition on "camping"—the use of "gay terms and mannerisms." Quoting from the New Hope program manual, Erzen notes the forms of clothing that were not permitted for men: "short shorts or tight pants, tank tops, spandex or biker pants, and cut-off or half-shirts." Nude sleeping was also prohibited.[55]

In large group settings such as Love Won Out and Exodus, staff and volunteers have been empowered to call attention to and discipline behavior that violates the movement's norms and ideology, and participants submit to this discipline in the hope that it will advance their healing from homosexuality.[56] In spite of our attempt to keep a low profile, when Jyl Josephson and I attended the Love Won Out conference in Minneapolis in 2004, we were scolded by a young volunteer for watching two young female protesters stage a "kiss-in" outside the door of the Lutheran Church in which the event was being held. The appropriate response, which was being modeled by other attendees, was to ignore the protesters, and our failure to do so attracted the young woman's attention. After the rebuke, we understood that the volunteer—who introduced herself to us with the words, "I'm an ex"—would be watching us and that any additional non-conforming behavior might result in our dismissal from the conference.

When they leave the context of group support and surveillance, strugglers and ex-gays are understood to be particularly vulnerable to temptation. Indeed, because of their private nature, sexual fantasies, sexual conduct, and reading and viewing habits constitute a constant challenge to the program of celibacy and sexual transformation. In response to this challenge, strugglers are taught and encouraged to practice forms of self-surveillance that recall Foucault's exposition of discipline, in which the individual becomes "the principle of his own subjection."[57]

One important site of vulnerability, and therefore of self-surveillance, is the internet. A number of filtering services on the market are endorsed by ex-gay leaders, including NetNanny, CyberPatrol, and Surfwatch. These services are marketed to parents as a way of protecting children from pornography and other dangers. Some of the same services advertised to parents for children also are marketed to adults who use them to bolster their self-control in avoiding sexual websites and chat rooms. However, as is often the case in ex-gay ministries, internet use is a case of the confluence of surveillance and self-surveillance, with mechanisms that provide a web of support and "accountability" for those who subscribe to the movement. Leaders in the ex-gay movement recommend internet services such as Hedgebuilders and CovenantEyes to "overcoming" women and men, who can choose between internet filtering, which blocks access to particular sites, and an accountability function, which automatically provides a record of websites the member has visited to a designated individual, usually an "accountability partner" who is more advanced in his or her Christian "walk."

The intent to protect adult members, and not just children, from immoral content is clear in the mission and service statements of the companies. "The HEDGEBUILDERS filtering cannot be uninstalled, deleted, or disabled without contacting HB support for a special uninstall code. This feature protects every member in the home including the person who is the computer administrator. Christian homes can feel secure knowing their children are protected. Christian men can protect themselves from messing up and viewing what they shouldn't. Christian wives can know their husbands are safe on the web."[58] CovenantEyes, which is frequently recommended to people struggling with same-sex desire, promises: "Our Accountability software monitors Internet use and emails reports to people you select. Our Filter Service blocks objectionable websites from your computer."[59] Products like these constitute a considerable advance in practical, as well as ideological, support for those who join the ex-gay movement.[60]

Many critics of ex-gay ministries have analyzed the movement's reliance on an addiction model to explain same-sex attraction and its similarities to twelve-step recovery programs.[61] Another model for ex-gay discourse that has received less attention is "positive thought," which, along with "positive theology" and the "motivation industry" Barbara Ehrenreich analyzes in *Bright-Sided: How the Relentless Promotion of Positive Thinking Has Undermined America*. Although Ehrenreich doesn't address the ex-gay movement directly, she documents the requirement in many institutional contexts that members engage in the "constant internal work of self-monitoring [to rid themselves of] 'negative thoughts' charged with anxiety or doubt" and that they "purge 'negative people'" from their lives.[62] Such exhortations are common in the literature and testimonies of the ex-gay movement. Key to reaping the rewards of positive thought is the mandate to claim a desired identity before it has become instantiated as reality; in cases Ehrenreich explores, this identity is frequently one of wealth/prosperity, while in the case of same-sex-attracted strugglers the identity is often heterosexuality. The declaration of heterosexual identity that strugglers have often made upon entering the movement confirms for them the hope and promise that the ministries will facilitate their transformation from gay to straight. Such declarations—which show up in academic research produced by antigay researchers—also complicate the process of discerning the efficacy of ex-gay ministries.[63]

While struggling women and men practice and consent to mechanisms of surveillance that promise to help them achieve their goal of overcoming homosexuality, an additional source of succor for strugglers often comes from "Transforming congregations." Transforming congregations constitute a "third way" between the exclusion of same-sex-attracted people from gospel churches and the inclusion of openly lesbian, gay, and bisexual people in "Reconciling" and "Welcoming and Affirming" congregations and church networks.[64] Exodus International practices outreach to theologically and politically conservative churches and denominations through affiliation with the Exodus Church Network and Exodus Member Ministries. Benefits for churches of becoming an Exodus Network Church include training and materials, conferences and seminars, a newsletter, and links to member ministries staffed by ex-gays or by trained and knowledgeable people whose friends or family members have been "involved in homosexuality."[65] Unlike in the early days of the ex-gay movement, today, strugglers can rely on a network of trained and compassionate believers whose task it is to help same-sex-attracted women and men negotiate the path out of homosexuality.

Leaving Homosexuality

The ex-gay movement provides a sophisticated set of ministries, therapies, publishing enterprises, and entrepreneurial opportunities. Having begun in the United States, the ex-gay movement is now international, but its theology and psychology continue to reflect its American roots. At the most basic level, what diverse venues of the ex-gay movement have in common is that they are motivated to help people in pain. Their purpose, in a familiar refrain, is to help same-sex-attracted people "leave homosexuality" by "speaking the truth in love" to people with a "homosexual problem" in a world "impacted by homosexuality."

Unlike the more explicitly political spheres of the Christian right's antigay movement, the ex-gay movement relies on what Jim Sidanius and Felicia Pratto call "the power of consensual ideology," a state of affairs in which attitudes and beliefs are reproduced and shared not only by members of dominant groups, but also by members of subordinated or less powerful groups, often to their detriment. Consensuality "helps to coordinate behaviors, makes social practices meaningful, gives people psychological security and provides standards for judging people's behavior or potential changes within the society. Consensual ideologies are therefore the thread that weaves the fabric of social relations together."[66] Although some consensual ideologies are hierarchy-attenuating, others are hierarchy-enhancing;[67] in the terms of social dominance theory, the ideology that undergirds the ex-gay movement qualifies as a hierarchy-enhancing consensual ideology. The racialized example of consensuality that Sidanius and Pratto offer in a chapter title is "let's both agree that you're really stupid"; the version of consensuality without which the ex-gay movement could not exist is "let's both agree that you're really sinful."

Some same-sex-attracted people who find their way to the ex-gay movement are delivered to it as adolescents by their parents or guardians. However, taking into account that many same-sex-oriented people are strenuously urged by family members or religious leaders to repudiate their same-sex attractions and relationships, most of those who enter the movement do so more or less willingly. These adherents may subscribe to any or all possible frames about same-sex desire in the movement's repertoire, including familial dysfunction, childhood molestation or sexual experimentation, sexual brokenness, sexual addiction, or simply a sinful human nature. Strugglers/overcoming women/men often seek out treatment by Christian therapists trained in reparative therapies; they remove themselves from networks of friends or lovers in order to facilitate their healing; they immerse themselves in settings that are consistent with their aspirations for sexual healing; they read the Bible and literatures associated with the ex-gay movement; and they consent to forms of surveillance and instruction that are calculated to bolster their own resistance to temptation at the risk of scrutiny and humiliation.

The key behavioral requirement of participation in ex-gay ministries is abstinence from sex, but as in abstinence-only sex education it is not only sexual behavior with partners that is proscribed. For example, strugglers and those who regard themselves as celibate ex-gays and ex-lesbians must contend with the movement's strict position on masturbation, which is disseminated in literature and in meetings convened by ex-gay groups.

An example is an essay entitled, "Masturbation and the Bible," by Lambert Dolphin, which is available through a link on the website of Exodus International. The essay's arguments against masturbation are consistent with the teachings of the ex-gay movement. These include the following: that secular psychological sources that define masturbation as harmless are unreliable; that guilt and shame effects of masturbation are inevitable; and that the biblical case against sexual impurity mandates that initiates foreswear masturbation.[68]

In ingroup contexts, participants in the ex-gay movement express interest in the possibility that masturbation might be a permissible alternative to same-sex sexual contact. In a session on "Top 10 Questions Overcoming Women Ask" held at the 2008 Exodus International conference, the subject of masturbation—designated as "the 'M' issue"—was raised by session facilitators Christine Sneeringer and Melissa Fryrear. Sneeringer and Fryrear proffered several responses to the M issue, including that shame would probably result from it, that all sexual behavior should be exposed to "trusted, mature confidants" in the movement, and that because masturbation is often accompanied by "pornographic" mental images that can entrench same-sex desire it is better to refrain.[69] Trusted leaders in the movement often share with followers their own spiritual struggles over masturbation and how, over time, God led them to give up the practice.

In another Exodus session for men entitled "Breaking the Cycle of Sexual Addiction," Cordy Campbell, of the organization Worthy Creation, suggested in literature he distributed that masturbation is "not a necessity like food, clothing, and shelter" and that it is "a way to avoid true recovery" from homosexuality.[70] He provided a "masturbation inventory" to attendees with questions such as: "Am I trying to avoid or medicate a feeling?" "Will I want to keep this a secret?" "Am I confused about what I really want?" "Will I feel guilty or badly afterwards?" Affirmative answers to these and similar questions suggest that the struggler answering the inventory is, in fact, avoiding recovery and needs to take decisive action to salvage it. The questionnaire lacks validity, but it shares superficial similarities with other valid and reliable psychological inventories.

The rhetorics and literatures of the ex-gay movement are diverse. In addition to scientific inventories that gauge strugglers' conformity to movement protocols they include ex-gay testimonies and books, pamphlets, and websites produced by a variety of ex-gay experts: psychologists, psychiatrists, pastors, lay ministers, and many others who have been called by God to minister to sexually broken and afflicted people.

As researchers, bloggers, and other interested parties have pointed out, like all aspects of the Christian right, ex-gay movement philosophy has not remained fixed over time. Instead, the messages and views of leaders in the movement have changed to respond to new lines of criticism, to accommodate shifts in leadership, and to take account of forms of knowledge that originate in the world outside the movement. These ongoing changes must be integrated into accounts of the movement in order to track the complexity and evolution of Christian compassion.

Taking the Ex-Gay Challenge

As I complete this book in the waning days of 2012, the ex-gay movement is undergoing what may turn out to be its toughest challenge yet. For some time, it's been clear that there are rifts in the movement that emanate from the question of whether same-sex-attracted people—especially those who cannot detect opposite-sex attraction in themselves—can become heterosexual. Besides validating the hopes of many who have some role in the ex-gay movement, the question has received attention because the belief that same-sex-attracted people can change their sexual orientation has been correlated positively with opposition to LGBTQ rights.[71] For many years, the two sides of this debate reflected the vigorous disagreement between the movement (mostly yes on the possibility of homosexual to heterosexual transformation, though with some caveats and deviations) and its pro-LGBTQ critics (mostly no on this possibility, though with some caveats and deviations). However, in recent years the consensus within the movement on the transformation of same-sex desire into heterosexuality has broken down, and with it the movement's hope of relative internal consistency.[72] To investigate this turn of events and to gauge the impact it is having on the rhetoric of Exodus International, Jyl Josephson and I met at the West Shore Evangelical Free Church in Mechanicsburg, Pennsylvania, on September 22, 2012, to attend our second Love Won Out conference.

As background, for years many people and organizations have tried to distance themselves from the exuberant promises of transformation of sexual orientation that characterized the early ex-gay movement of the 1970s. For the past several years, Exodus President Alan Chambers has signaled his discomfort with the term, "ex-gay" and suggested that those who live with unwanted same-sex attraction might never be free of those attractions. Even so, I was not prepared for the session I attended at Exodus' International Freedom Conference in 2008, a remarkable "special interest group" workshop on "Sexual Orientation Research" led by psychologist Warren Throckmorton. Throckmorton, who has made his name in part by debunking various studies that purported to demonstrate a biological basis for same-sex sexual orientation, explained to attendees at the session that research in the few years before 2008 did, in his view, demonstrate that sexual orientation is likely to be a consequence of prenatal effects that are not a result of environment or social learning.

The research Throckmorton referred to in that session included brain imaging studies performed by J. Michael Bailey, with whom Throckmorton had shared a panel at a Catholic University School of Law symposium in 2007 entitled, What's the Story? A Multidisciplinary Discussion of Same-Sex Marriage and Religious Liberty.[73] They also included Scandinavian research using PET and MRI technology that found "responses to putative pheromones and objects of sexual attraction" to "differ between homo- and heterosexual subjects."[74] In his rejoinder to Bailey at the Catholic University symposium, Throckmorton referred to the theme of "congruence" between values and sexual behavior that was also a theme of the session he offered at Exodus. Suggesting that people with exclusive same-sex attraction are not likely to change the direction of their sexual desire, Throckmorton argued that what such people do with their sexuality is nevertheless a moral decision. But he also clarified the difficulty of such a struggle: "[Y]our brain tries to bully you into doing things you don't value," and "it's not a fair fight."[75] Since 2008, research into possible biological determinants of sexuality has continued, with the most recent study identifying inherited "epigenetic markers" as a potential explanation for homosexuality.[76]

It was clear from what I observed at the Throckmorton session on "Sexual Orientation Research" that many aspiring ex-gays were deeply distressed that their long-standing trust in the motto "change is possible" might have been misplaced. What has happened since that time, far from assuaging those who have waited—patiently or not—for *healing* from homosexuality, has challenged the movement at its foundations.[77] Speaking at the Exodus International Freedom Conference in St. Paul, Minnesota, Alan Chambers made a definitive statement that Exodus no longer would support or encourage reparative therapy or the aspiration for a "cure" for same-sex attraction.[78] The announcement and subsequent statements received heavy coverage in Christian and mainstream media.

In the midst of the uproar, the Mormon Church also staked out a new public position, urging "love and understanding" for people with what the Church now concedes may be immutable same-sex attractions.[79]

In addition to the departure of Exodus board members and affiliated ministries, a predictable institutional response to the deviations of Chambers and Exodus has been the establishment of a new organization, conceived as an alternative to Exodus. That new organization, The Restored Hope Network (RHN), held its debut meeting on September 21 and 22 in Fair Oaks, California, on the same weekend that Exodus was staging Love Won Out in Pennsylvania. Well-known ex-gay leaders, and former Exodus associates, forming the new organization include Andrew Comiskey (founder of Desert Stream Ministries, now located in Kansas City, Missouri), Frank Worthen (founder of New Hope Ministries), Stephen Black (founder of First Stone Ministries in Oklahoma City, Oklahoma), Anne Paulk (ex-lesbian spokesperson and star of a 1998 newspaper ad, "I'm Living Proof that Truth Can Set You Free"), and theology professor Robert Gagnon (who has issued a public call for a "change of leadership at Exodus").[80]

Although he spoke as usual at the Exodus Love Won Out event in Pennsylvania, Joe Dallas, author and founder of Genesis Counseling, is also a founder of the Restored Hope Network. Dallas supports reparative therapy and the aspiration of same-sex to heterosexual transformation. In the "Counseling Services" section of the Genesis Counseling website, under the heading, "Reclaiming Godly Sexuality" we find the following statement:

> In the book of Genesis we read that when God surveyed all He'd created—including the sexual union between man and wife—He declared it to be very good. But sin, both through its inborn nature and its practice, has perverted what was once good into something that has become a source of tremendous pain and confusion. What was lost needs to be found, which is why "Reclaiming Godly Sexuality" isn't just a saying at Genesis. It's the God-ordained goal our clients strive for. And it's our pleasure to partner with them as they achieve it.

At Love Won Out in Mechanicsburg, Dallas didn't make the case for reparative therapy or sexual orientation change but, instead, spoke sternly against our "sexually idolatrous times," "moral compromises" such as adultery and use of pornography among believers, and the hostility of many Christians toward same-sex-attracted people.[81] During the final substantive session of the conference, How Should We Respond? Dallas reminded attendees that although homophobia is "evil," the goal of believers shouldn't be peaceful coexistence with a world that violates believers' understanding of God's law.

The new slogan of Exodus International, on which we heard variations at the recent Love Won Out meeting, appears to be: "the opposite of homosexuality isn't heterosexuality; it's holiness." For many ministry participants this is a welcome shift—one that enables them to feel as though they belong in the ex-gay movement even if their sexual attractions never change. One of these is Julie Rodgers, who serves on the leadership team of Living Hope Ministries in Arlington, Texas, and who delivered the "female testimony" at the Love Won Out conference in Mechanicsburg. As is the custom for ex-gay meetings, speakers tell their story; hers was a story of growing up in a Christian family, suffering sexual abuse, and acting on her sexual attraction to women.

But Rodgers also clarified that her story was "not about [her] going from gay to straight" but about the "miracle" of being able to be "a source of hope to others" and "a heart beating with compassion."[82] Rodgers' testimony on the Exodus website is "Making Room: A Shift toward Compassion," a title that suggests a desire to seize the mantle of compassion from those who continue to tout the efficacy of reparative therapies. There, Rodgers explicitly addresses the controversial change in Exodus's mission and underscores its value for those with tenacious, unwanted same-sex attractions:

> What a relief it was to hear Alan Chambers say Exodus was making some changes: the circle was becoming wide enough for people like me! I began hearing him say the goal was a more intimate relationship with Christ, not heterosexual attraction. While many people *do* experience *some* shift in their attractions, a significant percentage of us don't. And that's okay. Jesus never promised that our temptations or desires would be removed when we began to follow Him. We can be sure that we'll be more conformed to His image, exude more of the Fruit of the Spirit, and experience a softening of our hearts as we lose ourselves in His great story of restoration. But I might be solely attracted to women until I meet Him face to face. Luckily heterosexual attractions are not a prerequisite for passionately loving Jesus . . . I've embraced this (and am thrilled that Exodus has as well).[83]

Not all strugglers have responded so enthusiastically to Exodus's new position on curing homosexuality. Based on what I observed at Dr. Throckmorton's workshop in 2008 and the fallout from the course change at Exodus, many who have put their hopes in the movement as a support for becoming fully functional heterosexuals feel betrayed by the erasure of the ultimate goal of a cure for homosexuality from Exodus's discourse and agenda. Disenchanted with Exodus, perhaps these who remain affiliated with the movement will gravitate to RHN or to some other ministry that explicitly holds out hopes of heterosexuality and an end to same-sex attractions to those who persevere. On his blog, Warren Throckmorton sums up the choice provided by the new ex-gay market segmentation in this way: "While I disagree with the change paradigm (and won't recommend RHN for anyone), I think it will be helpful to have a way to identify organizations who hold to it. Traditional evangelicals who want that approach can find it, whereas those who affirm the congruence paradigm within conservative circles will move more toward Exodus."[84] A more accurate representation of the choice between the "change paradigm" and the "congruence paradigm" in the ex-gay marketplace would be that both Exodus and the Restored Hope Network offer strugglers the opportunity to practice congruence between their conservative Christian faith and their sexual lives. It is just that in addition, the RHN promises strugglers the possibility of life as a heterosexual.[85]

An important innovation wrought by compassion campaigns is that both ex-gay and postabortion ministries have incorporated churches and congregations into the process of supporting the healing of postabortive women and same-sex-attracted people. In addition to support and resources, these ministries function as conduits for the ideologies of the movements with which they are affiliated, absorbing and inculcating particular contours of compassion, freedom, and repentance. As a result of the recent splintering of the movement over the issue of changing sexual orientation, it may be that individual churches and ministries seek out different allies with different beliefs about the likelihood that same-sex-attracted people can experience change of their sexuality. These realignments may, indeed, change configurations of compassion and how Christian conservatives—strugglers as well as others—understand their own callings and efforts to minister to same-sex-attracted women and men.

As increasing numbers of Christian conservatives have received a call to "reach out [to struggling homosexuals] in love," so have many Christian conservatives received a call to reach out to postabortive women. These antiabortion Christians have worked to set aside their anger and outrage over the "holocaust" of abortion to minister to women they see as broken and needy, especially because of a past abortion. This shift—to a focus on adults instead of fetuses and emotional pain instead of death—is a significant one. It constitutes a quite different face of prolife politics in the United States than the one with which most Americans are familiar from clashes over clinic access and from news reports about threats to, and attacks on, abortion providers. In chapter 2, I focus on postabortion ministries, the compassionate side of Christian conservative antiabortion activism. Postabortion ministries are a more recent phenomenon than ex-gay ministries, and there is little overlap between the corps of activists who staff the two. Nonetheless, together they constitute an organized infrastructure of compassion that touches the lives of those who extend compassion and those who receive it. The compassion of these campaigns, which we will examine more closely in the chapters to come, is also a vehicle for antigay and antiabortion ideology.

2

What about the Women?

Compassion in Postabortion Ministries

From Abomination to Compassion

The right to obtain a legal abortion is a highly charged cultural issue in American public life.¹ Both supporters and critics of the right to abortion are galvanized by public opinion polls that suggest that in some ways the public is ambivalent or nearly divided on the issue. In 2008 the Pew Forum released the results of a public opinion survey entitled "A Slight but Steady Majority Favors Keeping Abortion Legal: But Most Also Favor Restrictions." The survey reveals a consistent pattern of weak support for a right to abortion, and it also reveals less support among people under thirty than those in the fifty to sixty-four category and that "most Americans harbor concerns about the morality of abortion and favor certain restrictions on its use." In addition, survey respondents distinguish between the justifications women often give for obtaining an abortion, being more willing to support abortions in cases of rape and incest and when the mother may experience health complications than in cases of financial hardship or other personal circumstances.² Just one year later, in "Support for Abortion Slips," Pew found that the election of a prochoice president had hardened the prolife views of conservative voters and undermined support for abortion rights.³ In the case of abortion, there is an incentive for advocates on both sides of the issue to try to move public opinion at the same time they work to obtain favorable policy decisions.

Even after all the public discourse that has surrounded the 1973 Supreme Court decision in *Roe v. Wade,* it is important to look back at this turning point in American morality politics. The usual narrative about *Roe* is that the decision took social conservatives by surprise but quickly catalyzed the movement by bringing Christian conservatives together and out of their political isolation and despondency. But this familiar narrative is disputed. Citing Christian right entrepreneur Paul Weyrich's own narrative of Christian right mobilization, Randall Balmer argues that it was another Supreme Court decision—*Green v. Connally,* decided in 1972—that actually brought those who become the leaders of the New Christian right together to form the Moral Majority. *Green* involved the federal government's attempt to rescind the tax-exempt status of South Carolina's Bob Jones University because of its racially discriminatory policies.[4]

For Christian conservatives, this challenge to segregated private religious schools represented "an assault on the evangelical subculture," and, like earlier federal government challenges to policies of racial segregation and racialized second-class citizenship, it motivated a political response.[5] If the federal government persisted in micromanaging the discriminatory behavior of states, organizations, and private market actors, then those who saw discrimination as a social good—or at least as a prerogative of private associations—had no choice but to respond with political mobilization. The familiar story of Christian right mobilization, widely cultivated and disseminated, is that *Roe* constituted the final insult and challenge to traditional morality, after which Christian conservatives could stand no more and began to organize themselves. This narrative is undeniably more ethically attractive, reflects better on the motivations of Christian right leaders, and has been effective as a rallying point for a movement that has gotten its bearings primarily from morality struggles over abortion and LGBTQ rights.

Even if most Protestant conservatives didn't become involved in the struggle against abortion immediately after the Court decision, throughout the 1970s they did begin to join conservative Catholics and effectively set in motion the contemporary antiabortion movement.[6] Maturing in the 1980s, the movement ignored the harm to women caused by the criminalization of abortion and focused its attention on the harm to, and suffering of, fetuses to enlist followers to the cause and to mobilize activism.[7] The most prominent organization in the struggle has been Operation Rescue, which was founded by Randall Terry in 1986 and calls itself the "leading pro-life Christian activist organization in the nation."[8] Mark Allen Steiner traces the genealogy of Operation Rescue's theology and rhetoric, central to which is the conception among prolife believers that the Court's decision in *Roe* was sudden and unprecedented, a renunciation of virtue and an installation of "child-killing" that would provide "the basis for God's judgment upon the nation."[9] Steiner finds the key points of the organization's theology in a videotape titled *Operation Rescue*, produced in 1989. There viewers are challenged to acknowledge and rectify their "bloodguiltiness" as bystanders to the more than "twenty-five million children . . . brutally murdered" as a result of the *Roe* decision.[10]

In 1996 Angelia Wilson conducted an interview in Dallas with Philip "Flip" Benham, who was then the national director of successor organization Operation Rescue National, about his views and activities, the prolife movement, and abortion in American politics. His responses provide a primer to the dominant wing of the movement, its focus on the fetus, and its murder rhetoric—the antiabortion movement's version of ingroup abomination rhetoric. In the interview Benham describes "a fight between two seeds": "the seed of the serpent and the seed of the woman." Violent imagery is Benham's stock in trade, as he moves from Jesus nailed to the cross to Jesus crushing the "head of the serpent" to "violence savaging the streets" of America because of the triumph of the human worldview, the worldview instantiated by the "seed of the woman" that has abortion as one of its signs.[11] Using a comparison that has become familiar from such initiatives as the Genocide Awareness Project (GAP), Benham compares Americans' failure to intervene in the practice of abortion to what "the Nazis did in Germany with the extermination of the Jews." Referring to the case of Susan Smith, who drowned her two sons in a lake in 1994, he said: "I just want you to know that it happens 4,400 times in our nation every single day as mothers do that. [That woman] did hers a little later than most of the moms."[12]

In none of his lengthy responses to open-ended questions did Benham suggest any compassion for women who have undergone an abortion procedure. But he does bear affection for Norma McCorvey, the woman behind *Roe*. Enjoining Wilson not to ask McCorvey any questions, Benham introduced her to McCorvey, who went to work in the Operation Rescue office after her high-profile simultaneous conversions to Christianity and the prolife cause. In the interview, Benham points out that McCorvey, "who was used to usher in this horrible thing [abortion rights], never had an abortion. She is a professing, confessing Christian." It is worth noting that in spite of his absolutist position on abortion, Benham resolves the clash of abomination perspectives on abortion and same-sex sexuality by privileging his horror of homosexuality over his hatred of abortion. After Wilson turned off her tape recorder, and as she prepared to leave the interview with Benham, she asked him if he could imagine any situation in which he would consider abortion acceptable. He replied that he would support abortion if researchers ever discovered a gay gene.[13]

Many students of the antiabortion movement have chronicled the varieties of tactics and rhetorics that have been crafted and deployed by activists who operate within the abomination paradigm. These have included "sidewalk counseling" that often involves accusing pregnant women of murder or begging them not to kill their babies; blocking access to clinics; picketing clinic employees' homes; acquiring and publicizing personal information about clinic workers and women who seek abortion services; stalking and making anonymous threats; disseminating personalized Wanted posters featuring clinic employees; and bombing and vandalizing clinics.[14] Although most leaders in the antiabortion movement have publicly eschewed violence, some activists have killed or injured those they charge with murder because of their role in the "abortion industry." In her study of the underlying logic of "killing for life," Carol Mason traces the apocalyptic thinking that justifies murders of clinic personnel, a logic that received renewed attention in the wake of the murder of Dr. George Tiller in Wichita, Kansas, in May 2009.[15] And harassment and threats of violence, especially directed toward clinic staff members, "pay off" for the prolife movement by diminishing the availability of abortion.[16]

However, these unequivocal forms of abomination rhetorics and direct actions were not the first responses of those who disapproved of abortion. Indeed, as Mason points out, from the 1960s, when many states liberalized their abortion statutes, into the 1970s, many opponents did not even characterize abortion as murder, or at least as killing on a par with the murder of a person after birth.[17] These forms of belief and political commitment needed to be constructed by those who emerged as leaders of the movement in a way that would resonate with groups of constituents, and they also needed to be seamlessly integrated into theologies through public rhetoric and biblical interpretation. At the same time that many of the most threatening and intimidating tactics of the pro-life movement were debuting in public spaces such as the streets and sidewalks outside abortion clinics and the residences of clinic staff members, a very different kind of argument about abortion was already coming into existence. Unlike the antiabortion version of abomination rhetoric—the claim that abortion is child murder and the woman who aborts a pregnancy, a murderer—this new argument focused on the harm to women who undergo the procedure.

It's about the Women, Stupid

Liberalization of abortion laws in the United States in the 1960s and 1970s created new opportunities for American researchers to study the medical and psychological consequences of abortion. One important collection of this research, published before the legal and cultural battle over *Roe* began, is *The Abortion Experience: Psychological and Medical Impact*, edited by Howard J. Osofsky and Joy D. Osofsky and published in 1973.[18] Contributors to the volume include psychologists, social workers, and MDs in the fields of obstetrics, epidemiology, and psychiatry; most of their research is concentrated on the United States, though some chapters include cross-cultural comparison using abortion data from other nations. In a preface to the volume, the editors note both their support for abortion legalization and their goal of providing "careful research and objective data collection" on the effects of abortion on women. Artifacts of the era before the rise of a national antiabortion movement, the articles do not presage the battle to come by concluding that women who procure legal abortions suffer psychological trauma. Indeed, including in their analysis women who sought and were unable to obtain abortion, women who bore unwanted children, and women who underwent illegal abortion, the authors suggest a relatively salubrious outcome for women who undergo safe legal abortion at the same time that they call for more data and more studies of the subject.

Psychological arguments *against* abortion began to be developed by abortion rights foes during the Reagan era. In 1987, in the context of conversations with antiabortion movement leaders, President Reagan tasked Surgeon General C. Everett Koop to issue a report on the effects of abortion on women. Reagan had every reason to believe that Koop would be pleased with the assignment, which was intended to document scientifically the harms to women of having an abortion. As a practicing physician, Koop had spoken out against abortion, and his 1981 confirmation hearings had been contentious because of his uncompromising prolife views. However, Koop disappointed both the president and the antiabortion movement by declining to issue the report that Reagan anticipated.

Instead of a formal report, in January 1989 Koop sent the president a letter in which he briefly summarized the landscape of the social struggle over abortion and the problems with gathering the kind of data that would answer Reagan's question definitively. "At this time," he concluded, "the available scientific evidence about the psychological sequelae of abortion simply cannot support either the preconceived beliefs of those pro-life or of those pro-choice."[19] Koop also outlined for the president what a valid scientific study of the mental and physical health effects on women of abortion would look like and what the likely cost of such a study would be. For his refusal to produce the kind of report Reagan and antiabortion leaders sought, Koop was vilified by the political right.

In fact, for conservatives, this was the second of Koop's major failures. In 1986 he had produced a brochure on HIV/AIDS that was medically accurate and that outlined methods of AIDS prevention beyond sexual abstinence. The brochure was mailed to all US households, as well as distributed to military personnel and to people incarcerated in American prisons.[20] Conservatives in organizations such as Concerned Women for America and the Southern Baptist Convention responded with outrage. When Koop refused to issue a report that might serve as a basis for overturning *Roe*, conservative activists speculated that he did not wish to be drawn back into bruising battles over abortion, but they were already disenchanted with the surgeon general. In contrast, many pro-choice advocates lauded Koop's intellectual integrity and took his rejoinder to the president as evidence that abortion is not a psychologically perilous procedure for women. Taking a less political perspective on the imbroglio, many medical researchers insisted that Koop's letter falsified the scientific evidence for women's well-being after abortion by ignoring conclusions from multiple studies that found no significant mental health threat from abortion.[21]

Oddly, the postscript to the stand-off over a report on the psychological sequelae of abortion was that the surgeon general's office did produce and issue a "Koop Report." Koop did not endorse the report, which in his view lacked scientific credibility, and in testimony before a House subcommittee he confirmed the views he had put forth in his letter to Reagan.[22] In retrospect, and whatever its dubious provenance, the Koop Report and the controversy surrounding was an important episode in the development of the post-abortion strategy of focusing on women and women's well-being. In other venues, outside the policy process of the US government, the development of this strategy was already underway.

A key progenitor and exponent of this new argument of abortion's harm to women is David C. Reardon, author of numerous prolife books and director of the Elliot Institute, a nonprofit postabortion organization dedicated to disseminating information on the negative effects of abortion on women. Reardon's first book, *Aborted Women: Silent No More*, was published in same year that President Reagan asked Koop to report on the effects of abortion on women, and it provided a different language for the prolife movement than the dominant rhetoric of abomination. According to Reardon, an "aborted woman" was "1: one of the class of women whose lives have been permanently altered by the experience of abortion 2: a woman who experiences self-alienation because of her ambivalence over terminating an unwanted pregnancy 3: a woman who, after an abortion, feels aborted herself, physically, psychologically, socially, and spiritually."[23]

In *Aborted Women*, Reardon teamed with the organization Women Exploited by Abortion (WEBA) to produce a compelling collective portrait of women harmed by abortion.[24] While he surveys both physical and psychological effects of abortion, Reardon's greatest contribution, in *Aborted Women*, and in later works, is to shift the frame of antiabortion discourse to a focus on the negative psychological effects of abortion for women. He accomplishes this reframing through the use of surveys and testimonies, but also by systematically confronting every prochoice argument and refuting it. For example, reflecting on the "hard" cases that are more likely to incite sympathy for an abortion decision—the need to save the life of the mother, rape or incest, or to prevent the birth of a severely disabled child—Reardon argues that these are the very kinds of abortion decisions that best predict postabortion mental health problems. Thus, compassionate citizens are bound by empirical evidence to use abortion hard cases as justifications for outlawing the procedure.[25]

While *Aborted Women* concentrates on firsthand testimony and the compassionate case for criminalizing abortion, *Making Abortion Rare* is a handbook for reconstituting the activist and policy arena of abortion politics. In his early book, Reardon rests the blame for abortion on "upper-class males who have dominated politics and the judiciary" and promises that as more women become involved in politics the false "freedom" of abortion rights, "imposed on women by men," will be repudiated.[26] In *Making Abortion Rare*, Reardon outlines a more politically savvy argument that focuses on using the tools of a prowoman approach to persuade the "ambivalent" or "middle majority" of the evil of abortion. The contemporary postabortion movement owes much to Reardon and his associates for the compassionate language, the research literature, and the policy articulations the movement relies on today.

In antiabortion discourse, as in antigay discourse, there is no neat "before" and "after" binary that relegates the abomination narrative to a time before a more sophisticated and obfuscating compassion narrative took hold. Instead, the abomination approach and rhetoric survives in a variety of settings and projects while compassion rhetoric mingles with it, sometimes partially displaces it, and signals to observers that therapeutic and political sides of the movement do different kinds of work in the struggle against abortion rights. The genealogy of antiabortion discourse and politics is not so much a shift from condemnation to compassion as a new bifurcation of discourse in which condemnation changes shape and compassion becomes a viable alternative foundation of the movement.

Although these two antiabortion narratives usually coexist as social and political alternatives, they can also conflict. While Reardon rebukes his comrades in the movement for their "exaggerated focus exclusively on the unborn child," some prolife advocates who emphasize the immorality of abortion as the killing of a human person believe that those who focus on the suffering and healing of women sidestep the moral core of the issue.[27] The most rigorous critic of the "new rhetorical strategy (NRS)" of harm to women is the philosopher Francis Beckwith, who subjects proponents' arguments to careful analysis and finds flaws in their assumptions, uses of social science data, and orientation toward moral philosophy. One aspect of Beckwith's withering critique focuses on the appeal to women's self-interest that's implicit in the compassionate approach. Responding to an "NRS" proponent, Beckwith declares that

> Nurturing an apparently unprincipled self-interested populace does not seem consistent with what pro-life activists would conceive as a pro-life culture, even if it results in fewer abortions. After all, [Paul] Swope and his allies admit that what is doing much of the moral work in the minds of women contemplating abortion is self-interest. Given that admission, it is not clear why they see that as a character trait to massage rather than as an impulse that needs to be disciplined by the exercise of moral judgment. Since the pro-life position affirms that one ought not to have an abortion in virtually every circumstance even if you judge it to be in your self-interest, it seems counterintuitive for the defenders of NRS to want to provide a cultural environment hospitable to the moral primacy of self-interest.[28]

For critics such as Beckwith, compassion for women is a poor foundation for the antiabortion movement even if it does work to diminish the number of abortions performed.

But Beckwith's objections were too recondite to function as guidelines for the prolife movement. Within the movement, psychological diagnosis and spiritual conviction have combined to propel a strategy of compassion for women that constitutes the other side of the antiabortion movement. That the diagnosis of "postabortion syndrome" is socially, rather than medically, conferred has not daunted those who embrace it. Indeed, in the case of postabortion syndrome the fact that medical and other authorities have not legitimated the diagnosis places it in the realm of "stigmatized knowledge."[29] This is not a deterrent to proponents of the syndrome, who are accustomed to developing knowledge claims in opposition to established authorities they understand as biased against biblical morality. However, when it comes to postabortion syndrome the irony is that advocates badly want the imprimatur of science on the diagnosis. And this struggle over what constitutes good medical science continues to the present.

Postabortion Syndrome

Antiabortion compassion is grounded in two arguments: first, that women who undergo abortion suffer from a kind of posttraumatic stress disorder (PTSD) and second, that as a result of this demonstrable harm to women, abortion should be outlawed. First named postabortion syndrome (PAS) in 1981, the checklist of responses advocates associate with the condition includes (but is not limited to): extreme sadness, anxiety, guilt, depression, flashbacks, a sense of hopelessness, low self-esteem, distrustfulness, substance abuse, impaired relationships, and propensity to self-harm and/or suicide.[30] Usually a checklist of symptoms is accompanied by the spiritual message that forgiveness and healing are available through repentance and a personal relationship with Jesus Christ, but the message can be rendered in more or less secular ways, depending on the context and audience. Because the syndrome is not recognized by the mental health profession, lay advocates diagnose themselves and others, finding in all who come forward with testimonies of postabortive distress some sign of the condition.

Since the 1980s a huge literature on the question of the mental health effects from abortion has accumulated. During the twilight of the Reagan administration, and under the influence of the public debates of the period, the American Psychological Association convened a panel of members to examine data that could be gleaned from relevant studies going back to the 1970s. The panel concluded in 1990 that there was no support for PAS.[31] However, it was only in the 1990s that proponents of PAS began to transform the antiabortion movement by using the syndrome and the argument for abortion's effects on women as a new social and political strategy. Thus, far from putting the matter of PAS to rest, statements such as the 1990 APA report confirmed for PAS proponents that educated prochoice professionals were firmly in control of elite discourse on abortion. In 2004 the APA released the "Briefing Paper on the Impact of Abortion on Women," in which it took what critics understood to be a political position: "that the ability of women to make decisions about their own childbearing (e.g., timing) is a necessary condition for their health and mental health, as well as for their families.' "[32] The paper denied negative mental health effects on women from abortion, finding that women tend to experience more stress before an abortion than after it and that "preexisting emotional problems" are at the root of postabortive mental health issues for women who experience them.

However, the Christian right received support from an unlikely quarter in 2006 when psychologists David M. Fergusson, L. John Horwood, and Elizabeth M. Ridder published an article that analyzed long-term "adverse mental health effects" as a result of abortion in young women. Using data from a twenty-five-year longitudinal study of New Zealanders, and analyzing data from other researchers, including David Reardon and his colleagues, the authors concluded that "abortion in young women may be associated with increased risks of mental health problems."[33] The article received intense scrutiny from Christian right proponents of PAS, not only because its findings confirmed those of prolife researchers but also because the authors explicitly criticized the APA for crafting a statement that overstated expert certainty about the emotional consequences of abortion.

After publication of the Fergusson study, the American Psychological Association pulled its "Briefing Paper on the Impact of Abortion" from its website, and Christian right organizations waited to see how the APA would respond. The answer came in 2008, when the APA posted its new "Report of the APA Task Force on Mental Health and Abortion." The report was a product of the APA Task Force on Mental Health and Abortion (the Task Force) and ran ninety-one pages. In it, the Task Force surveyed the literature going back to 1989, including the Fergusson study, and concluded that the research does not support a conclusion that "an observed association between abortion history and mental health was caused by the abortion *per se*, as opposed to other factors." Besides highlighting methodological problems in previous research, some "severe," the Task Force emphasized the importance of "taking pregnancy intendedness and wantedness into account."[34]

Christian right leaders struck back immediately after the new report was published. The Family Research Council (FRC) criticized the report in a statement and distributed email alerts to FRC members that impugned the APA for poor research and liberal politics. In an interview with anti-gay and prolife psychologist Warren Throckmorton, David Fergusson, who served as a reviewer for the report before its publication, noted that the Task Force had "drawn strong conclusions on the basis of weak evidence." Fergusson recommended that, in the absence of the kind of research that could settle the issue of abortion's harm to women once and for all, psychologists should forbear from drawing the possibly erroneous conclusion that abortion *does not* harm women. What is striking about the furor is that even though twenty years have passed since C. Everett Koop claimed that extant science could not definitively make the case for abortion's harm to women and called for more research, the positions of those on either side of the debate have hardly changed at all.

What has changed since the 1980s is that in many quarters PAS now is taken as a fact; information about the condition is readily available from Christian right antiabortion websites and publications. Many of these publications are constructed to mimic scientific sources. The National Right to Life (NRL) Educational Trust Fund publishes a small booklet, entitled "Abortion: Some Medical Facts," that looks like the kind of booklet a patient might pick up in a hospital. The only decoration on the cover is a caduceus—a winged staff surrounded by intertwined snakes—that most readers are likely to identify with the medical profession. Each section is illustrated with a medical clip art image: pills, needles, or surgical instruments. The website Abortion Facts makes the scientific case for the existence of PAS and highlights the refusal of mainstream medical researchers and associations to confirm it as a medical syndrome.[35] Sources that address the absence of a medico-scientific imprimatur explain the disjunction between prolife and scientific opinion on PAS as a function either of liberal cultural elitism or of the stranglehold of the "abortion industry" or prochoice views on the media and educational institutions. Others avoid political recriminations and simply address themselves to their audience, laying out the tenets of PAS and giving listeners a vocabulary with which to express feelings. It is these feelings that Emily Bazelon related in her 2007 *New York Times* article, "Is There a Post-Abortion Syndrome?"

Bazelon talked with Rhonda Arias, who calls herself an "abortion-recovery counsellor" and ministers to women in prison who have had an abortion. After considering the women who respond to the finding of PAS and the history of the syndrome, Bazelon concludes by saying that "there is the relief in seizing on a single clear explanation for a host of unwanted and overwhelming feelings, a cause for everything gone wrong. When Arias surveyed 104 of the prisoners she had counselled in 2004, two-thirds reported depression related to abortion, 32 percent reported suicide attempts related to abortion and 84 percent linked substance abuse to their abortions. They had a new key for unlocking themselves. And a way to make things right." Bazelon quotes psychologist Brenda Major on what PAS does for women: "The therapists and crusaders offer a diagnosis that gives meaning to the symptoms, and that gives the women a way to repent. You can't repent depressive symptoms. But you can repent an action." Major is the chair of the APA's 2008 Report on Mental Health and Abortion, and Christian right critics accuse her and other frequent debunkers of PAS, such as fellow Task Force member Nancy Russo, of feminist ideological commitments that make it impossible for them to be objective on the subject of abortion's harm to women.

In fact, a subset of academic researchers is concerned with harm to women related to abortion but not with the kind of harm abortion opponents would affirm. These researchers study abortion stigma, defined by one team of scholars as "a negative attribute ascribed to women who seek to terminate a pregnancy" that marks these women "as inferior to ideals of womanhood." Anuradha Kumar, Leila Hessini, and Ellen M. H. Mitchell argue that abortion violates three particular "cherished 'feminine' ideals: "perpetual fecundity; the inevitability of motherhood; and instinctive nurturing." Although the specific forms abortion stigma takes depend on local conditions—including social attitudes, modes of access to reproductive services, and gendered power relations—Kumar and her colleagues argue that its broad consequence is predictable: abortion stigma is associated with "negative health outcomes" for women.[36] Scholars investigate many dimensions of the consequences for women of abortion stigma, including the psychological effects of concealing abortion and the stigma-mitigating effects of social support for an abortion decision.[37]

But it is not just the mental health establishment that is biased on the subject of postabortion effects, according to proponents of PAS. Even secular sources outside the medical profession that acknowledge that some women may experience negative psychological effects from an abortion decision come in for criticism because of their prochoice politics. In February 2009, *Glamour* magazine published an article in which eight women out of more than two dozen interviewed were invited to contribute their answer to the question, What was the abortion experience like for you? Though the personal stories vary, none of the published accounts reflects a belief in PAS or the conviction that postabortive women need to repent their decision in order to experience forgiveness. In addition, as PAS advocates point out, the support organizations mentioned in the article—"resources that can help women navigate this choice"—are all prochoice groups, including the National Abortion Rights Action League (NARAL Pro-Choice America) and Exhale.[38]

In terms of the politics not only of PAS but also of compassion, Exhale is fascinating because it is a compassionate project that acknowledges the possibility that women may experience sadness, grief, or guilt, as well as relief, after an abortion. Founded in 2000, Exhale launched its "pro-voice movement"—a talkline for women who have had abortions—in 2002. The counselling model adopted by Exhale "respects the cultural, social and religious beliefs of all callers"; although "most, though not all" of the founders of the group were prochoice, the organization does not impose a particular interpretation of abortion or a particular conception of what kinds of effects women may experience after an abortion. Exhale founders acknowledge that women may self-diagnose, or be "diagnosed," as suffering from PAS; they implicitly criticize the PAS diagnosis, noting that whether or not a woman identifies as someone with PAS, "having feelings about a significant life event doesn't mean that you have a major psychological condition that requires medical care. For many women, naming and expressing their emotions, and having the space and support to do so, can be more empowering than being identified as having a disorder. Whether or not you think you have PASS [postabortion stress syndrome], the most important thing is that you get support for what you're feeling, not what someone else thinks you should be feeling." This gently skeptical passage about PAS on Exhale's website is accompanied by a more direct rejoinder to Christian conservatives who champion the diagnosis: "Exhale follows the findings of the American Psychological Association, which has not found a link between feelings that follow an abortion and a psychological condition in need of medical care."[39] Not only does Exhale leave the choice to have an abortion up to women, but it also looks for its foundational principles to the very secular establishment that Christian conservatives charge with ignoring science and undermining women's well-being. For postabortion ministries, it's the wrong kind of compassionate project with the wrong politics, at least for the Christian right. Better, from the perspective of Christian conservatives, is the nonprofit infrastructure that combines compassion for pregnant women with the determination to encourage those women to carry their pregnancies to term. Because this nonprofit sector serves the purpose of preventing abortion, it combines two mandates that prolife advocates believe never should come into conflict: saving the lives of children and protecting mothers' psychological health.

Compassion before Abortion

The nonprofit sector dedicated to persuading women to carry pregnancies to term goes by a variety of names, including crisis pregnancy centers, women's help centers, pregnancy help centers, pregnancy resource centers, pregnancy decision health centers, and a variety of unique names that may sow confusion about the differences between these destinations and those that offer women the option of an abortion. Although they came into existence in the 1960s, these centers expanded and attracted wider attention starting in the 1980s, and in 2006 they were the object of a high-profile congressional investigation of their practices led by Representative Henry Waxman (D-CA).[40] Today centers are more likely to bear generic names that do not advertise the solution to a "crisis"; however, in referring to them in general I will use the term "crisis pregnancy centers" because it has been a common designator and because it has been used recently in literature generated inside the antiabortion movement.[41]

A 2006 National Abortion Federation (NAF) report on crisis pregnancy centers defined the centers as "exist[ing] to keep women from having abortions." Of course, this is the opposition's reading of the justification for the centers, but it diverges from prolife activists' own understanding primarily in its omission of theological and emotional context.[42] Ellen Curro, a former director of the Crisis Pregnancy Center in Laurel, Maryland, describes these centers as situated in a "marketplace where women are hurting and babies' lives are being threatened" and writes that those who work in these centers "beg God to send the abortion-minded women to us" so that "the tiny baby inside her" has "a chance to live."[43] Chronicler of the movement Terry Ianora confirms that "our first priority is saving all unborn babies from abortion."[44]

As critics, including the NAF, report, the commission to prevent women from having abortions has been executed in a variety of ways, including using nomenclature for centers that suggests the availability of medical treatments, including abortion; designing office spaces to mimic those of a medical facility; equipping nonmedical staff with white medical jackets; locating offices near facilities that provide abortions; disguising the religious provenance of centers; and furnishing, in the title phrase of the Waxman report, "false and misleading health information" about the medical and psychological effects of abortion for women. During the George W. Bush administration, both states and the federal government began to provide direct support for crisis pregnancy centers through, for example, funds allocated for abstinence-only education and revenue raised by state specialty license plates with the "Choose Life" or "Respect Life" caption.[45]

Many scholars who have studied the antiabortion movement have listened to the voices of prolife women, especially those who have been involved in some form of public activism.[46] Unlike the direct action side of the prolife movement, in which men have held more prominent leadership roles in addition to being visible activists, postabortion ministries have usually had a female face even when these ministries originate in or are linked to organizations with quite different goals and tactics. For example, the postabortion ministry Silent No More Awareness is a project of NOEL and Priests for Life. NOEL was originally an acronym for National Organization of Episcopalians for Life, although it has been renamed Anglicans for Life. The director of Priests for Life, Father Frank Pavone, is a frequent speaker at Christian right and antiabortion events and practices the rhetoric of abomination about abortion, including displaying "pictures of aborted babies" on the Priests for Life website and at Christian right venues.[47] Although women also participate vigorously in the direct action side of the movement that proclaims abortion to be the murder of a child, the compassion of postabortion ministries is coded as feminine.

So too is the labor in crisis pregnancy centers, where clients meet one-on-one with women volunteers or paid staff who administer pregnancy tests, and sometimes ultrasounds, and counsel women to carry pregnancies to term. Dedicated as they are to preventing the killing of preborn children, crisis pregnancy centers are not compassionate projects of the same kind as postabortion ministries, but they do share some features. In both contexts, engagement and attunement with individuals are central dimensions of the activism; in both an ethos of caring or compassion is widely understood to be the justification for the existence of such ministries. The gendered nature of antiabortion compassion is consistent with Carol J. C. Maxwell's findings on the gendering of antiabortion activists' motivations, including masculine themes of war and abortion as a threat to the nation and feminine themes of "expressions of gratitude to God [and] reflections of their love for God." Maxwell notes that women activists she interviewed were much more likely than men to cite their own experiences with abortion and their concern that women were being coerced into having abortions.[48]

In addition to the need to prevent the killing of children, themes of love and the desire to prevent harm to women are conspicuous in the literature of crisis pregnancy centers. Curro's book, *Caring Enough to Help: Counseling at a Crisis Pregnancy Center*, is written in epistolary form, as a series of letters to her sister on different topics and motifs that, by extension, are addressed to "[her] sisters and brothers everywhere." Writing of "discouragement" as a "temptation" sent by "the devil" in the struggle against abortion, Curro asserts that "the majority of [crisis pregnancy center] volunteers have great gifts of mercy and compassion. . . . [and] tender hearts for the wounded, the suffering, and the oppressed." Volunteers are "compassionate, caring people" whom Curro believes "would rather die than see that mother and baby undergo an abortion." Addressing readers directly at the end of her book, Curro describes crisis pregnancy center workers as "wonderfully compassionate giving saints who make substantial sacrifices of their time, money, and energies to be available to those in crisis," and she quotes her pastor, defining "compassion as 'helping one's heart around the corner.'" To those who might be skeptical about workers' compassion extending beyond the embryo or fetus that might be saved from abortion, Curro declares that "those of us working in crisis pregnancy center[s] can't be there just to save babies—that we must first be able to love women in crisis."[49]

Besides encouraging women to continue pregnancies, centers often also distribute literature that addresses "abortion after-care," or situations in which the question of how to deal with a pregnancy is no longer at issue. This literature may include a hotline number for those "hurting because of a past abortion decision" as well as information on PAS. The closest crisis pregnancy center to Ohio State University is the campus Pregnancy Decision Health Center at the corner of High Street and Seventeenth Avenue, just down the street from my office in the Department of Women's, Gender, and Sexuality Studies. It consists of a small second-floor office with a waiting room filled with toys and brochures, most of which address questions about pregnancy. The center's one brochure geared to postabortive women and men is consistent with other literature produced within postabortion ministries. It advertises a "free, Biblically-based seven week support group called H.E.A.R.T. (Healing the Effects of Abortion Related Trauma)." Explaining PAS, the brochure lists ten symptoms—shame, sadness/sorrow, secrecy, feelings of loss, anxiety, isolation, regret/guilt, anger/rage, suicidal impulses, and self-destructive behavior—and claims that any one or more of these is a sign of PAS and of the need to "come to peace with God and others in relationship to the abortion experience."

While for critics of the crisis pregnancy center movement, the centers are primarily foci of deceptive advertising and the dissemination of false information about contraception, pregnancy, abortion and the sequelae of abortion, for prolife activists and center workers they are spaces in which "compassionate friends" devote affective labor to the cause of preventing harm.[50] Unlike crisis pregnancy centers, postabortion ministries are not constructed to serve pregnant women or—at least in any immediate sense—to prevent women from procuring an abortion. As a result, the mandate to serve women is not subordinate or ulterior to the goal of preventing abortion. Women are the primary focus and constituency for these ministries, which constitute an unambiguously compassionate domain of the prolife movement.

Helping Hurting Women

Antiabortion cultural politics is complicated. The abomination narrative of the murder of the innocent coexists with a narrative of abortion's harm to women, men, and families. The public faces of this second, compassionate, form of antiabortion politics are those of women who have had abortions and their male partners. Today, the more punitive movement slogans, "abortion is murder," "abortion stops a beating heart," "it's (she's) not a choice, it's a child" are deemphasized by leaders and activists in the postabortion movement in certain contexts in favor of slogans that are crafted to appeal to pregnant women and/or to women who have had an abortion in the past. These newer slogans—"you gave us a choice, now hear our voice: abortion hurts women," "women hurt by abortion," "hurting from abortion?" "helping/healing hurting women"—avoid assigning blame to individual women. Yet another category of slogans seems to constitute a bridge between these two categories of narratives: "one dead, one wounded;" "every abortion has two victims." These slogans blame the woman who has an abortion for the murder of an innocent while reminding her and others that she is also a victim.

All these kinds of slogans and orientations are evident in diverse venues, such as the annual March for Life, which attracts different antiabortion constituencies to the Mall and adjacent areas of Washington, DC, on January 22 every year to demonstrate against the Court decision in *Roe*. This large public event features a wide range of rhetorics about abortion. In 2008, many of the slogans on signs held aloft by participants broadcast abomination rhetoric, although the single most common sign, sponsored by the Knights of Columbus, used the understated slogan, "Defend Life." Others were not as indirect: "no death penalty for the unborn (or anyone)"; "abortion is homicide"; "abortion stops a beating [heart symbol]"; "face it/ abortion kills"; "abortion neat, quick, easy way out . . . for men"; "47,000,000+babies missing"; "the democratic party/ the party of death"; "pro choice=pro death"; "abortion: the leading cause of death in America"; "abortion is a dead end"; "abortion b murder"; "abortion sucks the life out of you"; "doesn't everyone deserve a birthday?"; "stop killing babies"; "abortion America's holocaust (with swastikas in the "o"s of "abortion"); "mommy let me live"; "America why are you afraid of me? [featuring a picture of a baby]"; "If Mary had been pro-choice we wouldn't have Christmas"; and "give life don't take it."

Some speakers split the difference between abomination and compassion, noting, for example, the "two victims in every abortion" and that abortion is "death to children and the exploitation of women." I suspect that in cases where these rhetorics are mixed, the death/abomination message trumps the message of compassion for women both because of the force of negative imagery—the rally included pictures of aborted fetuses that are common in such settings—and because antiabortion followers historically have been primed for abomination rhetoric in ways that they have not been primed for compassion rhetoric. In addition to these mixed messages, however, there were some messages of compassion that did not remind viewers of the death of a fetus. These included signs that said, "abortion hurts women" and "hurting after abortion."

The most significant venue for compassion in the 2008 March for Life was a segregated time and space away from the rally on the Mall—the sidewalk in front of the Supreme Court building. The event was sponsored by the Silent No More Awareness Campaign, which engages in public outreach and travels to different cities in the United States, United Kingdom, and Canada to encourage women to share their personal testimonies of regret over their own abortion decision. Public gatherings organized by the group feature women holding signs that say, "I regret my abortion." Those who concur with the values and aspirations of Silent No More can also purchase merchandise that advertises their beliefs: banners, book marks, bumper stickers, t-shirts, magnets, and other goods display the slogans, "I Regret my Abortion," "Women *Do* Regret Abortion," and "I Regret Lost Fatherhood."[51] Unlike slogans of abomination campaigns, these have in common their undeviating focus on adults touched by a past abortion decision.

At the Silent No More speakout I attended, the testimonies of those who came to the microphone emphasized that abortions cause life-long pain to the women who have them and that the unborn children are still alive and one day will be reunited with their mothers. Women shared the practice of naming their fetuses. Speakers reflected on invariant and complementary gender roles. Women are nurturers, and abortion violates the natural yearning of women for children; men are protectors, and men who acquiesce in abortion violate their natural role as the protectors of women and children. One man declared that "a mother's love for her child is stamped into her heart by God" and used the language scripted by Silent No More to describe the "pain of [his] lost fatherhood."[52]

By the time of the 2010 March for Life the compassion rhetoric of Silent No More Awareness was even more in evidence. Signs that carried the message "Women *Do* Regret Abortion"—and, on the reverse, "Men Regret Lost Fatherhood"—were visible throughout the rally because the organization had produced them in the tens of thousands and made them widely available even to groups with no direct affiliation to the Silent No More Awareness Campaign. With a pro-choice president in office, the 2010 March and rally also featured messages crafted to the politics of the moment and to Obama's putative disdain for Life. One arresting sign noted: "Obama's mama *Saved/* Attorney son *Kills,*" and on the reverse side, "Obama's mother *Saved* him/ Yet he kills others." Referring to comments Obama made at Pastor Rick Warren's Saddleback Church Forum on Leadership and Compassion in July, 2008, one sign read: "President Obama/ Rise above your pay grade/ The question is not, 'When does life begin'/ But/ When does love begin?/ THE Audicity [sic] of Love." However, in spite of the full integration of compassion rhetoric and groups into the antiabortion movement, abomination rhetoric has not lost its sway. Buoyed by recent signs that the antiabortion movement is gaining adherents, Representative Scott Garrett (R-NJ) enthusiastically addressed the crowd assembled on the Mall in 2010 with this line: "Let us now shout out loud . . . that abortion is murder."

One common mode of advocacy at events such as the March on Washington is public testimony. Testimonies solicited in church and activist settings are likely to adhere to certain narrative conventions. In her excellent study of prochoice and prolife activism in Fargo, North Dakota, in the 1980s, Faye Ginsburg found patterns of plot, discourse, and counterdiscourse that illuminated opposing conceptualizations of "reproduction and nurturance."[53] Similar, though less comprehensive, patterns emerge in the testimonies of "aborted women" in Silent No More. A significant convention is the foreclosure of abomination rhetoric directed at women. Women who speak decry their sinful selves but project blame onto immoral abortionists whom they describe as physically brutal, verbally and emotionally abusive, and driven by the profit motive. This last descriptor is popular in the movement and is found, for example, in David Reardon's writings; physicians who perform abortions are routinely described both as profiteers and as incompetent doctors. In addition, the women describe and appeal to fully developed and living children: "I expelled a tiny human being with an immortal soul who already possessed the capacity to love"; "I had to find my children and seek their forgiveness."[54] Considered in the context of dominant forms of abomination rhetoric that fetishize the dead child, this insistence on the still and always living child is striking. In the compassionate scene, the woman is not a murderer but a forgiven sinner; her child is not dead but alive and awaiting reunion with her.

Project Rachel, some of whose supporters have attended recent marches on Washington, offers this compassionate construction of mother and child. With its slogan, "There Is Hope after Abortion," Rachel describes itself as the "post-abortion ministry of the Catholic Church," but neither the psychology it espouses nor its use of personal testimonies distinguishes it from similar projects with different theological foundations. Indeed, most of the personal stories on the Project Rachel website originated with David Reardon's Elliot Institute.[55] In late 2008 and early 2009, Project Rachel ads with the message, "hope after abortion" and contact information appeared in the Washington, DC, metrorail system, a space in the nation's capital that has also hosted ex-gay ads because it is ideal for reaching people who are involved in the policy process.[56]

Personal testimonies attest to the aftermath of an abortion decision and implicitly represent the signatory's support for revoking the right to obtain an abortion. Groups such as Silent No More, the Elliot Institute, and others collect and use personal testimonies in a variety of ways that go beyond encouraging other postabortive women and men to identify with the diagnosis of PAS and to support postabortion ministries. For example, the Justice Foundation, a conservative prolife, legal nonprofit organization, submits personal testimonies such as those collected by postabortion ministries with amicus briefs in court cases or to state legislatures considering laws that would limit or ban abortions.[57] In the 2007 Supreme Court case that upheld the Partial-Birth Abortion Ban Act, *Gonzales v. Carhart*, Justice Anthony Kennedy cited such testimonies and concluded that "severe depression and loss of esteem" were risks of abortion.[58]

Whether the objects of concern are babies in the womb, pregnant women, or postabortive women, antiabortion Christian conservatives understand themselves as defending the cause of the helpless and vulnerable. For them, feminists are committed to an agenda of death and the destruction of the natural family. The accusation that feminists don't really care about pregnant women but, rather, use these women for their own political ends is not just the property of the compassionate side of the antiabortion rights movement. The charge of women's movement cynicism has been around throughout the life of the antiabortion movement. The charge often has been supplemented with the accusation or implication that lesbians are behind the abortion rights movement. In her recent book on the "abortion wars," Carole Joffe notes that protesters outside abortion clinics sometimes have reviled clinic patients by calling them lesbians.[59] A crude version of this accusation was Pat Robertson's infamous 1992 claim that feminists aimed to encourage women to "kill their children" and "become lesbians."[60] But the charge itself comes in many varieties, including that gay rights activists need the abortion rights movement to disseminate their self-interested ideology of "my rights, my body, my choice."[61]

However, the claim that proabortion rights feminists use women to accomplish their goals gained traction after Norma McCorvey went from being an abortion-rights activist to being an antiabortion-rights conservative evangelical. After her conversion, McCorvey—who lived for some time in a same-sex relationship—garnered media attention when she claimed that she had been used by the abortion rights movement to advance its agenda without concern for her well-being.[62] By all accounts, McCorvey knows she is an attractive prolife convert and spokesperson because of her abortion rights celebrity, but since her 1995 conversion she has consistently maintained that it is the prochoice community, including her attorney, Sarah Weddington, that used her for its own purposes.

Through postabortion ministries the Christian right currently is focused on taking up the cause of vulnerable women in a variety of ways. General purpose Christian right organizations such as Concerned Women for America, single issue groups such as the Elliot Institute, and activists disseminate well-coordinated critiques of abortion practice. These include poor regulation in the "abortion industry"; the failure of abortion providers fully to warn women about the medical risks associated with abortion (including a link between abortion and breast cancer that is not supported by medical research); and the probability that women are coerced into abortion by boyfriends or relatives.

Antiabortion leaders and activists consistently express concern about the vulnerability of poor women and women of color to abortion, and African American women receive particular attention. Two links connect racism and abortion in the ideology of post-abortion ministries. The first link is the argument that the foundation of the abortion rights movement was laid by the racist and eugenicist beliefs of the founder of Planned Parenthood, Margaret Sanger. The second is the conviction that the contemporary abortion rights movement is actively racist, a conviction that's been vindicated for Christian conservatives by the willingness of targeted Planned Parenthood offices in several states to accept anonymous contributions for abortions of "black babies" from antiabortion activists posing as donors.[63] In her study of African American women's reproductive rights, Dorothy Roberts traces the deep concern in the black community throughout the twentieth century with birth control and abortion being wielded by white people and institutions against African Americans.[64] Although many African American women leaders and organizations have supported the availability of birth control and safe, legal abortion, the vulnerability of black women to abortion has been a consistent theme of the majority-white antiabortion movement. In her personal account of work in a crisis pregnancy center, Ellen Curro writes of speaking at an all-male Catholic high school with a predominantly African American student body and pointing out to the students that "abortion is a great way to eliminate blacks"—a perspective on abortion that she reports "was news to most of them."[65]

One tactic of postabortion ministries that has migrated to the broader Christian right's antiabortion movement is reframing the decision to have an abortion in passive terms so that it is common now to hear of women "submitting" to abortion or being "victims of abortion" instead of women actively choosing or soliciting an abortion from a doctor or clinic. The consequences of this framing can be significant. Recent data show that Hispanic and African American women have abortions at three to five times the rate of white, non-Hispanic women.[66] For Carole Joffe, this disparity demonstrates "the 'two Americas' of reproductive health": women of color experience unplanned pregnancies at a higher rate than do white women largely because poorer women have less access to contraceptives and health insurance.[67] The passive language of women "submitting" to abortion has many uses, but it has become a particularly valuable tool for white Christian conservatives to use in creating common cause with people of color who have good historical reasons to fear white eliminationism. Christian right leaders speak movingly about the racism that motivates abortion providers as well as the high numbers of women of color who submit to abortion.[68]

Although they have not borne fruit in every arena as the Christian conservative movement might have wished, the movement continues to work toward "racial reconciliation." Racial reconciliation projects have occurred throughout modern US history, but some that gained popularity in the 1990s have operated in domains of same-sex sexuality and abortion to try to attract people of color to the morality politics of the Christian right.[69] Racial reconciliation also has another effect: engaging white Christian conservatives with racialized issues such as the "black genocide" of abortion in a way that enables them to "absolve [them]sel[ves] of the racist stereotype."[70] In this context, as in the ex-gay movement, the roots, aspirations, and activism are complicated by the interests of those who extend and practice Christian conservative compassion.

Sorting Out Compassion

There are many differences between the antigay and antiabortion compassion campaigns. One important distinction is that compassionate approaches to same-sex sexuality usually involve or accommodate instruction directed at Christian conservatives about the origins of same-sex desire. Postabortion ministries do not direct as much attention to questions of the origins of women's vulnerability to abortion as ex-gay ministries do to vulnerability to same-sex sin, although they do use psychological arguments after the fact to demonstrate the terrible impact of abortion on women. Another difference is that same-sex-attracted women and men are understood to be always in danger of backsliding into satisfying desires that they must fight, at least until God relieves them of their attractions. On the other hand, even if postabortive women have been multiple offenders, they are not regarded to be in continual danger of reoffending because of the exigencies of strong desires.

A third difference between the antiabortion and antigay movements is that while the antiabortion movement is explicitly motivated by religious convictions about the personhood and ensoulment of the fetus, the antigay movement contains a sector that purports to operate exclusively along secular and scientific lines. As the example of NARTH suggests, however, this claim to scientific legitimacy is highly compromised. Finally, there is a significant difference between the responses of mainstream psychological researchers to the psychological literatures deployed in the ex-gay and postabortion movements. For mainstream psychiatrists and psychologists, the linking of homosexuality to mental illness or emotional regressiveness is a biased remnant of the American mental health profession. By contrast, even though it is not recognized by psychiatrists and psychologists as a diagnosable mental health problem, the issue of a syndrome of psychological consequences after abortion has continued to be investigated and addressed by the mental health community.

There are also similarities in these two kinds of compassion campaigns. First, whether in the exgay movement or in the postabortion recovery movement, participants are expected to produce and deliver testimonies of healing that attest to the fruits of sinfulness and to a moment of grace that signals a turn away from sin, and hence from same-sex sexuality and abortion. In the ex-gay case, the testimony constructs and confirms the developmental failures that precipitated the damage to the afflicted person's natural heterosexual orientation. It describes the repudiation of homosexuality and continues to chart the subject's struggles with sexual desire and commitment to God (and, for some, to the possibility of heterosexuality). For women who have succumbed to the immoral choice to abort a fetus, the testimony explicates the painful life circumstances and spiritual void that precipitated the abortion decision. Its climax is a recitation of the dreadful consequences to which a woman is exposed as a result of her decision to abort. The turning point is the realization of the horror of what she has done and her turn toward God for redemption. In both cases, the willingness to bear the agonies of struggle with one's particular form of fallenness is a necessary condition of participation. Each movement relies on the repetition of this witness for its apodictic value and its political efficacy.

A second similarity is that both antigay and antiabortion compassion campaigns channel activism toward helping particular subsets of the afflicted—same-sex attracted people and women who are considering abortion—resist their baser impulses by removing the means by which they might realize their immoral ends. Like taking away the instruments by which vulnerable people might harm themselves, activists seek to end abortion and revoke gay rights and recognition in order to remove the public policies that might "stumble" others. Alan Chambers has spoken to this justification for opposing same-sex marriage when, in public talks and advertisements, he has expressed relief that this option wasn't available to him when he was living as a gay man.[71] Such concern is not mendacious in the sense that it functions as a cover for a motivation to harm, but it is a peculiar kind of rights claim: a plea to withhold a right from a specific set of citizens made on behalf of those who might exercise that right and some day come to regret having done so.[72]

Finally, both people who engage in same-sex sexual relations and women who have an abortion are subject to particular forms of stigma that reflect disapproval of those who transgress social rules. In Erving Goffman's typology, sexual minorities and postabortive women are understood to suffer from "blemishes of individual character" that distinguish them from putative "normals."[73] An important difference between those who support abortion rights and those who oppose them, those who support queer identity and nondiscrimination and those who oppose these goals, is that gay rights and abortion rights advocates consider stigma and social maltreatment eradicable features of social life. Christian conservatives generally see stigma, disgust, and misery as ineradicable, natural consequences of sinfulness.

I argue that the compassion that circulates in both the ex-gay movement and the postabortion movement is "real," that is, that it is not merely a kind of cynical elite discourse that functions to cover up more authentic, malevolent impulses. At the same time, I qualify this argument in many ways throughout this book. One qualification, which I will return to from time to time, is that in important respects Christian right compassion is aimed primarily inward toward members of the Christian conservative community: same-sex attracted believers who hail from Christian conservative families and foreswear homosexual lives and the families of same-sex attracted people; Christian women who regret their decision to have an abortion and the male partners who grieve that decision (and seek to atone for their role in it). Prominent ex-gay leaders and spokespersons testify about their Christian families of origin and/or their childhood salvation experiences. Postabortive women testify about accepting Jesus Christ as their personal savior or finding their way back to God after an abortion.

The consistency of this connection between the bestowing of compassion and membership in the Christian conservative community is not so much a matter of doctrine as it is a predictable empirical feature of the Christian right's projects. Although the ex-gay movement is open to all, it is oriented toward Christians who believe that refusing to renounce their sexual desires abrogates their relationship with God. Postabortion awareness and recovery ministries are also open to all who would participate in them, but the doctrine and practices of these ministries are religious and conservative. Thus, traditional Christian believers are the most likely consumers of the "goods" provided by ministries that are organized around conservative Christian principles, theology, testimony, and modes of worship.

A related characteristic of compassion campaigns is that they target and serve not only those who are the first objects of Christian conservative concern—women and men who struggle with same-sex desire and women who have had an abortion—but also their family members and loved ones. Ex-gay ministries provide literature, counseling, instruction, and support groups for parents and family members of same-sex-attracted people. Post-abortion ministries incorporate male partners, understood as representatives of lost fatherhood, into rituals and programs. Together, all these believers constitute a class of legitimate objects of compassion: the same-sex-attracted and postabortive women as well as the loved ones who have suffered the pain of emotional proximity to them. For this reason, it is accurate, though not sufficient, to say that compassion campaigns are vehicles through which those who identify with the Christian conservative movement can direct compassion to members of their own community— can, in effect, feel sorry for themselves. Through these campaigns believers express compassion for their own who, in turn, are encouraged to affirm Christian right doctrines on sexuality and to participate in programs that stigmatize same-sex sexuality and abortion.

Here is the limit to compassion, which consistently is constructed by pedagogical interventions aimed at followers. In the case of the ex-gay movement, this limit is defined by the refusal to renounce same-sex desire and sexuality, including the decision to publicly identify as lesbian, gay, bisexual, or queer. In the case of the antiabortion movement, the limit is defined by the refusal to renounce an abortion decision and/or support for a right to choose abortion.

The ex-gay movement directs compassion toward strugglers at the same time that it targets unregenerate queers for political intervention. The doctrine that justifies political intervention includes a number of elements, including God's opposition to same-sex sexuality, the harms that gay people are said to inflict on society, and the ineluctable misery of those who engage in same-sex relationships. Indeed, accounts of homosexual disease and misery constitute a mendacious baseline of information that is directed to strugglers and straight believers alike.[74] It is also standard for Christian right leaders to locate queer people outside the boundaries of Christian community with claims that Christian and homosexual identities are mutually exclusive. Positioning queers as outsiders to Christianity is a prerequisite to antigay rhetoric and politics. The antiabortion movement as a whole depicts women who have obtained, or are in the process of obtaining, an abortion as child murderers and as grotesque, unnatural women who can only be rescued and become proper objects of Christian compassion by turning to Christ, renouncing their abortion decision, and supporting an end to a right to procure an abortion.

Even though the ex-gay movement nurtures a public conception of its work as nonpolitical, ex-gay events and literature make a clear distinction between strugglers, for whom compassionate intervention is intended, and nonstrugglers, for whom decidedly noncompassionate political intervention is warranted. A significant portion of the pedagogy of the ex-gay movement is dedicated to clarifying what kinds of political positions those who minister to strugglers and ex-gays should support on issues such as same-sex marriage and domestic partnerships, safe schools initiatives that seek to protect minors from anti-LGBTQ bullying, and hate crimes legislation.[75] Activists in postabortion ministries refrain from indulging in abomination rhetoric and harassing tactics but, like their counterparts in ex-gay ministries, clarify the kinds of political positions it is acceptable for compassionate Christian conservatives to support.

Thus, while compassion campaigns claim to eschew politics and embrace theological and therapeutic aims, they are social enterprises that *also* buttress and inculcate political ideas. Their embeddedness in, and cooperation with, sectors of their movements that engage openly in politics and/or that deploy stigmatizing rhetoric overwhelms even the objections of some aspiring ex-gays who disavow, or are ambivalent about, the Christian right's political aims.[76] Whatever reservations individual members might quietly hold, ex-gay and postabortion groups are implicitly, and sometimes explicitly, committed to raising awareness about the social and personal ills associated with gay rights and abortion and supporting the elimination of queer civil rights and reproductive rights. Hence, though it makes sense to categorize different Christian conservative projects as either "political" or "therapeutic" for the purpose of understanding patterns of differences between them, the ideological functions of compassion campaigns underscore their implicit political functions.

In the chapters that follow I turn from the history and current facts about the ex-gay and postabortion movements and use theoretical sources as alternative modes of investigating the compassion that animates these movements and the role of compassion in politics. In chapter 3, I turn to a powerful critique of the consequences of compassionate forms of politics in the political theory of Hannah Arendt. Arendt's repudiation of compassion as a motivation for, and type of, politics looms large for students of democratic theory, and many scholars have criticized Arendt's vehement positioning of compassion in the private realm of the household and interpersonal relations rather than in the public realm of citizenship and action.

For her critics, Arendt's is a "philosophy of political heartlessness."[77] In addition to a pitiless repudiation of public compassion Arendt provides a timeless critique of the tendency of group members to indulge in love for their own group at great expense to others. By bringing Arendt's thought on compassion, the foundations of democracy, and the contradictory significance of group identities for politics to bear on the compassion campaigns of the Christian right I clarify how the Christian right's compassionate forays into divisive social and political conflicts over sexuality and reproduction vindicate Arendt's concerns about oppression and threats to public life.

3

Christian Right Compassion

What Would Hannah Arendt Do?

Identity in Politics

The first step in analyzing the meaning and significance of Christian right compassion is to establish the nature of this object, but this initial goal is more difficult to accomplish than it appears. The first obstacle to identifying the content and contours of Christian right compassion is left skepticism, which often identifies such compassion—or "compassion"—as a cover for normalization and punishment. Yet another obstacle is that in its early formulations compassionate conservatism was an articulation of the convergence between welfare provision and moral uplift: the site at which the provision of citizens' basic human needs intersected with a set of demands for citizens' moral virtue. However, Christian right compassion campaigns are not projects conceived to distribute or redistribute public revenue to needy citizens. They are something else; but what? In this chapter I address this and other questions about Christian compassion and its political shortcomings by applying the political philosophy of Hannah Arendt that centers both compassion and the prerequisites of citizenship.

As a political philosopher, Arendt had much to say about rights and about group-based discrimination. Arendt's work frequently has been employed in debates on stigma, marginality, and abject identity, often through the categories of pariah and parvenu that she used to examine the life of Rahel Varnhagen. Varnhagen was a late eighteenth-/early nineteenth-century Jewish writer and salon hostess, a prolific correspondent in the anti-Semitic milieu of nineteenth-century Europe, and a woman to whom Arendt referred as her "closest friend, though she has been dead for some one hundred years."[1] In *Rahel Varnhagen: The Life of a Jewish Woman*, Arendt sets out an argument about the choices and identity categories available to Varnhagen, and, by extension, to the bearers of other kinds of stigmatized identities.[2] These categories resonate with her later, and better known, analyses of the distinction between social and political that have so bedeviled political theorists. A number of thinkers have extended Arendt's categories to account for other kinds of group identities, including racial and sexual identities.[3] Applying Arendt's analysis of one kind of pariah identity, Jewishness, to another, same-sex sexuality, Morris Kaplan argues that "Arendt's analysis of the Jewish question leads us to be profoundly suspicious of the displacement of political equality onto the social domain and the characterization as 'private' of the denial of fundamental rights to an unpopular minority."[4]

In addition to the fertile line of inquiry of political rights and social marginalization, Arendt has been drafted into the debate on same-sex marriage. In 1959, Arendt criticized the Supreme Court decision in *Brown v. Topeka Kansas Board of Education*, arguing that antimiscegenation laws in the South were a more onerous affront to individual rights than were segregated schools. Her skeptical line of argument on the appropriate federal response to legal segregation shocked her progressive contemporaries, some of whom responded quickly, beginning with the issue of *Dissent* in which Arendt's essay was published.[5] But her argument has provided contemporary supporters of gay rights with a venerable voice in favor of same-sex marriage.[6] Arendt's "reflections on Little Rock" have been employed in the literature on the debate over abortion as well. Steven Maloney argues that the civil participation of prochoice clinic escorts who volunteer to buffer women entering clinics from prolife protesters is not accounted for by the "ruly" kind of participation imagined by theorists in the deliberative democratic tradition. Instead, Maloney suggests that such political acts are better explained by Arendt's more agonistic conceptualization of action—indeed, that abortion clinic escorting can be understood as a vivid example of the kind of contentious, decidedly nondeliberative political action Arendt believed was sometimes essential to upholding political freedom.[7]

For good reason, Arendt is not known as a theorist of identity or of identity politics. It may be inevitable, however, that her work frequently has been read through the prism of group identity even when she would not have approved of such readings and appropriations. For example, Jennifer Ring argues that while Arendt denied the significance of her gender for her philosophy, the reception of her work was marked and shaped by the fact that she was a woman. Ring concentrates on the reception of *Eichmann in Jerusalem*, especially the vehemence of the disapproval Arendt provoked by daring to be a Jewish woman who openly criticized male Jewish leaders "in public." Ring also makes a case that Arendt's arguments in *Eichmann* undermined the politics and constructions of masculinity of those who constituted the Jewish audience for the book.[8] Other invocations of Arendt, especially those touching racial identifications and attributions, most notably—but not restricted to—anti-Semitism, the implications for politics of class stratification, and the role of ideology in modern life, draw out themes that coexist with the more abstract theorizing on which her reputation rests.

If the Christian right's contemporary sexuality and reproductive politics are motivated by compassion in some form, Arendt's extensive considerations and critique of compassionate forms of political intervention will illuminate that intervention in a way that cannot be reduced to mere ideological disagreement. Here, I concentrate on Arendt's conception of compassion and the details of her opposition to it as a motivation for politics in order to generate insights that can help us interpret the compassion that operates in Christian right morality politics.

Caution: Hazardous Compassion Ahead

For people of quite different ideological stripes, compassion constitutes an inarguable motivation for political judgments and interventions. In the context of such conviction, Arendt's opposition to compassion as a mode and motivation of politics is a bracing challenge. Arendt articulated her critique of the role of compassion in political life incisively and generously throughout her writings. She regarded Jesus as a special moral exemplar, but George Kateb puts Arendt's view of compassionate politics starkly when he writes that, to her, "the goodness of Jesus destroys the world; the morality of love destroys the world."[9] Nonetheless, Arendt took love and compassion as her subject matter often throughout her career, writing of different forms of love, their intersections with less intimate forms of association, and their effects on politics beginning with her doctoral dissertation, *Love and Saint Augustine,* and ending with her unfinished manuscript that became *The Life of the Mind.*

Arendt's most complete consideration of the role of compassion in politics is found in *On Revolution,* her study of "the principles which underlie all revolutions."[10] There, she defines compassion: "to be stricken with the suffering of someone else as though it were contagious" and points out that compassion consists in "co-suffering" with "one person"—not a group or class. Thus, it is in the very definition of compassion that it is inconsistent with politics—a mass enterprise even when executed by individuals acting on a public stage. Compassion is characterized by "awkwardness with words," by which she means not maladroitness with language but speechlessness in the face of suffering.[11]

Arendt identifies the "passion of compassion" with the French Revolution rather than with the American. For Arendt, this is a compliment, but the distinction doesn't redound entirely to the benefit of the Americans. Pointing out that "it is by no means a matter of course for the spectacle of misery to move men to pity," Arendt offers a brief account of how American slaves were excluded from the sentiment of compassion by their free white revolutionary contemporaries. Arendt lauds one result of this exclusion—a revolution that wasn't driven by compassion for "sheer misery"—even as she conceptualizes a more appropriate and less destructive rationale for opposition to slavery than compassion: "if Jefferson, and others to a lesser degree, were aware of the primordial crime upon which the fabric of American society rested, if they "trembled when [they] thought that God is just" (Jefferson), they did so because they were convinced of the incompatibility of the institution of slavery with the foundation of freedom, not because they were moved by pity or by a feeling of solidarity with their fellow men."[12] Arendt uncovers a superior justification for revolution than compassion, explaining that even in circumstances that would more than warrant the sentiment of compassion, it is better for the polity for other—political, rather than social—reasons and motivations to prevail.

Arendt's rejection of absolute morality as a foundation for politics reveals her concern for the fragility of politics and of the world that politics secures. To engage with Arendt's critique of compassion it is necessary to tease out the meanings and connections between the concepts Arendt used to expose the dangers compassion poses to politics, especially pity, goodness (often rendered as "absolute goodness"), and violence. Students of Arendt's thought have given a good deal of consideration to her critique of compassion and its close cousin, pity. Kateb points out that for Arendt compassion and pity aren't the same (although she sometimes seems to conflate the two); pity is compassion perverted by its appearance in the public sphere. Pity results when people are called upon to feel compassion for the "suffering masses" rather than participating in relations with concrete suffering others.[13] Kathleen Jones agrees: "the problem with compassion for Arendt is that it soon deteriorates into pity; as such it is unable to distinguish among the masses and can only comprehend suffering in its sheer numbers."[14]

Also connected for Arendt are compassion and goodness, "related phenomena," although "they are not the same."[15] For Arendt, a problem with compassion as a source of political action is that it is often associated either with the incompatibility of goodness and politics or with the attempt of political actors to use political and other means to impose a particular conception of goodness on the world. Thus, a productive starting point for Arendt's perspective on compassion and love in politics is her attention to absolute morality and especially the incompatibility between politics and absolute morality.

In response to the widespread belief that only moral systems such as those found in religion could protect individuals from doing and suffering evil, Arendt countered with the value of institutions and of "action inspired by *public* principles."[16] As Margaret Canovan notes, Arendt was well aware of the common belief that political morality is a product of personal morality. But her study of totalitarianism persuaded her that because in Hitler's Germany and Stalin's Soviet Union, "conventional morality had been no impediment to political evil," it was necessary to look elsewhere for the foundations of action in a democratic republic. The answer was political: "[H]uman plurality offers us the possibility of . . . building and guarding political structures" by which we can "establish and maintain a republic based on equal rights for all."[17]

In addition to other sources, Arendt turned to literature to elucidate the problem of the apolitical nature of individual morality. Following Melville's description of the eponymous character Billy Budd—that "a virtue went out of him"—she represents him as a person of unworldly goodness and ultimately a figure of the sort whose virtues are irreconcilable with "laws and all lasting institutions."[18] So Arendt uses Budd to argue that personal goodness is not an adequate bulwark against political evil.[19] But she also uses *Billy Budd* to make a stronger claim that links "moral purity" with violence, though through association rather than causation.[20] "Arendt in effect congratulates Captain Vere for being a Machiavellian political actor; he may be tempted by compassion, but he does not abandon the virtue of his role in the political world for the moral purity of a supposedly higher one. . . . The danger of compassion is that, like spontaneous or unregulated violence, it destroys the conventions of political space."[21] In her historical analysis of compassion, Arendt's pivots to literary examples—Budd and Dostoyevsky's Grand Inquisitor—ultimately are unconvincing.[22] The turn to literature may signal that Arendt is unable to find historical examples of persons of absolute goodness thwarting the operations of "laws and all lasting institutions." She is more persuasive when she returns to her analysis of elites inciting violent mass fervor.

Arendt feared the ways in which compassion—or its pernicious cousin, pity—can quickly degenerate into some less benign reaction such as rage.[23] Drawing on Aristotle, Arendt argues that emotions such as rage can be rational or irrational, depending upon their context. Rage is natural in some circumstances, but it is not an ineluctable result of misery so much as it is a response to the foreclosure of possibility that misery can be ameliorated. Arendt adds that the "history of revolution" also demonstrates the role that compassionate "members of the upper classes" have in inciting the rage of the "oppressed and downtrodden" and in leading the rebellions that follow.[24] This course of events—compassion for the miserable leading to pity and from there, not inevitably but frequently, to rage and violence—clarifies the relationship Arendt posits between compassion and violence. It also clarifies the close relationship she finds between violence and the fascination with goodness that underwrites compassionate approaches to politics.

Arendt's critique of compassion in politics is no extraneous or idiosyncratic concern but is, rather, deeply embedded in, and often logically related to, core dimensions of her political thought. Throughout her work, she identifies a number of problems with the deployment of compassion in and as politics, all of which reinforce the untrustworthiness of compassion as a kind of *political* emotion. Many of these concerns emerge in some form in her extended analysis of the subject in On Revolution. There, Arendt lays out four political vices of compassionate politics. First, "pity . . . undermines solidarity"—a commitment to ideas and interests rather than to undifferentiated group identity or human neediness.[25] Second, to the extent that the conception of goodness upon which compassion is based is derived from a form of absolute morality, compassion can debase politics by turning it into a tool for the imposition of a particular version of goodness. A third, and closely related, issue is that the imposition of compassion driven by absolute morality easily leads to violence; Arendt's case, of course, is the Terror that followed the French Revolution.

Fourth, Arendt argues that compassion isn't a "natural" emotion that responds ineluctably to misery; rather, compassion selects its objects with great flexibility. Our compassion is guided by our own identifications and sentiments and excludes some even as it recognizes and validates the suffering of others. For Arendt, the failure of the American founders to respond with compassion to the suffering of slaves is both a laudable sign of the politics of the American Revolution and a demonstration of the untrustworthiness of compassion. This concern with the unavoidable partiality of compassion or, rather, with the partiality of those who would use compassion to ground their political sentiments and action is at work in Arendt's public correspondence with Gershom Scholem after the publication of *Eichmann in Jerusalem*.[26] When Scholem read passages in *Eichmann* as demonstrating that Arendt lacked "love of the Jewish people," Arendt replied that she did not—indeed, could not—love any group but could only love individuals. Further, she warned that "the role of the 'heart' in politics" was often "to conceal factual truth."[27] Individuals would be particularly tempted to conceal political truths in ways that would vitiate the bad acts and responsibility of their own groups. Loving their own groups, they would exonerate those groups of wrongdoing.

Arendt is hard on compassion in *On Revolution*, but opposition to compassionate politics is also a theme in her other writings. Indeed, a minor theme in her work is the unreliability of compassion—the flexibility with which compassion can be deployed by political actors. In *Eichmann in Jerusalem*, this flexibility is revealed by the fact that compassion is not always for the suffering other but, instead, can be turned back on the self. In her consideration of Nazi "psychology" (although she doesn't call it this), Arendt considers the question of conscience and argues that it's inaccurate to conclude that prominent architects of the Holocaust possessed no conscience because they committed mass murder. Rather, she says, we can see in prominent Nazis the permutations and inversions of conscience and the tactics by which many avoided enduring the moral responses of "normal men" to human suffering. One such "trick" "consisted of turning these instincts [of pity] around, as it were, in directing them toward the self so that instead of saying, "What horrible things I did to people!" the murderers would be able to say, "What horrible things I had to watch in the pursuance of my duties, how heavily the task weighed on my shoulders!"[28] Arendt is concerned with moral actors who administered the machinery of the Third Reich's mass extermination of European Jews, but the phenomenon she describes is more commonplace.

In the case of Christian conservative compassion, this practice of turning compassion on the self (and on one's own ingroup) is evident both in the ex-gay movement and in postabortion ministries. Although it advertises to those outside the movement, Christian ex-gay programs and therapies are almost entirely consumed by same-sex-attracted Christian conservatives, their families, and their communities.[29] Compassion pedagogy within the ex-gay movement encourages its audience to take themselves, and others with whom they identify most closely, as objects of compassion. Parents who dread the disappointment of a homosexual child become objects of compassion that the exgay movement serves, as do same-sex-attracted people who repent their desires and dread the dismay of their parents, friends, and religious communities. This is one way Christian conservatives learn that unapologetically gay people who are harmed by social stigma or discriminatory legislation are less deserving of compassion *or* political solidarity than those who suffer the close and unexpected proximity of queer friends and relations.

A final problem with compassionate politics is suggested in Arendt's other work, including *Beyond Past and Future* and *Lectures on Kant's Political Philosophy*. In *Lectures*, she responds to the belief that "critical thinking" is a function of "an enormously enlarged empathy" that captures the feelings, including the suffering, of others. Arendt disputes the value of empathy, putting in its place her interpretation of Kant's "enlargement of the mind": "To think with an enlarged mentality means that one trains one's imagination to go visiting."[30] For Arendt, empathy and compassion are not the same; however, even thinkers who are sympathetic to the importance of empathy may identify problems with it that resonate with Arendt's own.

One problem with empathy is that it is unreliable because it's not obvious to what purposes information—even accurate information—about what the other is feeling will be put. For example, Martha Nussbaum calls attention to the "empathetic torturer" problem, noting that it is plausible that sociopaths understand well the fears and feelings of their victims. Like Arendt, Nussbaum relies on Aristotle's definition of compassion as a corrective to the probability that empathy and compassion will not always be appropriately distinguished from each other.[31] But the larger problem with empathy is that it is presumptuous because, extraordinarily perceptive sociopaths aside, we cannot "know what actually goes on" in others—or, perhaps, we cannot ever be certain that we know. Even when we believe that we know what the other is feeling, the objects of compassionate intervention may be "mere figments in [our] imaginations."[32]

If this is so, then for Arendt we must decide for ourselves what conditions others inhabit and what kinds of judgments we will make about their situation, in part by putting *ourselves* in the place of the other and in part by "taking the viewpoints of others into account." This is Arendt's position: we cannot know what the other is feeling, but we may come to know what we would feel and think in the other's place—say, in the place of someone who lives in a "specific slum dwelling." The judgments we form as a result of the process of representative thinking are an important component of the broader category of political reason.[33]

Arendt's arguments on compassionate politics are clear, but they are less relevant to assessing the compassion campaigns of the Christian right than we might assume even if we do not dismiss outright Christian right compassion for same-sex-attracted strugglers and women who have had an abortion. The compassionate morality politics of the Christian right are dissimilar enough from the compassion politics that Arendt deplores to call into question the applicability of Arendt's concerns. Explicating differences between these conceptualizations of compassion also raises provocative new questions: about the meaning of Christian right compassion and about the ways in which Arendt's moral and political thought can speak to the theological politics of the movement.

The Miserable Ones

Two key differences between "Arendt's" compassion and that of the Christian right clarify that these two conceptions of compassion are meaningfully different and suggest what this distinction between the two might signify. These differences are the kind of group(s) that constitutes the object of compassionate politics and the relationship that prevails between the subjects and objects of compassion in each discourse. Arendt's critique of the destructive effects of compassion on politics requires two groups: a suffering group whose immiserated condition should not be made the raison d'être of political action and a political elite that is capable of acting on behalf of those whose misery effectively exiles them and their concerns from the political sphere. She is concerned with traditional forms of compassion that justify revolutions and mass movements: compassion for suffering groups with which revolutionaries and other political actors identify and in whose name they stage political interventions aimed at ending misery and enacting justice.

Surveying the French Revolution and subsequent political upheavals, Arendt treats compassion as a matter of sentiment for the indigent: "those who belong to the lower classes of society."[34] Action predicated on such sentiment substitutes the motivation of economic need for political freedom. The French revolutionaries made the happiness and "welfare of the people" the basis for politics. In the American Revolution, Arendt argues, it was not difficult for the revolutionaries to identify with the people; all lacked fundamental forms of political freedom such that the revolutionaries served as "representatives in a common cause" rather than having to "summon up" a useable construct of solidarity.[35]

Is this distinction between cohorts of eighteenth-century revolutionaries relevant to the Christian right's antiabortion and antigay compassion campaigns today? Not directly; even though individual churches and organizations sometimes engage in the delivery of social services, the Christian right doesn't target the poor for compassion or make their hidden neediness the object of its political agenda. Indeed, this difference between an emphasis on poverty and an emphasis on morality issues such as same-sex sexuality and abortion continues to define some portion of the boundary between Christian left (and center) and Christian right priorities. Evidence of this divide on poverty is available from many sources, but consider an exchange in a debate between Jim Willis, author and founder of Sojourners, and Richard Land, then president of the Ethics and Religious Liberty Commission of the Southern Baptist Convention at the 2007 Values Voter Summit in Washington, DC. When Wallis raised the issue of Christians responding to poverty, Land countered that poor children could not be helped out of poverty if they were killed by abortion before they were born. Moving the conversation decisively away from the issue of poverty, Land went on to compare abortion with slavery and to emphasize the importance of using the levers of law to end the right to abortion.[36]

However, compassionate politics does require an object on whose interests, and in whose name, political actors will act. As in Arendt's critique of revolutionary compassion, a precondition of Christian right compassion is the misery of those who will be its proper objects—those whose immiserated condition sets the stage for compassionate intervention. Instead of the traditional objects of compassion of whom Arendt writes, the Christian right produces quite different objects of compassion: same-sex-attracted strugglers and women who have undergone an abortion. Along with those objects, the movement produces ideology that sustains its own interpretation of misery and that defines the boundaries of these ostensibly suffering groups.

It's useful to consider the misery associated with the objects of sexuality politics more carefully. In the case of Arendt's (and the revolutionaries') lower classes, the finding of misery is an empirical matter: poverty is a matter of insufficient food, clothing, and shelter, and impoverished neediness and misery are overlapping, even if not identical, phenomena. In *On Revolution*, Arendt differentiates the French and American Revolutions by distinguishing poverty (a widespread condition in both nations) and misery (a condition widespread in France, she says, but not in the United States) and by clarifying the relationship between the two: for her, poverty does not ineluctably lead to misery. Arendt does not discuss American slaves or slavery in these passages, so it is possible to dispute the empirical accuracy of her claim that "the laborious in America were poor but not miserable." Setting aside the empirical accuracy of this distinction, however, Arendt clearly connects misery with economic "want" and the political invisibility that often does—though it need not necessarily—follow from it.[37]

In contemporary morality politics, by contrast, the misery of those who are members of the target groups is not really an empirical matter. Rather, it is an ideological assumption and a form of pedagogy that defines the terms of repentance for Christian conservatives. Antiabortion and antigay ideology works to produce the consequence it purports to discover. Four classes of people are relevant to this analysis because these distinctions are central to Christian right compassion: repentant women who have had abortions, unrepentant women who have had abortions; women and men who struggle against their same-sex attraction and reject a same-sex sexual identity; women and men who experience same-sex attraction, engage in same-sex sexuality and relationships, and do not repudiate their sexuality. Of these categories of persons, only the repentant are proper objects of conservative Christian compassion, because their repentance *and their willingness to embrace a miserable identity* situate them as deserving a compassionate response. So, for example, repentant women form new identities as women suffering from postabortion syndrome by embracing that diagnosis and understanding it as a moral consequence of their sinful behavior. Likewise, same-sex-attracted women and men who recite the unavoidable miseries of living a gay life—even if they have never actually lived such a life and are relying upon the reports of others—are appropriate objects of compassion.[38]

In this moral economy, unrepentant actors—women who have undergone abortion, lesbians, gay men, and (in the rare cases that they come in for attention from Christian conservatives) bisexuals—are read by the Christian right as miserable even if they do not experience their condition in this way. These heedless hedonists are "miserable individuals," objectively, if not subjectively.[39] Christian right descriptions of same-sex sexuality are lurid accounts of the miserable individuality of LGBTQ people. Even in the quarters of Christian antigay politics that combine compassion with traditional antigay politics, same-sex-attracted people who refuse to abstain from sexual activity and romantic relationships are described as leading unhappy lives dedicated to low pleasures for whom stigma, censure, social invisibility, and legal sanctions follow ineluctably from their immoral willfulness.[40] In the final analysis, members of these groups are all "miserable," but they are miserable in meaningfully different ways that justify and subtend the different consequences believers are called upon to expect and also to deliver.

Christian right compassion campaigns target groups that are not generally associated with material misery, though they may be associated with social stigma, organized discrimination, and/or legal jeopardy. In Christian right discourse, gay people are represented not as abject or in need of protective legislation but as both politically more powerful and economically more affluent than heterosexual citizens. Supreme Court Justice Antonin Scalia, whose sympathies lie with the Christian right on morality issues, cited the "high disposable income" of lesbians and gay men in his dissent from the majority opinion in *Romer v. Evans*, the 1996 case that voided an antigay amendment to the Colorado state constitution. To my knowledge, this mendacious characterization of queers as rich is never applied to strugglers, but the Christian right does locate strugglers and women who have had an abortion in the symbolic space occupied by the poor and powerless of other political ideologies. Not materially needy, they nevertheless remain in need of certain kinds of protections. Compassionate interventions of course include helping same-sex-attracted people avoid the temptation of same-sex marriage by outlawing such unions and obviating the possibility of women having to undergo the torment of having chosen abortion by making a legal abortion impossible to obtain.

Students of the Christian right have often called attention to the central importance of "emotions that matter" in the movement's ideology and pedagogy.[41] It is indeed crucial for critics of the movement to understand how the language of the heart works to constitute the belief system and the values and feelings of many Christian conservative followers. Many liberals and political pragmatists of all stripes ridiculed President George W. Bush's "incessant references to blood-pumping organs," but Bush's tendency to indulge in emotion language endeared him to Christian conservatives.[42] In contrast, Arendt's response to motivations of the heart is a muscular skepticism. Arendt's "unconsoling and austere" "relationship to suffering" requires that public forms of love and compassion be subjected to rigorous reality testing. As Deborah Nelson puts it, "the only way to become a realist, and for Arendt we all must do so for our mutual survival, is to cultivate a suspicion of intellectual and psychological comfort in whatever forms we find them."[43] This general characterization is well-applied to Arendt's thoughts on fellow feeling and compassion, not for the Other, but for members of one's own group.

Love among the Outcasts

What is at stake for Arendt in all her critiques of compassion in politics is the existence of politics itself. Kateb sums up Arendt's concern by noting that "a politicized love of humanity sponsors appalling ruin in political life" and that "compassion and pity are the fertile source of political crime and terror."[44] However, this critique is not as productive a guide to evaluating the ideology and rhetoric of the Christian right as it might at first appear to be. The sexuality and reproductive rights compassion campaigns do not provoke the critique of compassion Arendt mounts in *On Revolution* because these compassion projects are not aimed at immiserated populations. Rather, they are concerted attempts to discursively script a social and political reality in which particular groups deserve compassion while others who are understood as needing it—they're miserable whether they know it or not—do not deserve it. In terms of Arendt's thought, the distinction is crucial because a dominant anxiety about the realm of politics is that it is fragile and easily overwhelmed by the demands of material necessity, either from within the household or from needy and undifferentiated mobs.[45]

Instead, the variety of Arendtian compassion that bears the closest resemblance to the Christian right's campaigns is another form of non-intimate compassion with which Arendt grappled, one that's related to compassion for the suffering public Other but also distinguishable from it. This is the compassion that circulates among pariahs and that helps to solder bonds of group fraternity. This second kind of compassion circulates within a group, especially a group whose members share experiences of ostracism and suffering. In her essay "On Humanity in Dark Times: Thoughts about Lessing," Arendt examines closely the compassion and sense of fraternity that afflicted people bear for each other. There she suggests that persecution forces members of a group into an association that "produces a warmth of human relationships" that is "the great privilege of pariah peoples." However, Arendt rejects this compassion, in its turn, as unpolitical. For her, the very forced expulsion from the freedom of the public sphere that creates the possibility of warm humanity among the oppressed also guarantees their "worldlessness." The peculiar fraternity of the "insulted and injured" is meaningful in human terms, but it is "absolutely [politically] irrelevant" because it comes at the cost of participation in a world that's common to all.[46]

Christian right leaders often remind followers of the group's status as cultural victims of secular laws, mores, and practices. Ingroup Christian conservative discourse is rife with references to Christian martyrdom and the anti-Christian discrimination that is understood to characterize quotidian life in the United States. In response to pressures on the group and its core beliefs, Christian right love aspires to bind all believers together in adherence to theology and ideology, to keep same-sex-attracted and postabortive Christian conservatives from traversing the boundaries of the group, and to care for those affronted and violated by the unexpected proximity of same-sex-attracted people and postabortive women in their families and religious communities.

In the ex-gay movement the prominent role mapped out for friends, family members, and fellow congregants of gays and strugglers demonstrates the importance of these believers, both for reinforcing the ideology of the movement and for retaining the allegiance of the afflicted person to Christian conservatism. For these goals to be met, the movement must discourage competing ideologies of sexuality such as those available in liberal Christian traditions, agnosticism, and feminism. Ex-lesbian spokespersons often address their own former feminism and instruct followers about its inconsistency with Christian—by which they mean Christian conservative—belief. This includes reconciling women struggling with same-sex attraction to Christian conservative ideals of authority and submission. As one speaker at the 2008 Exodus International conference put it, as a feminist she had found it "repugnant" to consider being under the authority of, and submitting to, a man until she came to understand that God gave wives the "privilege" of displaying the relationship of Jesus to his church.[47] In her study of support groups for wives of Christian men struggling with same-sex sexuality, Michelle Wolkomir points out that ex-gay ministries provide an "ideological framework" for resolving their gender, marital, and spiritual crisis, and that this framework provides wives with resources for remaining in the Christian conservative community.[48]

In an attempt to expand the possibilities of political love beyond love for one's own group, Shin Chiba chides Arendt for rejecting *agape*, for early Christians, the unconditional love of God and the imperative to human beings to love as God does. One ground of Chiba's attempt to reclaim *agape* as a form of love that is consistent with political relations is his insistence that *agape* does not signal the end of ethical discriminations: "[A]gape is not merely a reconciling and forgiving love but also a willing resistance to evil at the same time." What's more, agape "aims at the betterment of an evildoer by 'containing' or 'defeating evil.'"[49] What easily may be taken for granted in such an argument is what kinds of acts and worldly consequences may be understood, and combated, as evil.

The love and compassion that circulate *among Christian conservatives* as a group does, indeed, identify evil and seek its demise. The problem is that those outside the movement often disagree vehemently with a Christian conservative assessment of evil, not in easy cases—such as the genocide in the Darfur region of Sudan that generated widespread denunciation in the United States across ideological differences—but in hard cases of morality politics such as same-sex sexuality and abortion rights. For the Christian right, same-sex sexuality is a master signifier of evil and abomination—"a demonic counterfeit for God's created design [for sexuality]."[50] Similarly, abortion (and sometimes even contraception) is routinely represented as murder and as an incitement to God's reckoning.[51] From this perspective, it's no consolation to know that Christian compassion is dedicated to defeating evil, rescuing its victims, and reconciling its perpetrators because its conception of evil and evildoers is ideological and sectarian.

Conservative Christians for whom the movement's pedagogy is intended are encouraged to respond with appropriate emotions and actions, delivering compassionate help to those struggling with same-sex desire or with a past decision to have an abortion and condemnation to those who reject the role that compassionate ideology scripts for them. Central to the aspirations of the Christian right movement is a reformation of moral categories that distinguishes moral from immoral, deserving from undeserving, citizens. The Christian right does not explicitly advocate hierarchies of citizenship. But as theorists who work in the sexual citizenship literature make clear, such hierarchies, and the obstacles to political inclusion, participation, and representation that go with them, are nonetheless goals of the movement.[52]

A World of Others

Christian right compassion bears little resemblance to the compassion for immiserated others that Arendt criticizes as destructive to politics and much resemblance to the fraternal compassion she worried constituted little more than love for our own. With that distinction established, her work can help us understand what kind of cultural and political work compassion campaigns perform. One dimension of her thought that's useful for evaluating these compassion campaigns is her emphasis on the meaning and value of plurality. "Plurality" is one of the central political categories in *The Human Condition*, where she defines the idea in its relation to political action: "Action, the only activity that goes on directly between men without the intermediary of things or matter, corresponds to the human condition of plurality, to the fact that men, not Man, live on the earth and inhabit the world. . . . Plurality is the condition of human action because we are all the same, that is, human, in such a way that nobody is ever the same as anyone else who ever lived, lives, or will live."[53] Plurality is essential for political action because action discloses the individuality of an actor to fellow citizens. Without these citizens, no action or political agency is possible, so plurality secures the possibility of a public sphere in which speech and other kinds of political action can take place.[54]

The concept of plurality might easily be read as a concern with the presence, absence, or collective "voice" of identity groups in public life, but this is not Arendt's plurality, at least in the first instance. For her, "a political community that constitutes itself on the basis of a prior, shared, and stable identity threatens to close the spaces of politics."[55] Her first concern, then, is with "the preservation of individuality in a common life"—"who" rather than "what" we are.[56] Even so, however, identity groups, socially constructed entities that they are, are "politically relevant" because all actions take place in the context of particular political contexts—contexts in which group identifications have effects and in which individuals may challenge the meaning, if not the fact, of their belonging to identity groups.[57]

Of course, individuals may also challenge, or deny, their identification with ascriptive identity groups, but Arendt is strenuous in rejecting this alternative. Arendt's biography of Varnhagen is a meditative analysis of Jewish identity in anti-Semitic Europe before the bloody twentieth century. After fleeing the Nazis, and before immigrating to the United States, Arendt spent her years in Paris writing and working for the Jewish Agency, an organization and Jewish quasigovernment that helped refugees resettle in Palestine. And when provoked, she wrote personally of her own Jewish identity, for example, in her public correspondence with Gershom Scholem.[58] Arendt did consider being a woman irrelevant to her political theorizing, and she thus challenged the significance (but not the fact) of biological sex.[59]

Arendt famously proclaimed that "when one is attacked as a Jew one must defend oneself as a Jew. Not as a German, not as a world-citizen, not as an upholder of the Rights of Man."[60] As Margaret Betz Hull points out, this is a "conditional statement" in which defending oneself from the standpoint of membership in an oppressed group becomes necessary because of the nature of the attack on the group, or on oneself as a member of a group.[61] Far from being an essentializing statement about group identity and the disappearance of the individual into the group, it is an argument about the role of the individual in the public realm in conditions of group-related oppression. It is this recognition of the significance of group identity that encourages Hanna Pitkin to read Arendt's concerns with plurality and citizenship in two quite different ways. The first, and the one that Arendt herself would endorse, is the course of individuality; as Pitkin puts it, "Be who you uniquely are!" The second—perhaps most, but surely not only, relevant to the pariah—is "Maintain solidarity with 'your people'!" As Pitkin notes, there is more than a little conflict between these alternatives, neither of which is sufficient on its own as a guide to negotiating the course of membership in a polity.[62]

Plurality has implications for these individuals, but it also has implications for political movements and the forms of politics these movements advance or foreclose. Students of the Christian right have often noted that the movement's discourse most often excludes LGBTQ *people*, though not repentant strugglers, from its representation of homosexuality.[63] Of course, mass movements frequently substitute broad categories and characterizations of adversaries rather than grapple with the vagaries of individuals and their stories. Thus, movement discourses abound with rapacious elites, warmongers, capitalists, rabble-rousers, racists, and the ungodly. The Christian right is certainly not distinguished from other social/political movements in its tendency toward undifferentiated representation of its adversaries. However, it remains useful to examine movement discourse for such tendencies and to consider some of their social and political consequences.

Critics of the Christian right's antigay politics have pointed out "the strange absence of gays" in Christian right discourse. Scott Barclay shows that Christian right leaders often substitute sex and gender difference for sexuality and sexual orientation in rhetoric about same-sex sexuality, a move that discloses anxieties about changing gender roles and their importance in stabilizing or undermining heterosexuality. But he also notes that when they are mentioned, lesbians and gay men usually appear in the abstract—for example, as a group that poses a threat to Christian conservatives. Another common form of representation is to conflate gay individuals with the "faceless political actions" of LGBT civil rights organizations that, like homosexuals as a group, threaten heterosexuals, Christians (and Christianity), and America.[64]

Political speech that excludes queer people in favor of the abstraction of homosexuality may reveal widespread discomfort with sexuality. Shame and discomfort about sexuality or specifically about minority sexuality may be found in many venues, and it may be the reason why even Christian opinion leaders who do not adopt the most punitive of perspectives toward lesbians, bisexuals, and gay men tend toward abstraction when dealing with same-sex sexuality. In interviews with mainline clergy that they conducted in 2000, Laura Olson and Wendy Cadge found that ministers in mainline Christian denominations "who choose to speak on homosexuality tend to frame the issue in terms of the diffuse notion of 'homosexuality,' rather than talking about gay men and lesbians as people."[65]

It would be possible that Christian right discourse exhibits a similar use of abstraction to mask shame and discomfort about sexuality but for the fact that the Christian right movement has often marketed graphic and negative depictions of same-sex sexuality to Christian conservative followers. The existence of this ingroup abomination rhetoric suggests that the exclusion of lesbians and gay men is not a side effect of discomfort with public talk about matters presumed to be properly private but is, instead, a deliberate tool of political pedagogy. Taking such ingroup rhetoric into account suggests that one way to interpret abstraction is that it helps Christian conservatives disidentify with those who are disadvantaged by public policies aimed at sexual minorities. Both opprobrious descriptions of same-sex sexuality and characterizations of homosexuals as a nihilistic and destructive bloc would perform similar work, discouraging Christian conservatives from identifying with same-sex-attracted people.

The psychological process of identification (or disidentification) is not pertinent to an Arendtian perspective. Arendt abhorred substitutions of psychology and psychological processes—the darkness and interiority of the human heart—for political ones. What her work would recommend instead of a concern with identification, and corollaries like empathy and the unconscious, is representative thinking, the enlarged mentality that is thereby enhanced and its related political faculty of judgment. The demands of exercising an enlarged mentality are strenuous, including, for example, "disregarding . . . self-interest" while "taking the viewpoints of others into account." Arendt's conception of this process differs from

Kant's own in the sense that Arendt does not embrace the idea of a "general standpoint of 'any' man." Instead, she insists on the importance of hearing from concrete others and imagining the many standpoints that would emerge from different situations: "The more people's standpoints I have present in my mind while I am pondering a given issue, and the better I can imagine how I would think and feel if I were in their place, the stronger will be my capacity for representative thinking."[66]

Other theorists have found Arendt's concept of representative thinking useful even as they have rearticulated it and applied it to particular contexts. Iris Young expands its scope by arguing that what is taken into account when we practice representative thinking is not only the interests and perspectives of the other but also "the collective social processes and relationships that lie between us."[67] Such a reconceptualization is consistent with Ange-Marie Hancock's analysis and critique of "the public identity of the welfare queen." Relying on Arendt, Hancock finds frequent failures of representative thinking in public debates and media discourse about welfare recipients that she associates with structural inequalities and a bias of powerful actors toward evaluating situations without regard for concrete information about the effects of inequalities. As Arendt would predict, the absence of information that reflects the standpoints of welfare recipients and the persuasive force of racialized antiwelfare ideology vitiate the possibilities for representative thinking.

As David Gutterman points out, the process of representative thinking is inextricable from listening to and reflecting upon the stories that people tell about their situations, traditions, and identities, though most of this "listening" is likely to take place at a remove from personal, face-to-face interaction. This capacity and practice is essential to democratic politics in a "plural polity" because to successfully share the world with others, citizens must be willing to defamiliarize their own sacred stories and to encounter the unfamiliar. Indeed, Gutterman contrasts Christian left and right orientations toward democratic politics in part by outlining the ways in which Christian right groups like Promise Keepers encourage their members to minimize contact with fellow citizens who do not share their views. Those "who are different—be they worshippers of holy cows, radical feminists, or any other unbelievers" pose "a risk to one's own purity."[68]

Not surprisingly, Christian right compassion campaigns do not encourage followers to develop enlarged mentalities. Indeed, Christian right compassion pedagogy discourages representative thinking that runs the risk of violating conservative Christian doctrine. If this is so in general, it is particularly true of rhetoric directed to or about members of sexually stigmatized groups. Instead, Christian right antigay pedagogy aims to cultivate compassion for, and perhaps even identification with, those who suffer because of the unbidden appearance of same-sex-attracted people in their midst. This group includes parents, siblings, and other blood relatives of lesbians and gay men and members of churches and religious communities who find themselves worshipping with and ministering to same-sex-attracted women and men.

Indeed, I have yet to encounter any example of Christian conservative developmental or ex-gay discourse that invites heterosexual readers or listeners to imagine what it would be like to discover same-sex sexual attraction in themselves as some young Christian conservatives do. Same-sex desires and those who come to understand themselves as same-sex attracted are always "other" to the Christian conservative, even when Christian conservatives minister to same-sex-attracted people who hail from Christian conservative families and consider themselves conservative believers. Likewise, antiabortion discourse does not situate Christian conservatives to imagine themselves in the position of being confronted with an unwanted pregnancy or in conditions that would make childbearing frightening or dangerous. Instead, the discourse cultivates conservative moral proscriptions against abortion and conservative religious prescriptions for sinners of repentance, public testimony, and political activism.[69]

The Christian right aspires not only to hold the line against the erosion of sexual stigma in the United States and elsewhere in the world but also to reverse its course and to reaffirm traditionalist Christian principles regarding sexual morality. To this end, movement leaders formulate political discourse that treats homosexuality as an abstraction and avoids information about the lives of LGBT people, including the consequences of sexual stigma and antigay public policies. Also relevant to Arendt's concerns with plurality and representative thinking is the fact that large percentages of Christian conservatives successfully minimize contact with openly queer people.[70] As researchers have established, those who do not have contact with lesbians and gay men are more successful at retaining antigay beliefs, while those who report contact with gay people also report lower levels of antigay beliefs.[71]

In Arendtian terms, the motivation of compassion does not insulate political actors from criticism; indeed, Arendt sees in compassionate politics a threat to politics itself. One possible—albeit unlikely—response of those who champion compassionate approaches to abortion and same-sex desire could be to relate their efforts to Arendt's own distinction between categories of the social and the political. In this scenario, compassion campaigns do not threaten the integrity of democratic civil liberties because they are confined to private relationships, decisions, and activity, from social supports for women who have had an abortion to therapies and support groups for same-sex-attracted strugglers. Although this distinction is plausible, it is not consistent with the reality of compassionate projects and their integration into the broader Christian right movement. Hence, both Arendt's concerns with compassion and her arguments for plurality as a condition of politics remain.

Revisiting Compassion Campaigns

In Arendt's terms, the Christian conservative movement's compassion campaigns often operate in what she understood as the "social," rather than the political, sphere. The category of "the social," what Hanna Pitkin dubbed "the blob" in Arendt's oeuvre, has always been a sticking point for scholars of her work. As Pitkin points out, what Arendt meant by "the social" is "far from obvious," but included economic relations, the bodily necessities usually subsumed in intimate relations and the household, and social relations in the sense of "oppressive conformity to mainstream values." Pitkin concludes that "the social" is a "complex composite, somehow involving both economics and normalization."[72] This insight is valuable because Arendt is not always read as a critic of normalization even though she anticipates many contemporary arguments in this genre at the same time that she stamps them with her own unique concerns. Consider, for example, this rumination on "the Jews and Society" in *The Origins of Totalitarianism*:

> Whenever equality becomes a mundane fact in itself. . . . there are ninety-nine chances [in a hundred] that it will be mistaken for an innate quality of every individual, who is "normal" if he is like everyone else and "abnormal" if he happens to be different. This perversion of equality from a political into a social concept is all the more dangerous when a society leaves but little space for special groups and individuals, for then their differences become all the more conspicuous.[73]

In any case, what is clear is that Arendt regarded "the rise of the social" in the modern world as a threat to politics in the sense that this process effected the "displacement of politics by routinized, bureaucratic, and administrative regimes."[74]

Acknowledging that most activities associated with the ex-gay movement and postabortion ministries exist in Arendt's domain of the social does not mean there is nothing more to be said of them, even from the perspective of Arendt's own thought. It is clear that Arendt was not opposed to training analytical scrutiny on social processes we would now conceptualize as normalizing. Although she understood the realm of the social as a threat to politics, she did not take social needs and relations, their present and their history, to be beyond the scope of political theorizing. More specifically, Arendt's incisive dissection of pariah identity and the choices available to those who are bearers of a "despised" "social condition" in her biography of Varnhagen is as painfully discerning today as when she wrote it in the 1930s.[75]

But the most powerful rejoinder to the characterization of compassion campaigns as "social" *as opposed to* "political" is their allegiance to political projects that suppress difference and that seek to maintain hierarchies of citizenship. Nor does such a perspective necessitate valorizing Arendt's categories of the social and the political. Although many compassion campaigns exist as free-standing social projects aimed at the healing of same-sex-attracted and postabortive individuals, they are closely linked to other forms of antigay and antiabortion politics. State, regional, national, and international Christian right organizations engage in lobbying, publishing, talk radio, television broadcasting, policy scorecards, and ballot initiatives. They host strategy sessions for movement insiders and hold conferences that serve as "beauty contests" of conservative candidates for political office. Some groups and individuals engage in compassionate projects in the area of sexuality without direct ties to national organizations that operate in policy arenas to deny rights to individuals. However, even for independent groups and their compassionate projects, tight cooperation and associative networks between compassion campaigns and traditional forms of conservative politics are the norm.

Major Christian right policy and lobbying organizations, such as Concerned Women for America and Focus on the Family—and its "completely [legally] separate" lobbying organization, Focus on the Family Action—engage in both explicitly political and ministerial activities. That is, some campaigns specifically formed for the purpose of engaging in compassionate forms of intervention on behalf of same-sex-attracted people and women who have had abortions are projects of national organizations that also engage in more traditional forms of antigay and antiabortion politics. An example of a national organization that engages in both compassionate and traditional forms of antigay politics is Focus on the Family, which developed the ex-gay Love Won Out conferences that have now been absorbed into the operations of Exodus International.

Another antiabortion organization with intertwined therapeutic and political dimensions is Operation Outcry: A Project of the Justice Foundation. The Justice Foundation, originally the Texas Justice Foundation, is a conservative litigation firm that takes cases in the areas of "limited government, free markets, private property, school choice, parental rights in education, and enforcing laws to protect women's health."[76] In the category of women's health, the Justice Foundation submits amicus briefs in abortion cases and sponsors Operation Outcry, a project that appears unrelated to the group's litigation focus.

> OPERATION OUTCRY is the project of THE JUSTICE FOUNDATION to end legal abortion by exposing the truth about its devastating impact on women and families. We believe that this will be accomplished through prayer and with the testimonies of mothers who have taken the life of their own unborn babies and of others who have suffered harm from abortion. We are working to restore justice and to protect women, men, and children from the destruction that abortion causes[77]

Even as it gestures toward the broader agenda of its parent organization, the motto of Operation Outcry replicates the slogans of other compassion campaigns: "Touching Hearts, Changing Lives, Restoring Justice."[78] Unlike the Justice Foundation website, which features icons of law and patriotism—American flag, gavel, legal scales, and the Declaration of Independence—set against a dark blue background, the Operation Outcry website is sky blue with a logo comprised of a line drawing of two women's silhouettes. The Operation Outcry appeal to women promotes an agenda of "hope and healing for those hurting from abortion" in part by concealing the legal and political agenda of the Christian right.

One initiative of Operation Outcry (and The Justice Foundation) is the television program *Faces of Abortion,* which has aired on the Sky Angel Satellite television network. Conceptualized through the prism of abomination rhetoric, one might guess that the "faces" of abortion featured in programming would be those of babies and children, perhaps even those spared from abortions. But the faces of abortion are those of postabortive women. Consistent with the conventions of postabortion ministries, *Faces* "features the personal stories of women—many after years of silence—about the long-lasting and harmful effects that exercising their right to choose has cost them. The cost has been high: grief, fear, shame, physical and emotional problems, broken relationships and marriages, and destructive and addictive behaviors. It also features stories of others hurt by abortion."[79] Operation Outcry also coordinates strategy with other antiabortion projects such as 40 Days for Life, a national clinic vigil campaign with origins in Texas. David Bereit, 40 Days for Life founder and national director, is a veteran of many prolife projects, including the American Life League's STOPP program, dedicated to the demise of Planned Parenthood.[80]

Cooperation between compassionate and traditional political arms of the Christian right movement is evident in such venues as the Family Research Council's Values Voter Summit, held in Washington, DC, in September 2006. The 2006 Summit featured an appearance by Georgette Forney, president of NOEL and cofounder of the Silent No More Campaign. Forney spoke to the crowd of Christian conservatives about her mission to serve women in the "post-abortion community"—to "reach out to those who are suffering in silence" because of an abortion in their past. Forney spoke of the specifically Christian and compassionate underpinnings of her work, noting that her mission on behalf of women who have had an abortion was founded on the love of Jesus Christ. Forney also related the variety of marketing tools used by the postabortion community, including billboards, public service announcements, buttons, help lines, and the formation of public gatherings at which testimonies can be delivered.

In her contribution to the Values Voter Summit Forney focused on the compassionate social campaign that she helped to found, its theology of repentance, and the community-building value of public witness, not on antiabortion laws and public policies. Other speakers supplemented Forney's compassionate approach with more recognizable conservative political rhetoric about abortion, a division of labor that exposed the links between compassion campaigns and antiabortion discourse as two complementary forms of Christian conservative politics. Rick Scarborough of Vision America linked *Roe v. Wade* to stem cell research and said of both that "Adolf Hitler would be proud." He charged that behind sham moral and political arguments in favor of abortion rights were financial interests that stood to gain from the abortion industry. Gary Bauer, Ann Coulter, James Inhofe, former Kansas attorney general Phill Kline, and current governor of Kansas Sam Brownback all spoke out against abortion rights. Of these speakers, Bauer fused compassion discourse with antiabortion politics when he noted that the Christian right doesn't hate women as its critics often charge but merely "wants the exploitation of women to stop."[81]

Bauer's claim affirms a consequential dimension of the expansion of abomination rhetoric into multiple rhetorics of abomination and compassion: the rearticulation and reemphasis on Christian forgiveness even in this vexing realm of sexual law and transgression. For Christian conservatives who endorse and employ abomination rhetoric, both those who have lived, or merely desired, satisfaction of same-sex sexual and romantic desires and those who have aborted a pregnancy are already indicted and bound for punishment. By contrast, proponents of compassion minister to the least of these: the guilty, afflicted, desolate, and spiritually broken. These Christian conservatives strive to enact the forgiveness of Jesus, who, once her accusers and would-be executioners had withdrawn from the scene, told the woman taken in adultery to go and sin no more.[82] As we shall see, the interplay between punishment and forgiveness, rather than the replacement of punishment by forgiveness, continues to characterize Christian right politics as compassion resituates both sexual sinners and those who minister to them in relation to Christian love and law.

Arendt and Christian Love

Throughout her scholarly life, Arendt was fascinated by dimensions of Christian theology and the relationship between that theology and the account of politics and citizenship that she was developing. Arendt was particularly interested in love and forgiveness, and in her dissertation, *Love and Saint Augustine*, she extracted from Augustine's writings different conceptions of love. The conception that intrigued her most was *caritas*, or charity, which she used to theorize about the bonds that form the basis of respect and equality in political communities. Arendt's Augustine establishes common sinfulness as the original basis for neighborliness; as she explains it, "humanity's common descent is its common share in original sin. This sinfulness, conferred with birth, necessarily attaches to everyone. There is no escape from it. It is the same in all people.... This equality is the predominant fact that wipes out all distinctions."[83] But a sinful nature is only the beginning of *caritas*. More important than what from a Christian perspective is a theological brute fact, Arendt finds in

Augustine an account of social embeddedness and an individual sphere of action that she translates from a theological register to a political one. This account provides a foundation for Arendt's unique conception of politics and citizenship.

A key issue for Augustine, for Arendt, and for contemporary Christians is the question of neighborliness: who is the neighbor Christians are commanded to love?[84] The question is important for Arendt because it intersects with her own concerns about individuality, political community, and a solidarity that's not reducible to group identity. Here Arendt reveals her own theoretical agenda, locating in Augustine an understanding of neighborliness that isn't confined to fellow believers. Joanna Vecchiarelli Scott finds Arendt's reading of Augustine on this point unpersuasive, but it is clear why this is such a crucial issue for Arendt. At stake for her is an equality that reconciles the givenness of identity with membership in a community that features plurality and scope for the exercise of political judgment.[85] Concluding that Augustine "loves his neighbor in sublime indifference regardless of what or who he is," Arendt cites Augustine's famous dictum that "he who lives according to God . . . will not hate a man because of this vice nor love the vice because of a man, but he will hate the vice and love the man."[86] Inconveniently, some translations of *The City of God* offer a version of the dictum that suggest quite a different guide to the vicissitudes of caritas: "[H]e who lives according to God ought to cherish toward evil men a perfect hatred, so that he shall neither hate the man because of his vice, nor love the vice because of the man, but hate the vice and love the man."[87] It's not surprising that Christian conservatives locked in moral combat with organized sinfulness have made use of this ambiguous principle.

Augustine also preached forgiveness of one's neighbor, and Arendt retrieves and incorporates into her political thought this part of the Christian tradition.[88] Although Arendt's forgiveness is not Christian forgiveness that relies upon and reflects God's grace toward sinners, Arendt traces forgiveness to the teachings of Jesus: "The discoverer of the role of forgiveness in the realm of human affairs was Jesus of Nazareth. The fact that he made this discovery in a religious context and articulated it in religious language is no reason to take it any less seriously in a strictly secular sense."[89] In *The Human Condition* Arendt presents forgiving as one of two "modes of redemption" that helps to mitigate the unanticipated consequences of political action.[90] Arendt recommends it to citizens as a "remedy" for "the predicament of irreversibility," one that can serve "to undo the deeds of the past." Though an unlikely political category, for Arendt, forgiveness is necessary both because of the irreversibility of human action and because of the likelihood of unforeseen consequences.[91]

A marker of the disagreement between Arendt and the Christian right is that while Arendt makes forgiveness a political relationship between citizens, the Christian right makes expiation of sin and the conditions for God's forgiveness central to its theological, social, and political missions. Critics of the Christian right accuse the movement of crafting compassionate rhetoric in an attempt to obscure the punitive, theological, anti-individual rights foundations of its politics. These critics are not completely wrong, of course. Like other carefully constructed and executed forms of political rhetoric and action, compassion can function as a strategy that immunizes political actors and ideologies against accusations of hatred and extremism. However, compassion campaigns have other effects besides such political payoffs. These include calling forth compassion from Christian conservative followers and defining for these followers the appropriate form and boundaries of compassion. The wide variety of goals and effects of compassion rhetoric and projects should encourage those who are concerned about the personal and public significance of compassion campaigns to assess them carefully. Hannah Arendt's critique of compassion in, or as, politics is one starting point for such an assessment.

Arendt has been taken to task for defining politics in such a way as to stigmatize compassion, to diminish its role in politics, and to leave in its place a conception of politics that is agonistic, masculine, and amoral. Expositors identify a severe tone or perspective in many of her works. Even her treatment of Varnhagen, which Arendt cast innocently as a "narrat[ion of] the story of Rahel's life," has been described as cleansed of "compassionate depth" and "as ruthless as it was insightful."[92] Arendt's theoretical attention to love and compassion helped to define the contours of her particular controversial conception of the public sphere and politics as a space of action, assertion, and freedom. However, her theorizations of love, neediness, and the body have seemed disturbing and in need of redress. It seems that many readers have been uncomfortable with a woman so hard and unfeeling.

It's a tribute to Arendt's depth as a thinker that we continue to have these arguments about her and that readers continue to find in her work resources for alternative conceptions of politics that are neither amoral nor perhaps even entirely heartless. In any case, however Arendt theorized the likely effects of compassionate forms of politics, not all forms of mass compassion are equally subject to Arendt's critique. Christian conservatives associate compassion with efforts to fight sexual sinfulness for the benefit of those who are caught in its grasp. At the same time, the political instruction that accompanies compassion clarifies a second goal: to contain sexual sinfulness so that the behaviors and political commitments associated with it—abortion and LGBT rights—do not contaminate American culture and politics. As a movement, the Christian right seeks to shore up and restore traditional sexual identity and gender roles, the stigmatized status of same-sex sexuality, and a particular kind of reproductive order. Related goals include reinforcing its own version of Christian morality in believer-activists, enacting antigay and antiabortion—"family values"-friendly—public policies; transforming American culture in ways that are consistent with the movement's conception of sexuality and sexual immorality and; in eschatological terms, turning God's wrath away from an America that is perceived to court divine judgment with every cultural and political shift.

However different from each other, these goals are inconsistent with the kind of compassionate politics that so worried Arendt. They are, however, vulnerable to being analyzed and criticized from the perspective of other aspects of her political thought. Arendt worried about attempts to impose regimes of absolute morality and the havoc wreaked by figures like Robespierre who confuse moral ideals for political ones. For Arendt, "the human condition is a condition of plurality . . . that . . . is inhospitable to the rigid moralism of single truths. Public life or politics thrives on debate, conversation and compromise, not on absolute truths, imagined or real."[93] Compassionate or not, political efforts to diminish plurality, foreclose representative thinking, and install a particular ideal of goodness as a basis for citizenship are a problem for Arendt and for us all.

Hannah Arendt calls into question the role of compassion and love in public affairs. In the next chapter, I introduce Ayn Rand, the spokesperson and avatar of selfishness, as a thinker whose work is surprisingly useful in deciphering the compassion politics of the Christian right. Though they were very different thinkers, Rand and Arendt did not disagree on everything. Both renounced group-based discrimination. Both held that compassion is appropriate to aim at individuals rather than at groups and that public life (as each understood it) is deformed by attempts to use compassion as a justification for policies, whether nationalist, racialist, or economically redistributive. Both found the subject of evil compelling and even theorized about its nature in some similar ways. In "The Age of Envy," Rand defines as the "naked face of evil" the "pure, 'nonvenal' hatred of the good for being the good."[94] Similarly, for Arendt, "evil is not just the privation (absence) of good, but the willful destruction of good because it is good."[95]

However, there the comparison ends. Arendt and Rand could not have diverged more on the subject of what constitutes "the good" for human beings. Arendt was a champion and expositor of a sphere of politics that never should be reduced to economics. Rand, however, did not acknowledge an independent sphere of the political and defined her preferred political system as "capitalism."[96] In spite of Arendt's protests to the contrary, I suspect that Rand would have cast Arendt as a communist as Rand did so many others who failed to share her vision of "man." For her part, Arendt might have refused to validate Rand's pretensions to the label of "philosopher." Neither was a Christian, and neither would have trucked with the contemporary Christian right, which was still in its formative stage when the two thinkers died in 1975 (Arendt) and 1982 (Rand). Nonetheless, by helping to clarify what Christian right compassion is *not* and what it *is*, both thinkers can help us make sense of our contemporary politics and, more specifically, of the compassionate projects spawned by contemporary culture wars.

4

Just Deserts

The Compassion of Ayn Rand

Who *Is* John Galt?

In the wake of the collapse of the housing market and the Great Recession that followed, the tea party movement launched in 2009. The movement attracted many Americans with its official mission of reducing government regulation of business and industry, diminishing the size and scope of the federal government, and as Tea Party Express, one of the largest of the tea party umbrella groups, put it, "return[ing] our country to the Constitutional principles that have made America the 'shining city on a hill.'"[1] The narrow mandate of constitutional fidelity and individual liberty from government interference was echoed by tea party activists as well as by policy makers who allied themselves with the tea party movement. What was left out of this public transcript, however, was a less well-advertised hidden transcript of social issues that included opposition to abortion and LGBT rights.[2] Although the movement claimed as its source and genealogy the founding period of the American republic and a strict interest in matters of government and the economy, many observers of the tea party quickly identified the tea party as drawing upon other sources for its philosophy and personnel. These sources included Christian conservatism and the thought of novelist and putative philosopher Ayn Rand.[3]

Since 2008 the ideas of Ayn Rand have undergone a remarkable renaissance. Advanced by spokespersons of the right such as Glenn Beck, Pamela Geller, and Michelle Malkin—and with her vehement distaste for religion often conveniently excised or downplayed—Rand has come back into fashion. I do not argue that the Christian right uses Rand's ideology openly; given Rand's disdain for superstition, a category that for her would include mainstream Christian doctrines, such a public appeal to her thought by Christian right elites would be extremely unlikely. But in his recent foray into the world of Rand admiration and appropriation, Gary Weiss finds evidence that Rand's ideas are alive and well in the overlapping tea party and Christian right movements. Having located "Christian Objectivists," as well as Christian conservatives who would not call themselves by the name of her philosophy even though they have been influenced by her, Weiss "found [him]self admiring [their] sound political sense, which could serve as a bridge between the Christian right and the doctrinaire free-market atheists of the Randian persuasion. The formula was simple: politely disagree with Rand's beliefs that are repulsive to devout Christians, such as her atheism and approval of abortion, and rationalize her disdain for charity, altruism, and other Judeo-Christian principles."[4] Rand would not have approved of these "loopholes," but neither her most consistent fans and expositors nor the think tanks and media outlets they control can enforce ideological consistency on those who find elements of Rand's thought persuasive or compatible with their existing beliefs. Indeed, as Weiss suggests, such appropriations and reconciliations with existing attitudes and convictions help to explain the ongoing expansion of Rand's influence and its impact on American life.

In surveying the current landscape of Rand's influence in the United States, it is important to remember that Rand was not always the champion of complete laissez-faire capitalism that she eventually became. Before she was the foremost American apologist for the morality of capitalism, her thought was characterized by a more generalized "Nietzschean fixation on the superior individual" that lead her to reflect positively upon the selfishness and individualism of criminals such as the murderer William Hickman, whom Rand complimented as "a man who really stands alone, in action and in soul."[5] A central tenet of Ayn Rand's thought is the distinction that can, and should, be made between individuals based on desert, the terms and conditions of which Rand was happy to expound in fiction, nonfiction, and her personal relationships. This distinction does not operate only in arenas of financial competition and transactions but, rather, pervades other dimensions of Rand's worldview.

Given her contempt for religious habits of mind, it is striking how closely many of Rand's ideas articulate with both the political economy and the sexuality politics of the contemporary Christian right. For example, Rand's thought is productive for studying the the ideology of the Christian right because of the movement's own embrace of laissez-faire capitalism.⁶ Rand's strenuous defense of the purest versions of unregulated market capitalism can be found today among Christian conservative elites who read the Bible as a brief for capitalism and forge what William Connolly calls "the evangelical-capitalist resonance machine."⁷ Multiple continuities—modes of setting boundaries for compassion, a consistent defense of laissez-faire capitalism, as well as socially conservative positions on gender and sexuality—inspire a return to the Randian canon as a resource for contemporary American political ideology, including that of the Christian right.

Most Americans have discovered Rand's philosophy through her novels, especially *The Fountainhead* or *Atlas Shrugged*. Published in 1957, *Atlas Shrugged* is Rand's monumental work of fiction: "the astounding story of a man who said that he would stop the motor of the world—and did."⁸ In *Atlas*, Rand uses the sphere of industrial manufacturing as a backdrop for the philosophical, social, economic, psychological, and political conflict between two great "isms": individualism and collectivism. In the years immediately following the novel's publication, Gore Vidal delivered a testimony to Rand's broad appeal when he noted that Rand "was the one writer people knew and talked about" in 1960 when he was campaigning unsuccessfully for a seat in the US House of Representatives. Vidal was startled to find Rand's "philosophy" "nearly perfect in its immorality," and he argued that this reversal of traditional morality "makes the size of her audience all the more ominous and symptomatic as we enter a curious new phase in our society."⁹

As numerous histories and commentaries demonstrate, Rand—or at least her ideas, if not her official philosophy of objectivism—was present at the birth of conservative "fusionism" and the new right. In the 1960s, as now, a key obstacle to the consolidation of the diverse philosophical strands of conservatism revolved around the question of Christianity as a moral basis for the movement.¹⁰ But the fact that the atheism of Rand and objectivism could not be reconciled imminently with a new Christian conservatism that was just beginning to be brought into existence didn't prevent Rand's ideas from making their way into the consciousness of Americans. As Lisa McGirr explains in her study of "the origins of the new American right," Rand's objectivism, traditional libertarianism and social conservatism "shared a belief that the tendency toward liberal 'collectivism' undermined older moral principles and what they perceived as fundamental truths."¹¹ As a result, adherents to these ideologies could engage in "joint mobilization" over their distrust of the federal government, their equation of freedom with economic freedom, and their repudiation of "egalitarianism."¹²

These arenas of agreement were in evidence in Senator Barry Goldwater's campaign for president in 1964, which Rand supported enthusiastically. Memoirist Jerome Tucille relates that Goldwater was understood by Rand's followers as a "Randian character" and 'hero straight from the pages of *Atlas Shrugged*" who, before his election defeat, "belonged in Galt's Gulch."[13] Considering Goldwater's religious views and the beliefs of many Christian conservatives who supported his candidacy, Rand reconciled herself to endorsing him in spite of religion—that is, to picking and choosing the parts of Goldwater's philosophy that were consistent with her own and that she believed constituted the core of his platform.[14] Today, it appears as though Christian conservatives are returning the favor. The fact that Rand "declared war" on Christ and Christian morality—or at least on a particular conception of them—has not prevented the integration of Rand's "romantic capitalism" into the foundations of the conservative movement.[15] And her stringent criteria of good and evil easily articulate with the uncompromising moral distinctions that form the basis of Christian conservative compassion in ex-gay and postabortion ministries.

The devout manner with which many Randians have approached the texts, principles, and pronouncements of the author has struck many observers of Rand and her objectivist movement. Tucille argues that for young people from a "regimented, religious background," Rand's thought provides a "dogmatic" and "closed system of ideas" and that her philosophy shares key characteristics with doctrinaire forms of Protestant, Catholic, and Jewish faith (as well as Marxist ideology).[16] Having fallen out of favor with Rand, libertarian Murray Rothbard denounced the "Ayn Rand cult" in an entertaining and irreverent 1972 article, noting that an "ideological cult can adopt the same features as the more overtly religious cult, even when the ideology is explicitly atheistic and anti-religious." Rothbard skewered the movement as a religious cult whose hidden agenda—its "esoteric creed"—represented the opposite of all it ostensibly stood for. With *Atlas Shrugged*, as a sacred text, Rand possessed a network of true believers, a hierarchy, and an implicit threat (and sometime reality) of excommunication.

Rothbard recognized that the mechanism of control that Rand wielded over her immediate group of followers was objectivist psychotherapy, which provided interpretations about members' psychological states that accorded with objectivist doctrine. But he also points out that Rand's heroes—wooden, posturing, and one-dimensional as they might be—were intended to "serve as role models for every Randian. Just as every Christian is supposed to aim at the imitation of Christ in his own daily life, so every Randian was supposed to aim at the imitation of John Galt."[17]

Rand concluded *Atlas Shrugged* with an unusual first-person statement entitled, "About the Author." The final paragraph, often reprinted as a telling epigram for Rand's oeuvre, reads: "I trust that no one will tell me that men such as I write about don't exist. That this book has been written—and published—is my proof that they do." It is a stirring statement, but it's not true in the sense that Rand intended it. The fact that Rand created her characters does not, of course, prove that such specimens of objectivism exist.[18] Neither does the fact that there has been such a prodigious market for Rand's fiction prove that the reading public is stocked with Dagney Taggarts, Howard Roarks, and John Galts.[19] Since only two basic kinds of characters exist in Rand's fictional world, the rational and the irrational—"the able . . . and the incompetent"—her fiction encourages readers to identify with, and aim at, virtue as Rand understands it.[20] This pedagogical and aspirational dimension of Rand's work suggests quite a different psychology and motivation than the one Rand attributed to those who embrace her writing.

I argue that Rand's own rejection of religion is not dispositive on the issue of her usefulness as a guide to contemporary Christian right thought. Like the foundational ideas of other modern thinkers, Rand's ideas have passed into popular discourse, many having become detached from their origins in the specific texts of their idiosyncratic creator. In this chapter I argue that there are two kinds of link between the Christian right's compassionate sexuality politics and Rand. The first is Rand's own conceptions of same-sex sexuality and gender, which she wrote into her fiction and philosophy, while the second—and even more productive—is a set of foundational ideas that encompasses, but is not exhausted by, Rand's market fundamentalism. Together, these dimensions of Rand's thought help to construct a blueprint for understanding Christian conservative compassion.

Rand, Sex, and Gender

Unlike the Christian right, Rand was libertarian on reproductive rights; she advocated the view that the bodies of women belonged to nobody but themselves and that, as potential rather than actual persons, fetuses could not have rights. Heller finds evidence that Rand procured an abortion sometime in the early 1930s after her marriage to Frank O'Connor.[21]

Rand also held libertarian views with regard to proscriptions and prosecutions of same-sex sexuality. However, like the Christian right she was harsh in her assessment of homosexuals, noting in her most public statement on the subject that homosexuality "involves psychological flaws, corruptions, errors, or unfortunate premises. . . . Therefore I regard it as immoral . . . And more than that, if you want my really sincere opinion. It's disgusting."[22] With regard to gay male sexuality, Rand's second, and final, "intellectual heir," Leonard Peikoff, describes Rand's view of love between two men in this way: "[T]his relationship . . . can exist between two men who are both healthy; it would not include sex—because, she thought, they won't have the desire for that form of expression of their love."[23] Although she did not express her views on the subject often, Rand's perspective on same-sex sexuality has had a long life and occasioned a good deal of discussion among her followers and interlocutors. A key text in this debate is *Ayn Rand, Homosexuality, and Human Liberation*, by Chris Matthew Sciabarra, Rand's most persistent academic expositor.

In his brief monograph, originally published as essays in an objectivist magazine, Sciabarra surveys past and present objectivists on the subject of Rand's and her movement's orientation toward same-sex sexuality.[24] What he finds is that the history of objectivism has been marked by bias against lesbians and gay men in the name of the founder's own beliefs and of the morality and rationality she championed. Using the narratives of respondents and his own interpretation of objectivist philosophy, Sciabarra denounces this bias. He argues that human liberation can be achieved through adherence to the precepts of Rand's philosophy, even when those precepts diverge from Rand's own flawed personal judgment and taste. Even though respondents attest that antigay bias in the movement has diminished since the 1960s and 1970s, not everyone is persuaded that the shift toward greater tolerance is consistent with objectivist thought.

So, for example, Reginald Firehammer's *The Hijacking of a Philosophy: Homosexuals vs. Ayn Rand's Objectivism* is a response to Sciabarra and to a putative "homosexual agenda" within the ideological precincts of objectivism.[25] An objectivist reviewer of Sciabarra's book points out that while Sciabarra rightly calls upon Rand's principles of privacy and autonomy for his reconciling of objectivism with same-sex sexuality, he risks substituting a "liberal and permissive narrative about sexuality" for Rand's sexuality of "majesty and meaning."[26] It seems that many of Sciabarra's testimonials to the harms wrought by objectivist antigay bias are produced by people who engage in sexuality for pleasure (or pay) rather than for "majesty and meaning." This disagreement over the correct objectivist position on same-sex sexuality is plainly a struggle over Rand's legacy. Still, assuming that pure reason does not dictate antigay morality, the struggle helps to clarify the continuing relevance of antigay social conservatism among many of Rand's admirers.

Rand did not arrive at her conclusions by way of religious belief, yet there are deep similarities between Rand's understanding of sexual orientation and the positions expounded by the Christian right in the years since Rand's public statement. Rand's view that homosexuality could be summed up by noting its immorality, the psychological problems of its practitioners, and the natural disgust of heterosexuals toward same-sex sexuality is still common in the conservative Christian movement. However, as the movement has become both more politically sophisticated and more integrated into governing institutions, rhetoric about same-sex sexuality has softened and become bifurcated. Abomination rhetoric about immorality and disgust is preserved in ingroup contexts dedicated to political activism, and compassionate rhetoric about psychological struggles with predispositions to same-sex attraction and the imperative for Christians to overcome their disgust in the service of ministry is featured in ex-gay ministries.

In addition to the congruence between her views and those of the Christian right on same-sex sexuality, Rand's gender essentialism and gender complementarity are also closer to those on the Christian right than we might think given her stance against religious belief. It is clear from Rand's writings and the memoirs of her companions that Rand's views of same-sex sexuality were closely linked with her conception of gender, and especially of gender complementarity. If Rand's perspective on gender as a binary system is not obvious enough in her novels, her close companions testify to this aspect of her thought and autobiography.[27]

A prominent detail of Rand's personal conception of gender difference often has been the subject of discussion in her work: that the natural orientation of women toward men is hero worship. Elaborating on Rand's public and written comments on Rand's conception of gender, Nathaniel Branden, her young lover and the man she first publicly identified as her "intellectual heir," confirms that Rand often referred to herself as a "man-worshiper."[28] By this she meant, no doubt, the worship of "man" in the abstract sense celebrated in her novels but also "man" in the sense of the particular male hero to whom she longed to submit sexually. Branden reports that when he challenged Rand on this point, she clarified that she understood "man as superior to woman" and, further, that women seek a man to "inspire them to sexual/romantic surrender."[29] In Rand's novels, the belief that by nature a heroic woman seeks to submit herself to a suitably heroic man is fully instantiated. Indeed, Branden cites the scene in *Atlas Shrugged* in which Dagny Taggart, the woman who runs a railroad, appears in an evening gown: "[T]he diamond band on the wrist of her naked arm gave her the most feminine of all aspects: the look of being chained."[30]

In her biography of Rand, Barbara Branden relates the course of Rand's intimate relationship with Barbara's husband, Nathaniel. There, Rand's "psycho-epistemological" assumptions about heterosexual sexuality and female gender identity emerge in the context of Rand's relationships with Nathaniel and with her husband, Frank O'Connor. Barbara relates the ways in which Rand used charisma and the tenets of her philosophy of reason to elicit consent for the affair from O'Connor and the Brandens and to use her relationship with Nathaniel to construct the epic sexual relationship she believed was a direct consequence of both her and Nathaniel's superior nature. When Branden later ended his sexual relationship with Rand and fell in love with a younger woman, Rand took it as evidence that he was not the heroic character she had scripted him to be and ejected him from the movement. Rothbard characterizes the episode as Satan being "ejected from Paradise."[31]

Rand's heroic female protagonist, Dagney Taggart, becomes romantically and sexually involved with two of the novel's male protagonists, Francisco d'Anconia and, later, Hank Rearden. But ultimately she falls in love with John Galt, whose superiority over the other heroic males is legible even to the least discerning readers. Given that the two men Taggart loves before she loves Galt embody reason, it is only natural that both understand and support Taggart's love for Galt. Setting aside the polyamory and sexual self-determination of her characters, Rand's doctrine of emotion has much in common with the doctrine of emotion of the contemporary Christian right. For Christian conservatives, emotions are God's messages to believers, either delivered directly or through the intervening mechanism of natural law. In objectivism, emotions are a product of premises, rational or otherwise. In neither ideology is it possible to conceptualize emotion in terms of unconscious motivation, interpersonal experience, or social context or in any way that violates the core tenets of the belief system. In both, emotions enact moral standards and measure the distance between an actual state of affairs and the doctrinal ideal.

The passage in Rand's fiction that is most revealing and controversial on the point of gendered femininity and women's sexuality is a scene in *The Fountainhead*. There, the male protagonist, architect Howard Roark, rapes—or "rapes"—the female protagonist, Dominique Francon. The scene has inspired a prodigious amount of commentary on Rand's work. Rand's own reading is that unspoken consent underlies the encounter between Roark and Francon and, thus, that the sex is "rape by engraved invitation."[32] Following Rand, many critics have denied that a rape occurs, preferring to read the scene as an episode of "rough sex" onto which feminists have projected their own contrary conception of appropriate physicality and consent. Wendy McElroy makes this case, noting that in reflecting on the event later Francon defiantly recalls her enjoyment. For McElroy, Francon's pleasure nullifies the interpretation of rape.[33]

If the author's reading does not exhaust the possibilities of interpretation, and given the prima facie evidence at the "scene," it is possible that Rand staged and then disclaimed the rape of Dominique Francon. In any case, Rand's reading of the violent sexual encounter she created is consistent with her personal conception of sexuality. As Mercer notes, "sex to [Rand] was an elevated union between two outsized personalities, who are united in values and life force; a savage yet spiritual act of conquest. Sex to Rand had little to do with sexual expression and affirmation per se. Both are concepts that belong in the collectivist arena of gender and identity politics."[34] In sex, as in many other aspects of her philosophy, Rand set her own preferences as standards for aspiration, rationality, and right conduct.

Christian right narratives of same-sex sexual development are also grounded in consistent binary conceptions of feminine and masculine gender. These conceptions are taught and modeled by ex-gay and -lesbian spokespersons in the ex-gay movement, who are taught during their own struggles against homosexuality that a damaged gender identity lies at the root of same-sex desire.[35] Sometimes this instruction is cosmetic, focused on external characteristics such as dress and deportment.[36] But more phenomenological forms of instruction offer a better sense of the stakes of gender difference and what Christian conservatives understand as natural in gender and sexual difference. One form of instruction defines femininity as fundamentally receptive, an orientation that includes receptiveness to the teachings and gifts of God, but also emotional and sexual receptiveness toward a husband.[37] In the context of the ex-gay movement, it is assumed that some women may have to learn the appropriate, though still always natural, virtues of receptiveness and submissiveness, both to elicit and to accommodate male heterosexual desire.

Christian conservative women write frequently on the issue of submission, a concept they argue is often misconstrued by those who do not share their traditionalist faith. Beverly LaHaye speaks for many when she writes that biblical teaching on women's submission is that women are "subordinate, but not inferior." Hence, for LaHaye, popular meanings of submission that suggest inferiority or slavishness are not appropriate and demean women.[38] For Christian conservative women, the requirement of submission, to God and to one's own husband, is grounded in women's nature and in biblical admonitions concerning sexual difference, women's relations to their husbands, and women's role in public life. An additional dimension to women's submission is documented by Michelle Wolkomir in her work on marital crises of Christian women married to same-sex-attracted Christian men: women using submission as "a strategy to advance their own interests, invoking God's authority to imbue their demands with credibility and power." In such circumstances, Wolkomir finds women experiencing submission as "liberating, transforming, and empowering" and relying on it to assert control in painful circumstances.[39]

Of course, Rand did not rely on the Bible as an authority, but she did regard the feminine desire for submission to be physiologically and "psycho-epistemologically" scripted. Her protégé, Nathaniel Branden, summarized the objectivist view in this way: "While a healthy aggressiveness and self-assertiveness is proper and desirable for both sexes, man experiences the essence of his masculinity in the act of romantic dominance; woman experiences the essence of her femininity in the act of romantic submission."[40] The key distinction between the forms of submission that Rand repudiates throughout her work and the form she valorizes between the men and women who exemplify her ideal of heroism is that the latter is freely chosen rather than a result of manipulation, false consciousness, or convention. Indeed, gendered dominance and submission are markers of the individualism Rand celebrates.

For Christian conservative women, gendered submission is freely chosen as well. Indeed, freedom itself is usually contrasted with license and defined as the willingness to fulfill the nature God has created for us. It is in this spirit of freedom from the bondage of sin and licentiousness that women in the postabortion movement embrace gender scripts that specify female nurturance and male protectiveness as a prelude to healing from abortion. For these women gendered submission is a marker of a Christian woman's relationship with God and a celebration of womanhood rather than the outward sign of an abject identity. And both Christian conservative and objectivist perspectives provide similar explanations of this key difference between feminine and masculine gender identities.

To Barbara Branden, Rand asserted that "a man [is] defined by his relationship to reality, while a woman [is] defined by her relationship to a man," or man is to reality as woman is to man.[41] This relational logic is consistent with Rand's views as she articulated them. The parallel construction for Christian conservatives is derived from, among other biblical passages, 1 Corinthians 11:3: "But I would have you know, that the head of every man is Christ; and the head of the woman is the man; and the head of Christ is God," or man is to Christ as woman is to man.[42] This conception of "headship" or, as it is often rendered, "servant leadership," is at the core of Christian right doctrine on marriage and on forms of leadership outside the household.[43] A recent public articulation of female submission comes from reporting of Representative Michele Bachmann's statement in a 2006 talk at Minnesota's Living Word Christian Center that, because she believes in women being submissive to their husbands, she became a tax attorney because her husband told her to.[44] Clearly, the Christian conservative demand for married women's submission, at least as it is presently interpreted, is consistent with women being strong and commanding in a way that is consistent with Rand's tough Dagny Taggart. For Rand, as for the Christian right, strong women can and should be submissive. Of course, in real life, Christian conservative women may employ a "repertoire of strategies for negotiating, reinterpreting, and subverting this doctrine of female submission" that includes following biblical prescriptions and their own consciences as they are led by God.[45]

The particulars of gender scripts and female submission in Rand's work and in the ideology of the Christian right still vary considerably. I am not suggesting that gender conceptions are exactly the same in these quite different modes of thought but, rather, that the structure of the gender system that each constructs is similar enough to the other that both can be, and frequently have been, contrasted to a morally inferior feminist ideal of gender egalitarianism and neutrality with regard to the superiority of heterosexual desire. Both Rand and the Christian right understand gender as a binary system and one that upholds women's value at the same time that it scripts natural submission to men in intimate relations. This binary system of gender in turn underwrites the abjection of same-sex sexuality as unnatural and morally grotesque.

Writing in an organ of the objectivist movement, one admirer asks the question: should Ayn Rand have been a feminist? He answers: "While her own account of sexuality is in many ways quite traditional (and thus anti-feminist), her individualist ethics suggests an antitraditional resolution to the questions of sex."[46] Susan Love Brown suggests that the problem is deeper than this distinction between Rand's thought and her personal consistency will allow when she argues that "Rand's thinking itself is compromised" by her insistence that a woman should not occupy the position of president of the United States. In her essay, "About a Woman President," Rand clarified her objection to a woman president by saying that "a properly feminine woman does not treat men as if she were their pal, sister, mother—or leader." As Brown points out, in the essay Rand is at pains to make the case that this position is not a statement of personal discomfort with women's leadership but, rather, is a logical outcome of the application of her philosophy.[47]

It is common for Rand's commentators to position her as feminist in the ways that matter, especially in terms of her strong female characters and her strenuous defense of individualism. Her indifference or hostility to feminism and the women's movement is explained by the deep intersections between feminism/the women's movement and collectivism as Rand understood it. But not all of Rand's ideas are easily resolved by this strategy. Rand's conceptions of gender and sexuality are certainly antitraditional in many important respects. But it is the common ground they share with traditional views that suggests ways in which they can underwrite other forms of individualism (and conservatism) than those Rand herself would have associated with her thought.

Objectiv(ist) Compassion

Even with these similarities between Rand's thinking and the ideology of the Christian right, it is not necessary to rely on autobiographical details to see how it is that Rand's work and ideas are compatible with Christian right compassion. Indeed, comparing her broader philosophy with the doctrine and mechanics of Christian conservative compassion enables a different perspective on the ideology that grounds the compassionate sexuality politics of the Christian right. This ideology consists of six key principles: first, compassion is a valuable form of personal and social relations; second, compassion can only function properly if the boundary between appropriate and inappropriate compassion is demarcated; third, those who are marked as morally undeserving are wicked and deserving of punishment; fourth, collectivist "special" rights for victims of moral and social castigation must always be rejected; fifth, the good and morally worthy should not be held responsible for harm suffered by the undeserving; and sixth, leaders and intellectuals who represent morally undesirable people and ideals should be held more responsible for the misappropriation of compassion than the ordinary undeserving. In the sections that follow I consider each of these areas of similarity between Rand and the Christian right.

The Value of Compassion

Because of the emphasis she places on individual striving in her fiction, Rand is often read to scorn the helping hand of compassion altogether. Although he is sympathetic to objectivism in many respects, W. Teed Rockwell seems unaware of passages in Rand's work that address compassion directly and mounts a defense of compassion against Rand's repudiation of altruism.[48] But even Nathaniel Branden, who is more than familiar with the Rand canon, criticizes Rand for her dearth of attention to compassion, accusing her of limiting consideration of it to "the context of self-sacrifice and/or . . . the context of government coercion."[49] Yet there is more to Rand's treatment of compassion than is revealed by Branden's 1984 critique.

Rand invites such readings of the deficit of compassion in her work through her recurring critiques of liberal compassion, both in her fiction and in her nonfiction: "If anyone ever believed (or tried to believe) that the motive of altruism is compassion, that its goal is the relief of human suffering and the elimination of poverty, the state of today's culture now deprives him of any foothold on self-deception. Today, altruism is running amuck, shedding its tattered rationalizations and displaying its soul."[50] But the conclusion that Rand has nothing to say about compassion that is not pejorative fails to account for the explicit treatment she gives the subject in her work. For Rand, compassion can be immoral, but only when it is extended to the undeserving. As she put it in a famous 1964 interview with *Playboy*, "there is nothing wrong in helping other people, if and when they are worthy of the help."[51] It would be inaccurate to regard the phrase "nothing wrong" as merely a cliché in this passage because Rand always made clear that she did regard the inappropriate dispensing of compassion to constitute a moral wrong. And the words and actions of her novels' heroes attest to her interest in extending compassion only to those she deemed worthy of it.

For Rand, compassion is positive under two conditions: that the individuals who extend compassion do so willingly and not as a matter of compulsion and that those who are recipients of compassion are deserving by the standard of morality Rand offers—a standard she claims is objective and universal. For Rand, as for compassionate conservatives, liberalism fails as a governing philosophy for three reasons. First, liberalism subjects citizens to compulsory giving through taxation and various redistributive schemes. Second, liberalism sanctions the expenditure of inappropriate compassion on undeserving objects. And third, liberalism incites and tolerates the leveling of rage and *ressentiment* at deserving objects, especially those who exemplify individualism and produce society's goods.[52] As many scholars have pointed out, the distinction between deserving and undeserving has a long history in politics. Feminists have traced the history of the welfare state, for example, by examining the evolution of the distinction and using it to track the expansions and withdrawals of American social benefits.[53] This literature demonstrates the significance of race, gender, and class in constituting entrenched categories of "desert." However, they also show that these dimensions of power and identity do not exhaust the possibilities for binaries that can distinguish between deserving and undeserving. For example, in their study of the tea party movement, Theda Skocpol and Vanessa Williamson find a generational dimension to the movement's moral distinctions such that "overly entitled young people" constitute a new class of the undeserving for very conservative older Americans.[54]

The split between deserving and undeserving in American history has frequently revolved around distinctions of status, as in boundaries drawn around gender, racial, ethnic, or socioeconomic class identity. Behavioral characteristics presumed to adhere to groups, for example distinctions between the hard-working and the lazy—which roughly map onto John Locke's famous distinction between the "industrious and rational" and the "quarrelsome and contentious"—are also invoked as a basis for hierarchies of benefits and social status.[55] Such behavioral distinctions are often parasitic on status distinctions, however. Perceived group-linked behaviors have often been premised on group identity or perceptions of identity. Examples include stubborn beliefs about the moral and/or intellectual inadequacies of a number of groups in American history, most notably African Americans.[56]

Rand's perspective on compassion runs through both her fiction and her nonfiction. Indeed, one fruitful way to read her work is as a set of guidelines about the appropriate moral grounds for compassion. As a thinker, she rejected the kinds of status distinctions that have been common in American history as a measure of individual value or deservingness, sanctioning neither raced nor most gendered hierarchies. However, in spite of the significance of behavior as a marker of the boundary between characters that embody reason and those that embody its opposite, ideology is a key component of that distinction. We can read Rand's fiction to discover the conditions under which compassion emerges among the characters in her fiction, the discrete qualities that animate it, and the importance of ideology in its circulation.

The Boundary of Compassion

In ideology as well as novelistic complexity, *The Fountainhead* serves as the dress rehearsal for Rand's masterwork, *Atlas Shrugged*. In *The Fountainhead*, the male protagonist, Howard Roark, is an architect in the aesthetic mold of Frank Lloyd Wright, whom Rand admired. Idealistic, naïve, and nearly martyred by those who hate his purity and unwillingness to compromise, he passes through a variety of trials—including an actual trial for destroying a building that represents a corruption of his work—before emerging victorious, his integrity intact. Another of the main characters of *The Fountainhead* is Ellsworth Toohey, Rand's most compelling villain and a character she describes as having "all the sorry fragility of unhardened bones." Toohey is a journalist who exemplifies the evil of social collectivism and the personal absence of values, a destructive and resentful parasite. Through the figure of Toohey Rand fleshes out the profile of the "moocher"/"rotter"/"looter"/"second-hander," terms Rand uses to denote those who make claims on others for spiritual and material goods they have not produced and do not deserve. And she uses him to limn the threat posed by the appeal of compassion, an appeal he wields to indoctrinate the vulnerable and defeat the strong. Toohey is also a figure in a small but memorable scene that establishes his standing in comparison to the hero, Roark. When Toohey puts himself in Roark's way in a deserted location and asks Roark, "[W]hat [do] you think of me?" Roark responds, "But I don't think of you."[57]

But Rand works out the theme of compassion most fully in *Atlas Shrugged*, her most famous work. Never a subtle storyteller, Rand expounds her account of desert and the mind of those who speak for undeserved compassion in a chapter entitled, "Anti-Life."[58] As usual, she subordinates plot and character to didactic commentary; the chapter itself consists of a series of confrontations that clarify the values that underlie the story and move the novel toward its denouement. In "Anti-Life" the looters are seizing control of the world's governments and economic system. Bragging of his pending victory over the industrialist achievers,

Dagny's brother, James Taggart, exposes his contemptible ideology to his wife, a woman he had married because he believed she would be incapable of understanding and judging his moral ignominy. When Cherryl Taggart flees from her husband she goes to Dagny to apologize, and Dagny reaches out to her desperate sister-in-law: "I feel terribly sorry for you, Cherryl, and I'd like to help you—not because you suffer, but because you haven't deserved to suffer." Later, Dagny, experiencing a foreboding spasm of concern, invites Cherryl to spend the night with her instead of returning home. Cherryl declines, and at the conclusion of the chapter, Dagny's anxiety about Cherryl's fate is vindicated. Having realized the nature of the evil that motivates her husband and his comrades, Cherryl commits suicide, plunging into the river to her death.[59]

As the climax of the novel approaches, a sentimental scene unfolds that reveals the conditions under which it is morally acceptable for compassion to come into existence. The collectivist regime is moving to appropriate the productive apparatus of the novel's protagonists, and a young man Hank Reardon has dubbed "the Wet Nurse" defies the looters and is shot as he flees to warn Reardon about their designs. As the Wet Nurse lies dying from a chest wound, Reardon hears his story, which includes a lengthy confession of previous ideological error and the Wet Nurse's repentance. Reardon responds to this change of mind by humanizing the young man—calling him by his real name—cradling him in the manner of a pietà, and tenderly kissing him on the forehead. Throughout the novels, Rand has heroic characters to whom compassion is extended express concern that they are being presumptuous so that she can define the terms by which compassion is (now) deserved. So it is with Tony/the Wet Nurse: "The boy's head dropped on Reardon's shoulder, hesitantly, almost as if this were a presumption. Reardon bent down and pressed his lips to the dust-streaked forehead. The boy jerked back, raising his head with a shock of incredulous, indignant astonishment. "Do you know what you did?" he whispered, as if unable to believe that it was meant for him.'Put your head down,' said Reardon, 'and I'll do it again.'"[60] For Rand, appropriate compassion emerges between hero-protagonists because they embrace a common morality/ideology. She stages compassion for the reader by reminding the reader of its boundaries. When Cherryl Taggart says to Dagny, "That I happen to suffer doesn't give me a claim on you," Dagny responds predictably: "No, it doesn't. But that you value all the things I value, does."[61]

One sign of Rand's commitment to right thinking, even over right acting, is the character of Dominique Francon, perhaps the most fascinating of Rand's characters precisely because she spends much of *The Fountainhead* not hewing to the heroic path that Rand sets our for her superior "men." Although she allies herself with Roark's enemies out of despair that goodness cannot triumph, Francon loves all that is good and rational in the world. Regardless of what she does, she knows the good, and her reason remains intact. This temporary inversion of Francon's alliances allows Rand to use her to mouth the dangers of compassion: "Compassion is a wonderful thing. It's what one feels when one looks at a squashed caterpillar. An elevating experience. One can let oneself go and spread—you know, like taking a girdle off. You don't have to hold your stomach, your heart or your spirit up—when you feel compassion. All you have to do is look down. It's much easier. When you look up you get a pain in the neck. Compassion is the greatest virtue. It justifies suffering."[62] Yet even though Dominique Francon engages in actions that make her an effective conduit for Rand's disgust with misplaced compassion, we know her heart isn't in it. She remains a heroic figure, the only worthy mate for the much-injured Roark.

Like Rand, Christian conservative leaders also teach their followers how to distinguish the deserving from the undeserving. As a political movement, the Christian right draws a bright line between those who are objects of legitimate concern as fellow persons and citizens and those who are not. By contrast with distinctions of status and behavior that often provide a framework for the treatment of LGBTQ people, the Christian right's compassion campaigns make ideological distinctions based upon the beliefs/convictions of potential objects of compassion. Proper objects of compassion believe that what they want to do (queers) or have done (queers/women who have had abortions) is morally wrong, and they commit themselves to a slate of convictions that's consistent with conservative Christian theology. This is not to say that their behavior is unimportant, but behavior is not the most important standard by which they are to be judged.

The priority of ideology over identity becomes most clear when we focus attention on those designated as undeserving. Conservative Christians who are involved with the ex-gay movement understand that same-sex-attracted people in the movement may have engaged in homosexual behavior and may even continue to experience sexual "falls" while struggling with same-sex desire. Tanya Erzen documents this dynamic of struggle in her ethnographic study of New Hope Ministry when she finds that sexual "brokenness" and falls serve the pedagogical purpose of reinforcing the wonder of God's grace and the distance between sinfulness and obedience. They also provide the material for a more fascinating public witness.[63]

What is intriguing about the ex-gay movement, and particularly about the way it is often understood by many outside critics, is that in spite of the emphasis on *change* of sexual orientation, there has been wide latitude for the tenaciousness of same-sex desire and for the substitution of a right relationship with Jesus Christ for a transformation of proscribed sexual desires. This is true of both Catholic and Protestant arms of the movement. The Catholic ex-gay project, Courage, has long emphasized celibacy in the presence of what is assumed will be continuing same-sex desire, while until very recently Protestant projects have held out the hope for transformation of these desires into normative heterosexuality. But both—often in the private precincts of the movement—acknowledge that the positioning of individuals within the boundaries of compassion is conditioned neither on the absence of same-sex desire nor on the absence of even sexual acting out. Rather, it is a matter of conviction and testimony: of being willing to attest to a moral system in which same-sex sexuality is morally anathema.

If same-sex-attracted women and men who renounce their desires and commit themselves to abstinence from same-sex sexuality are proper objects of compassion, same-sex-attracted people who claim a gay or queer identity are outside the boundary of appropriate compassion. Similarly, with regard to abortion, medical personnel who perform the procedure, women who stubbornly refuse to renounce a previous abortion, and those who support the right to abortion (regardless of whether they have actually undergone the procedure) are all undeserving of compassion. Not only is their repudiation rehearsed explicitly in the political pedagogy of the Christian right's antiabortion movement, but it is also implicit in the way the boundary of compassion is constructed around those penitents who grieve their sinful decision and claim a new identity as sinners suffering from postabortion syndrome.

Sacrificing the Guilty

The Christian right is rightly identified with the theological position that God may punish the ostensibly innocent for his own greater purposes. One specific version of this belief came to public awareness in September 2001 when Jerry Falwell appeared on Pat Robertson's *700 Club* television program and commented about the recent attacks in New York City and Washington, DC, that "God continues to lift the curtain and allow the enemies of America to give us probably what we deserve." Falwell was specific about the identities of those who called down the attack on America, including lesbians, gay men, abortionists, and feminists. Other Christian conservatives who received less attention made similar claims, which were consistent with a conservative Christian reading of God's special covenant with America and with some versions of Christian eschatology.[64] In more complete versions of the moral indictment that escaped attention from the media, Christian right leaders drew parallels between God's depopulation of the earth in Noah's flood and his destruction of Sodom and Gomorrah, and the September 11 attacks on the United States. However, D. James Kennedy pointed out that, unlike these Old Testament cases, those killed in the conflagrations of September 11 were not guiltier than those who were spared.[65] Rather, they were as guilty—or as innocent—as their fellow citizens. Their deaths confirm that widespread tolerance of cultural evils such as same-sex sexuality and abortion have corrupted American life and require the cleansing fire of God's wrath.

Objectivist readers of Rand would no doubt reject any comparison between her strict adherence to a doctrine of individual desert and the belief in collective sacrifice and punishment that animates the sexuality politics of the Christian right. However, there is less light between the two than readers might at first believe. Thomas F. Bertonneau points out that in *Atlas*, Rand operates on a "borrowed premise" (a common term of derision in her work)—an embrace of the very "sacrificial imagination" she repudiates.[66] Bertonneau analyzes the telling descriptors Rand uses throughout the novel to encourage identification with her protagonists and contempt for their vicious foils. But his main focus is a particular scene in the novel, the Taggart Tunnel disaster, in which three hundred travelers are killed by smoke inhalation because a corrupt official uses his clout to force hapless railroad employees to drive a coal-burning engine into the tunnel.[67]

As Bertonneau points out, Rand introduces the scene with an uncharacteristic omniscient narrator expatiating on the themes of fate and desert: "It is said that catastrophes are a matter of pure chance, and there were those who would have said that the passengers of the Comet were not guilty or responsible for the thing that happened to them."[68] In what follows, Rand interposes her proofs of guilt as commentaries on the passengers, distancing herself and her readers from them by using the numbers of their cars to refer to them: "The woman in Roomette 10, Car No. 3, was an elderly schoolteacher who had spent her life turning class after class of helpless children into miserable cowards, by teaching them that the will of the majority is the only standard of good and evil. . . . The man in Bedroom A, Car No. 16 was a humanitarian who had said, 'The men of ability? I do not care what or if they are made to suffer. They must be penalized in order to support the incompetent.' "[69] There seems to be a clear contrast between this scene—including the satisfying annihilation of all the train's occupants—and Rand's own philosophy. With the authorial gesture of stocking the train with the guilty and sending all to their deserved deaths, Rand executes a "grand fantasy of godlike revenge, a theater of resentment assuaged, a daydream of limitless ego." As Bertonneau remarks of the disaster, "every Jack and Jane of the mean-spirited wretches painfully asphyxiates."[70]

It is easy to be reminded of the graphic descriptions of the demise of the wicked in Tim LaHaye and Jerry B. Jenkins' *Left Behind* series of novels, in which great swaths of the inhabitants of the end times die hideous deaths.[71] Indeed, reading *Atlas Shrugged* in light of *Left Behind* suggests ways in which Rand shares an apocalyptic imagination with premillennial Christian conservatives, with the collapsing world economy giving the looters their just deserts and a kind of secular Second Coming in the long-awaited appearance of the savior, John Galt. Without recourse to more recent articulations of Christian right eschatology, in his 1957 review of *Atlas Shrugged*, Whittaker Chambers describes its "primitive" plot as "The War between the Children of Light and the Children of Darkness." Chambers imagines Rand imagining herself as the "bringer of a final revelation," and suggests that the mind that created *Atlas* revels in "grotesque and excessive" punishment of those who resist the "Message."[72] The barely disguised pleasure that many Christian conservative leaders appear to take in the fantasy of the destruction of their immoral adversaries finds its match in Rand's grand fantasy of revenge.[73]

Special Rights

A fourth way in which Rand's thought anticipates and converges with that of the Christian right is her rejection of "special privileges" for identity groups alleged to have been victims of discrimination. Rand often wrote and spoke against what she understood as collectivist special rights, and her main arguments are on display in an essay entitled "The Age of Envy," originally published in *The Objectivist Newsletter* in 1971. There, Rand applies her anticollectivism and her denunciation of pressure groups to issue a harsh indictment of the women's movement, pointing out that while "every other pressure group has some semi-plausible complaint or pretense at a complaint as an excuse for existing" "Women's Lib has none."[74] Indeed, her reading of the early Second Wave women's movement is one that could have been produced by many in the Christian right but for the appearance of the key Randian term, "premises" and the absence of any overt reference to God: "The sex views professed by Women's Lib are so hideous that they cannot be discussed—at least not by me. To regard man as an enemy. . . . to proclaim spiritual sisterhood with lesbians, and to swear eternal hostility to men—is so repulsive a set of premises from so loathsome a sense of life that an accurate commentary would require the kind of language I do not like to see in print."[75]

Rand's essay on the women's movement was first published before the Supreme Court's decision in *Roe*, and at a time when the US women's movement was involved in campaigns against state laws that criminalized abortion procedures. In spite of her objectivist support for abortion rights and the debates about the constitutional right to privacy that surrounded the 1965 Supreme Court case *Griswold vs. Connecticut*, in 1971 Rand could imagine no justification for a women's rights movement.

Although she did not address the gay rights movement as she did the women's and African American civil rights movements, her discussions of New Left movements reveal what they have in common. These movement characteristics, which Rand repudiates in the strongest terms, are public claims based on the weakness and vulnerability of group members, an elevation of collective characteristics (for example, race, gender, sexuality) over the differentiating characteristics of individuals, and policy designs that violate the rights of private property. Because of her concern with property rights, Rand opposed passage of the Civil Rights Act of 1964, calling it "the worst breach of property rights in the sorry record of American history in respect to that subject."[76] Nor would Rand's opposition to the Civil Rights Acts necessarily embarrass her today among social conservatives. In his book, *The End of Racism: Principles for a Multiracial Society*, Dinesh D'Souza calls for the repeal of the 1964 law, arguing for a market-based approach to discrimination that does not unduly limit the freedom of corporations.[77] And in the months before the 2010 Congressional midterm elections, Tennessee Senate candidate, later Senator, Rand Paul revived Rand's critique of the 1964 law.

The anti-"special rights" campaigns of the Christian right are well known and unnecessary to rehearse at length. Beginning in 1977 when Anita Bryant launched "Save Our Children" to reverse an antidiscrimination ordinance in Dade County, Florida, the conservative Christian movement has constructed and been mobilized by an antigay agenda that is explicitly fueled by arguments that queer people seek rights not available to heterosexual Americans. These campaigns have employed many public and private justifications. One is that they recognize and fix forms of identity that do not objectively exist, either because homosexuality is merely a construct that reifies behavior or because all people are naturally heterosexual, whatever the nature of their sexual desires—the "homosexual myth" noted by some in the ex-gay movement. Another justification is the argument that protection of LGBT rights functions as a reward for immorality and, thus, operates as a kind of moral hazard that undermines public virtue.

Finally, like Rand, the Christian right also advances an argument for individual rights, though the Christian right's version of this argument has two prongs: the argument that antidiscrimination policies that specify sexual orientation undermine religious freedom—a prominent theme in the 2012 presidential election—and the argument that these policies undermine the right of individuals to use their property in ways that are consistent with their own values.[78] Recent court cases have tested the right of Christian conservative individuals and businesses to withhold services from openly gay customers or to those in same-sex relationships in jurisdictions with either antidiscrimination laws or relationship recognition. While conservative organizations support conscience protections for Christian conservatives who want the right to withhold their services from LGBT people or those in same-sex relationships, LGBT civil rights groups argue that actors in the economic marketplace should be held to conformity with nondiscrimination laws.[79]

Public arguments for free speech and religious exercise have become particularly salient in recent years in court cases and in public dialogues about gay rights. These arguments are also influential in ingroup settings; they instruct Christian conservatives that their own freedoms decline proportionately as the rights and protections available to LGBTQ people and women who seek a right to abortion and contraception increase. The most recent issue to galvanize arguments about the decline of religious freedom is the Obama administration's Patient Protection and Affordable Care Act, known across the conservative movement as "Obamacare." The law's requirement that companies and organizations—including those that have religious affiliations and are not churches—must cooperate with healthcare insurers to provide access to contraception without employee cost sharing is understood by Christian conservatives to be the most egregious violation of religious liberty in US history. Ayn Rand likely would not have supported the many discriminatory antigay laws and policies that have been promulgated in recent years, but her economic arguments provide a template for the kinds of public rhetoric the Christian right has adopted to redescribe discrimination as individual liberty and equality as a violation of religious liberty.

Responsibility for Harm

Fifth, Rand's whole philosophy is premised on political and methodological individualism. Throughout her work, Rand rejects the possibility of structural harms and either indirect or collective political responsibility for repairing the continuing effects of these harms. In this respect, Rand's discussion of racism in her essay of the same name is instructive. She utterly excoriates racism as a doctrine "of, by and for brutes," and perhaps more important for her, a "version of collectivism" that is at odds with the very core of her philosophy. However, Rand was unable to imagine any kind of oppression that cannot be reduced to the prejudicial acts of some specific individuals against others. Such bias is easily remedied through the application of her philosophy: "There is only one antidote to racism: the philosophy of individualism and its politico-economic corollary, laissez-faire capitalism."[80]

Even if we leave aside Rand's own bias against same-sex sexuality and those who identify as gay or homosexual, such an interpretation of the nature and limits of group-based bias is incorrigibly short-sighted. For example, she does not acknowledge unconscious bias, including the effects of stereotypes injurious to group members. Nor does she acknowledge the continuing effects on group members of institutionalized bias that rewards particular forms of gender or sexual relations and modes of existence without the intervening vehicle of individual prejudice. Finally, she fails to recognize ways in which institutionalized—and not merely individual—bias confers "positional goods" on members of dominant groups that these citizens may be loathe to relinquish through changes in policy or social status.[81]

Indeed, once Rand dispenses with the problem of individual racism, it is clear that she has little else to say about the problem of group-based oppression and bias. The essay "Racism" is brief; approximately half of it is taken up with a denunciation of racial bias itself, while the other half of the essay is as vociferous a repudiation of liberals and "Negro leaders" for violating principles of individualism and for penalizing white men *"for the sins of their ancestors."*[82] While Rand's defense of judging an individual—in her writing, a man—by the content of his character is laudable, it was not a lonely position for a prominent American intellectual to take in 1963. But her refusal to consider the breadth and subtleties of the harms inflicted by social and political bias position her as a thinker whose work easily could be drawn upon by social conservatives today, particularly in public discourse that seeks a palatable alternative to explicit bias and exclusion.

The early conservative Christian narrative of development of the 1970s focused on the misery of a homosexual lifestyle while denying the consequences of harms inflicted on gays through discriminatory laws and social practices and punitive family relations. For the most part, Christian conservatives have continued to reject the idea that LGBTQ people are harmed primarily by social oppression rather than the fruits of their own nonnormative gender or sexual behavior. This position constitutes a point of divergence between many mainline Protestants and traditional conservative Christians (Protestants and Catholics, as well as Mormons and others) on the issue of responsibility for identity-based harm. In the face of intrachurch and intradenominational conflict on the issue of sexuality, many moderate Christians across denominations acknowledge harms caused by antigay social sentiment and legal discrimination.[83] As Dawne Moon shows in her ethnographic study of two churches in a Midwestern city, one "liberal" and one "conservative," the conservative church proscribes any discussion of "gay pain," while the liberal church—which includes a range of members from theologically liberal to theologically conservative—actively discusses social harms and the effects of prejudice.[84]

In recent compassionate discourse Christian right leaders increasingly concede that LGBT people may be harmed by the natural social effects of their lifestyle and that people who suffer from unwanted same-sex desire are certainly harmed by the revulsion that Christians may experience toward the bearers of such proscribed desire. These leaders urge Christian conservatives toward compassion as a way to avoid being implicated in that oppression. Nevertheless, they reject the idea that social stigma and marginalization constitute a primary cause of harm because to do so would be to undermine the idea that God is in control of his creation and that violations of the moral law bring natural and appropriate consequences. If queers suffer social exclusion and legal discrimination, these losses and deprivations follow inexorably from their violation of natural law and not from state policies or the acts of their fellow citizens. These Christian conservatives agree with Paul's writing in the book of Romans that people who engage in same-sex sexuality "receive in themselves that recompense of their error which [is] meet."[85]

In venues where ex-gay leaders speak to overcoming women and men as well as to straight family members and those engaged in church ministries to homosexuals, Christian conservative leaders *do* instruct followers to hold themselves responsible for caring for homosexuals inadequately; signs of inadequate care include failing to minister to homosexuals with God's word against same-sex sexuality and allowing feelings of disgust to interrupt that ministry. However, compassionate pedagogy does not implicate its subjects in destructiveness toward others. It does not acknowledge, for example, histories of targeted violence, police harassment, family rejection, harmful therapeutic interventions, and the continuing need of many to remain closeted in their daily lives. And it does not explore ways in which heterosexuals benefit from the abjected status of LGBTQ people in the construction of their own identities and the social provision of ready targets for projection of shame. Instead, it carefully positions Christian conservatives as purveyors of God's law on sexuality and exonerates them for harm-doing against LGBT people.

Focus on the Intellectuals

A final similarity between Rand and the Christian right on compassion is that both reserve their most scathing denunciations not for undeserving individuals themselves—for conservative Christians, the unrepentant lesbian or the unrepentant woman who has undergone an abortion—but for those who organize, represent, and propagandize with/for the unrepentant. Hence, the characters in Rand's fiction who serve as the most loathsome recipients of her (and her protagonists') contempt are not ordinary moochers who ask for a handout, destroy themselves with drink, or shift responsibility away from themselves and bow to the whims of corrupt superiors. Instead, the figures of contempt are powerful spokespersons for a particular brand of ethics, personhood, and government action. For Rand, these characters, inevitably politicians or intellectuals, constitute the true face of evil. Consumed by the envious drive to destroy goodness and elevate unworthiness, they know what evil they do, and they do it remorselessly.

In her novels, Rand does not equivocate in representing these characters as malign, noting their simmering *ressentiment* of their moral superiors, their will-to-power, and their unheroic behavioral excesses. In case anyone has missed these more elusive pointers, she gives them first or last names that mirror their cunning, superficiality, and corruption: Toohey, Cuffy, Kip, Mouch, Balph, Tinky, Chick, Scudder. Ordinary losers/looters, meanwhile, remain nameless. Politicians and intellectuals, including academics, writers, and social workers, come in for particular scorn. Social workers and their ideology of help for the have-nots and scorn for the haves are unambiguously identified as "profiteers"—"haters of the good" who produce a slave revolt in morals.

In both *The Fountainhead* and *Atlas Shrugged*, Rand endows a social worker with the voice of selflessness and *ressentiment*. For Rand, the social work profession produces particularly nefarious characters, who profess compassion at the same time they exemplify a vicious strain of contempt for those who stand as independent achievers and not as the recipients of handouts. In *The Fountainhead*, the social worker is the villain Toohey's niece, Catherine Halsey who, having been systematically undermined and corrupted by her uncle, becomes a destroyer afflicted with a morbid compassion that feeds off its victims. In *Atlas*, it is an anonymous social worker whose exhortations to selflessness drive Daphne Taggart's sister-in-law, Cherryl, from the edge of a pier to her death.

Teachers and academics have an even more basic function in Rand's ideology: to serve as the (mis)shapers of children's and young adults' view of good and evil. Rand did not fare well at the hands of many book reviewers, and most academics ignored her during her lifetime. Those who didn't, such as the philosopher Sidney Hook, dissected her philosophy and pointed out her fallacies and misreadings.[86] No doubt her academic characters are Rand's revenge for the way her work was received by the intellectuals who were gatekeepers to intellectual legitimacy during her lifetime. In any case, Rand's educators are intentional proponents and propounders of evil. After all the dispossessions he suffers at the looters' hands, when Reardon finally comes to the point of murderous rage, Rand offers this explanation: "The desire [to kill] was not directed at the unknown thug who had sent a bullet through the [Wet Nurse's] body, or at the looting bureaucrats who had hired the thug to do it, but at the boy's teachers, who had delivered him, disarmed, to the thug's gun—at the soft, safe assassins of college classrooms who, incompetent to answer the queries of a quest for reason, took pleasure in crippling the young minds entrusted to their care."[87] Was there ever a time when it was not so? Rand constructs a fantasy of a righteous founding from which we as a nation have drifted and to which we must return. After entertaining his murderous thoughts against the teachers, Reardon reflects, "But a different breed of teachers had once existed . . . and had reared the men who created this country."[88]

Christian conservatives also rely on the fantasy of a righteous founding. Christian dominionist David Barton has had a significant impact on the Christian right movement through his writings and through Wall-Builders, an organization he founded that has as its mission "presenting America's forgotten history and heroes."[89] Books and materials for the Christian home-schooling movement project contemporary Christian conservative ideology backward to the founding period, finding there contemporary Christian evangelical beliefs and a political system founded, not on secular and Enlightenment ideals, but on the truths of the Bible.[90] In fact, although Rand embraces a reason she understands as inhering in the nature of man, and the Christian right embraces truths they understand as inhering in the nature of God's creation, both share a particular kind of anti-intellectualism that Richard Hofstadter noted in American self-help literature and other popular discourses. This anti-intellectualism minimizes the value of a liberal education and preaches the importance of right ideas and values against the knowledge and pretensions of educated elites.[91]

By comparison, the Christian conservative stance toward objects of blame is actually more complicated than Rand's. On the one hand, Christian right leaders in the ex-gay movement denounce "gay activists," and this term suggests a position toward leaders of gay politics rather than gay people themselves. However, by activists, many conservative Christian leaders mean those who embrace their same-sex attraction and name themselves as "gay," "lesbian," or "queer" rather than those who preside over organizations or engage in deliberate interventions to change political attitudes or realities. Even ordinary citizens who seek to marry or do marry a same-sex partner in jurisdictions where the possibility exists, may be reviled as "gay activists" and not distinguished, for example, from those who actively participate in political projects or in the work of civil rights organizations. Even so, Christian right elites still reserve particular venom for individuals—whether politicians, intellectuals, or other opinion leaders—and groups that advocate for LGBTQ rights or represent queer people in a positive light in culture and media.

In the arena of abortion politics, Christian right leaders even more obviously bypass women who have had abortions to focus attention and blame on apologists for abortion. These include politicians, intellectuals, and activists who rally support for the cause of legal abortion and for women's right to choose to terminate a pregnancy. The framing of women "submitting" to abortion suggests that the natural reservations of distraught women are overcome by the influence of more powerful actors, including medical personnel and proabortion ideologists. It is morally wicked leaders, those who wield the tools of status, ideology, and medical expertise, who bear the real guilt for the immoral acts of vulnerable women. This stance lends some credibility to the common Christian right refrain that if abortion were criminalized the movement would not seek criminal penalties for women who obtained one, though not all abortion opponents make such a pledge.

With regard to the deserving and the undeserving, Rand is every bit as convinced and, to her admirers, convincing as those who advocate for conservative Christian sexuality politics. Rand distinguishes between "hatred of the good for being the good"—"the naked face of evil"—and its alternative when she writes, "Do not confuse this response with that of a person who resents someone's unearned success, or feels pleased by someone's deserved failure. These responses are caused by a sense of justice, which is an entirely different phenomenon, and its emotional manifestations are different: in such cases, a person expresses indignation, not hatred—or relief, not malicious gloating."[92] Rand's ideology creates vivid placeholders, categories of good and evil constructed to condition readers and followers to a system of morality whose primary reference points are distinctions of deservingness. Acknowledging as a "hazard" of Rand's philosophy her "appalling moralism," Nathaniel Branden wrote after her death: "I don't know of anyone other than the Church fathers in the Dark Ages who used the word 'evil' quite so often as Ayn Rand."[93] That there are discrete differences between Rand's and the Christian right's conceptions of justice and desert should not erase the structural similarities that dictate the terms of compassion and, indeed, respect for fellow citizens.

Ayn Rand Always with Us

Why turn to Rand to elucidate the role of compassion in the sexuality politics of the Christian right? After all, like Nietzsche, Rand was an unrelenting critic of Christian morality, including an ideal of unconditional Christian love or charity.[94] But this distinction between Rand and Christian ethics supposes a homogenous conception of Christianity that cannot be reconciled with the contemporary landscape of theological politics. In the United States today, Christian doctrines and denominations are distributed across the economic and political continuum, identified with a broad range of policies and ideologies from left progressivism to right conservatism. More important, these versions of Christianity are not only products of differing interpretations of scripture, as important as these diverse modes of exegesis are. The doctrines of sects, denominations, and other kinds of Christian groups are profoundly influenced by a variety of factors, including demographic shifts, social changes, perceptions of threat, American political ideologies, and popular culture.[95] As ubiquitous as Rand has become in debates over governmentality and the role of government in economies, it's useful to remember that many of her own positions on issues such as gender complementarity and same-sex sexuality bear a strong resemblance to those of the Christian right. But even more important is the way in which Rand teaches a conception of compassion and its boundaries that is virtually indistinguishable from that of the Christian right.

This distinction between deserving and undeserving citizens provides intellectual purchase on the contested doctrine and strategy of compassion as it is practiced today by the Christian right. In the spaces and discourses of compassion constructed by the Christian right, compassion that might be targeted to those who are treated with indignity and/or politically oppressed is routed away from queers through the use of narratives of deserved suffering, miserable individuality, subversion of Godly normality, and/or the "natural repulsion" that queer identity and sexuality inspire in others.[96] Likewise, compassion is routed away from those who advocate for abortion rights (including unrepentant women) through narratives of the murder of the helpless, lesbian seduction, gender violation, racism, and the death of the biblical family. Narratives such as these protect traditional believers by vividly contrasting them with the aggressively unredeemed and unregenerate. In political terms, such narratives, and the political projects they facilitate, help to justify a range of public policies that define those others as second-class citizens and a threat to the nation. But they also have other effects, such as shoring up defenses against the possibility of guilt, identification and ambivalence.

In chapter 5 I use relational psychoanalytic thought, and especially the work of Melanie Klein and her interlocutors, to explore the Christian right's compassion crusades. Both using and departing radically from the Freudian tradition of psychoanalysis, Klein did most of her clinical and theoretical work at the level of the individual. However, her ideas have been translated by subsequent scholars into a system that critically investigates group psychologies. Addressing itself to questions of care for others, guilt, and responsibility for harm, the psychoanalytic theory of Klein and those who have used her work offers an alternative to a Randian theory of desert and a provocative account of the psychology that is expressed by the Christian right's ex-gay and postabortion compassion crusades.

5

Drawing the Compassionate Line
Love, Guilt, and Melanie Klein

The Psychoanalytic Turn

In this final theoretical chapter I turn to psychoanalysis to construct an account of the moral psychology of the Christian right's compassion campaigns. American psychoanalysis has played a major role in antigay thought by formulating most of the ex-gay movement's foundational claims about gender and sexuality. Repudiated by the psychological establishment beginning in the 1970s, Christian conservatives repaired to a subset of mid-twentieth-century American psychodynamic literature for intellectual support in their condemnation of same-sex sexuality and nonnormative gender.[1] In many respects it's ironic that Christian conservatives have relied as heavily as they have on psychoanalysis given the staunch secularism of most leading psychoanalysts and the sexual permissiveness that's been identified with psychoanalysis from its origins. Nevertheless, not only did psychoanalysis erect the infrastructure of antigay conservative Christian thought, but it has occasionally been used more broadly by social conservatives to bolster traditional ideals of "family values."[2]

In using relational psychoanalysis to interpret the Christian right, I don't claim that particular theorists have outlined a truthful and exhaustive theory of human nature to which Christian right doctrine can be contrasted. Rather, relational psychoanalysis furnishes a robust system of psychological thought whose key contributions to studies of reparative morality, group identity, and the psychodynamic underpinnings of group ideology are particularly helpful in understanding the Christian right's infrastructure of compassion.

As the progenitor of object relations theory, Melanie Klein's thought revolved around categories that she understood as universal: emotions (such as love, hate, envy, guilt, and greed) and psychic defenses (such as splitting, denial, and the projective defenses). For her, these emotions and defenses were life-long processes that constituted the self or subject—not just the Western liberal bourgeois self, for example, but selves in their rich diversity. Object relations clinicians and theorists "see the human self as something constructed out of social relationships; . . . aspects of these relationships become 'internal objects' for the self, helping to constitute its very nature."[3] A frequent criticism of psychoanalysis, and one that includes relational theorists of Klein's generation as well as those who later appropriated and duly rearticulated relational thought, is that it mistakes particular subject formations for the human, thus overlooking and eliding the hegemony of particular kinds of race, gender, sexual, and national identities. In their turn, relational thinkers insist that the "logic of object relations" holds that "there may be more than one form of 'human nature'; as social relations change, so too . . . would 'human nature.'"[4] Object relations theory does, indeed, treat "human nature" as both historically and contextually malleable. Theorists in this tradition use tools such as clinical explications of the operations of defenses to trace these changes and to analyze their effects.

Because she did not address political debates directly in her work, it's not possible to ascertain Klein's perspectives on the politics of reproductive rights, but her views on same-sex desire and sexuality are well documented in her writing. In a general way, her conception of same-sex sexual identity followed Freud's in positing a trajectory of development in which "in the ordinary course of events," early homosexual feelings are sublimated or transmuted into mature, nongenital same-sex friendships.[5] In clinical writings such as "A Contribution to the Psychogenesis of Tics" and *Narrative of a Child Analysis*, Klein is clear about the developmental failures associated with male homosexuality. In "Tics," Klein analyzes the hapless "Felix"—actually her own son, Hans—a thirteen-year-old boy whose repressed (and, later, not-so-repressed) homosexuality she interprets as a symptom of oedipal conflicts.[6] In "Envy and Gratitude," Klein takes up the issue of lesbianism and argues that oedipal disturbances such as "envy of the mother's breast" can result in "impairment of genital potency, compulsive need for genital gratification, promiscuity, and homosexuality."[7]

It is not surprising that Klein has had many critics among feminists and LGBTQ theorists. Noreen O'Connor and Joanna Ryan examine closely Klein's rebuttable assumptions about femininity, lesbians, and lesbian desire and show how Klein theoretically maroons lesbians in a developmental phase that precludes mature morality and relationality.[8] But other critics insist that Klein's specific assumptions and clinical interpretations should be read through the lens of her innovative challenges to psychoanalysis: "[I]n the face of th[e] pervasive and prejudicial psychoanalytic understanding of homosexuality, Klein's account of the Oedipus complex offers a reading of sexuality that could be considered queerer, less orthodox, and even anti-oedipal (in the Freudian sense)."[9] However we regard Klein's perspectives on nonnormative sexuality today, they no longer are widely shared among theorists and clinicians in the object relations tradition. The shift represents one of the many ways in which contemporary psychoanalysts and scholars who make use of psychoanalytic theory deplore the profession's complicity in bias against gays and same-sex relations.[10]

Relational psychoanalysis directly addresses the coconstructing relationship of individual and group and the role of emotions in constituting individuals' and groups' relationships with the outside world. Here I argue that concepts and processes drawn from the work of Melanie Klein and theorists influenced by her help to explain the ideological contours and content of antigay and antiabortion compassion campaigns. Turning from a direct focus on compassion, I show how Klein's conceptualizations of developmental positions, reparation, "mock" reparation, and the defenses illuminate such central features of Christian right compassion campaigns as the boundaries they draw between good and evil and the relationship between guilt and the particular kind of compassion on display in these projects.

More Narratives of Development

As conjectural and provisional as they often may be, developmental narratives and trajectories occupy an important place in psychoanalytic theories. Indeed, psychoanalytic theories and traditions can be distinguished from each other by the differences between the developmental stories they tell. In crucial respects, object relations theory subverts the foundations of Christian right sexual and reproductive politics by occluding the importance of gender-specific developmental pathways. Even though

Klein herself had a good deal to say about what she took to be the essential components of gender identity, relational psychoanalysis does not rely on the reification of gender roles and traits to create a set of binary and distinct developmental trajectories. In this respect, object relations theory is an alternative to Freudian and Lacanian traditions that generate stricter gendered modes of development.[11]

By contrast with object relations, any excavation of compassion campaigns finds at their core a set of explicable and relatively stable traits and dispositions associated with male and female sex. In Christian conservatism, assertions of the social construction of gender, empirical attention to cross-cultural or historical regimes of gender, and politicized refusals of gender alike threaten the ideology upon which the ex-gay and postabortion movements are erected. In Christian right ideology the delinking of gender from biological sex is itself evidence of radical political ideology. More radical still is any challenge to the contents of the categories of "masculine" and "feminine." Women are created by God to be feminine: receptive (often substituted for the more contentious, "passive"), nurturing, and submissive (in the normative, rather than the pejorative, sense). Men are created to be masculine: virile, protective, and leaders in intimate and spiritual arenas. These bundles of gendered characteristics are natural and, at the same time, extremely fragile.[12] They underwrite compassion campaigns by enabling Christian conservatives to frame same-sex desire and abortion not as a sinful violation, as abomination rhetoric and politics would have it, but as the entirely predictable consequence of a subject's tragic failure to claim and enact a fundamental and God-given identity as a woman or man.[13] Healing, both from abortion and from same-sex attraction, thus requires reclaiming and reaffirming the gender identity held out by the movement.

In place of a fundamental set of gendered traits and characteristics, Klein proposed "positions" that undermine the primacy of gender for individuals. This theory of positions would be used by later analysts to describe the moral orientation of groups. For Klein, individuals attain, and then move back and forth between, the paranoid-schizoid and the depressive positions. These positions are neither strictly functions of physiological development nor of libidinal drives; instead they are like syndromes: constellations of anxieties, defenses, and object relations that often are manifested through emotions and recognizable patterns of fantasy. By the term "paranoid-schizoid" Klein means a condition characterized by fear of disintegration, fantasies of persecution, and defenses against these anxieties. The signal defenses of the paranoid-schizoid position are splitting and projective defenses. Unconsciously, the self splits good and bad, loving and hating, images and fantasies and tries to project the bad, malevolent, hating parts of the self away and "into" others. The inevitable result is an experience of the external world as aggressive and threatening. The attempt to protect the self by rigidly segregating the good and loving feelings and images and claiming them all for oneself creates the dangerous object world that the defenses are mobilized to guard against.

The central impetus for the depressive position is a cognitive integration that makes possible the knowledge that "the loved object is at the same time the hated one," that "the bad mother who frustrates [us], and whom [we] have destroyed in phantasy a thousand times, is also the good mother who tenderly meets [our] needs."[14] Symptomatic of the depressive position is depressive anxiety, the fear that we are not strong enough, that we lack the "capacity to make restitution" for our aggression and for our fantasized destructiveness.[15] Although the paranoid-schizoid position always comes first in individual development, Klein didn't hold the attainment of the more mature depressive position to represent a secure and irreversible achievement. Rather, the constellation of anxieties, defenses, and object relations that prevailed would depend on the developing perceptions and psychodynamics of the self as well as the stability of a "good enough" external world.[16] The paranoid-schizoid and depressive positions name "different relations to loved objects."[17]

In Klein's thought, the defenses, prominent among which are splitting, projective defenses, introjection, and idealization, are both the building blocks of the self and the processes by which the self defends against anxieties that originate in the paranoid-schizoid and depressive positions. Many of Klein's commentators regard her most unique contribution to psychoanalysis to be her clinical and theoretical elaboration of the projective defenses. Projection proper has been defined in slightly different ways by different theorists, but generally it is the externalization, or ascription to another, of a painful or undesirable feeling, desire, or mental representation.

But the projective defense that has received most attention in the Kleinian canon is the version of projection she called projective identification.[18] Projective identification is "the prototype of an aggressive object-relation."[19] Klein described it most simply as "the impulse to intrude into another person," but it is more complicated than this, both psychically and socially.[20] Klein's briefest definition does not suggest the range of motives and purposes that projective identification serves, including, "to control the object, to acquire its attributes, to evacuate a bad quality, to protect a good quality, to avoid separation."[21] Many theorists and clinicians also include in its scope the effects of the projection on its object because recipients often come to internalize the traits, feelings, images, or motivations attributed to them.[22] The process that relational psychoanalysts describe as projective identification has often been simplified and redescribed by feminists as some form of internalized bias that operates against the self, such as, for example, internalized sexism or racism.[23]

Projective identification has been taken by many students of psychoanalysis as shorthand for malign, paranoid-schizoid, modes of relating. It is this, but it is much besides. Kleinians understand it as a process at work more generally in the development of the self: "[T]he processes of splitting off parts of the self and projecting them into objects are . . . of vital importance for normal development as well as for abnormal object relations."[24] In terms of normal, and indeed, normative, development, projective identification may be "the underlying mechanism of the capacity for empathy (putting oneself in someone else's shoes)."[25] As Klein put it, "to be genuinely considerate implies that we can put ourselves in the place of other people: we 'identify' ourselves with them."[26]

Like the compassion with which it is closely related, empathy has been understood to occupy "the center of the progressive moral worldview."[27] Yet a Kleinian account of projective identification can warn us that the positive moral virtue of empathy is complicated by a number of possible hazards. The benign take is that projective identification "modifies perception of the object and, in a reciprocal fashion, alters the image of the self," a process that's crucial to empathy as it's typically understood.[28] However, this generic explanation is cast somewhat differently by Klein, who suggests that the psychic process so basic to empathy is one that "leads to a strong confusion between the self and the object, which also comes to stand for the self."[29] The prospect and reality of such confusion may help to explain why projective identification is often cast by theorists in negative terms that overshadow its constructive role in empathy.

From this perspective, it makes sense that Hannah Arendt is troubled by the facile confidence that characterizes empathy, "as though [one] tried to be or to feel like somebody else."[30] Even though Arendt was dismissive of "the pseudo-scientific apparatuses of depth-psychology, psychoanalysis,"[31] it is easy to read Arendt's representative thinking as a plea for what more psychodynamically oriented theorists would call reality testing. With its foundations in "different viewpoints" and "thinking in my own identity where actually I am not," representative thinking is a bid to make conscious, and thus to try to discipline, the boundary-confusing vicissitudes of projective identification.[32] By consciously weighing both the testimony of others and one's own process of evaluating the situation of those others, Arendt hopes to enhance the capacity for an enlarged mentality.

Arendt wrote of coming to "valid . . . final conclusions" as a result of the process of representative thinking, and here her own confidence seems overstated. However, she also made clear that conclusions drawn from representative thinking are always susceptible to new information and are, thus, provisional. In her essay, "Reflections on Little Rock," Arendt had condemned what she understood to be the inappropriate politicization of African American children in struggles over school desegregation. Later, after hearing Ralph Ellison's criticism of her position Arendt conceded his point and adjusted her understanding of what black parents and children faced in the segregated South.[33] She did this not as a matter of empathy but as a consequence of exercising representative thinking in the context of new information about the differences between racism in the United States and her own childhood experience of anti-Semitic discrimination in Germany.

Overlooking the exploration of themes such as the psychodynamic roots of empathy, one critique of psychotherapeutic discourses has been that they are essentially amoral and apolitical, therefore either of little use to feminists and progressives or subversive of egalitarian goals and aspirations.[34] Certainly Klein's psychoanalysis is not political in any immediately identifiable way, but it doesn't have to be to be consistent with many political projects that would recommend equality of rights and access to respect. I take up the question of the politics of Klein's object relations when I turn to a relational theory of groups, but for now suffice it to say that Klein's work is "saturated with terms which embody moral discriminations[,] . . . categorizations of dispositions and states of feeling which have ethical significance."[35] Because she didn't hesitate to integrate moral assumptions and reasoning into her clinical and theoretical writing, some contemporary readers might find her a pedant and scold.[36] Nonetheless, her system is grounded in a recognizable system of moral and ethical standards and aspirations. The "essence of morality" is in intimate relations, the maintenance of a balance and love and hate that can foster caring and nondestructive forms of attachment. Especially as other theorists have translated her ideas, in broader social relations the essence of morality lies in containing and modifying group identifications in ways that diminish the destructiveness of individuals acting under the influence of group identity.

Making Good

For Klein, the foundation of morality is a human "wish to make good," an impulse she identified clinically in the contradictions of early love-hate relationships.[37] Klein made theoretical sense of this wish to make good through a concept she referred to as "restitution" and "restoration" before she settled on the term "reparation." For Klein, reparation is a developmental achievement that arises in the depressive position from the need to protect loved ones from harm. Thus, it is in the first instance a process directed toward immediate love objects and only later a process that includes others and the wider world.

The difference between Kleinian reparation and a more generic urge to protect intimates is that reparation describes a process in which unconscious elements of love, hate, and guilt precipitate the desire—and in propitious psychological circumstances, the ability—to protect objects of love *from our own aggression*, and not from the depredations of strangers or the outside world. "Side by side with the destructive impulses in the unconscious mind both of the child and of the adult, there exists a profound urge to make sacrifices, in order to help and to put right loved people who in phantasy have been harmed or destroyed."[38] It is the hating self that is key to Klein's moral vision, not only what the self does and feels but also what the self fears from its own internal aggression: "Love as the concern for an object other than ourselves only gains its meaning when approached against the background of the power of destructive instincts."[39] R. D. Hinshelwood points out that in reparation it is "primarily . . . a repair of the internal world that is intended, through repairing the external."[40] This insight is key because it reflects Klein's view that when we care about another we do so in a context of depressive anxiety that our caring is too weak to overcome our capacity for harm.

Although reparation emerges through, and in some respects is always tied to, relations with love objects, in Klein's view neither reparative nor other kinds of urges remain bound to specific loved ones forever. In adults the repertoire of feelings, defenses, and motivations becomes displaced, and other attachments, including group identifications, form. The result is "the development of culture and civilization," with all its opportunities for hostility and aggression as well as for cooperation and reparation, not only between individuals but also between groups.[41]

Both for Klein and for later analysts and scholars in the relational tradition, reparation is one of only two basic foundations for a morality of relationships. The other is the "talion morality" of the paranoid-schizoid position—the morality of dread, preemptive aggression, and revenge.

Talion morality is the moral system of those who have not yet navigated the depressive position, but it is also the moral system of those who, because of vicissitudes of psychic life or stressful external circumstances, experience a reemergence of paranoid-schizoid processes and modes of feeling.[42] For social theorists influenced by Klein, talion morality is one predictable consequence of group psychology. But it is also the likely morality of groups, which is to say, of people feeling, thinking, and acting as members of groups.[43]

Yet if talion morality is premised on paranoia and revenge, and therefore threatens its objects with disgust, contempt, hatred, or violence, even depressive reparative morality can be more complicated than it first appears for two reasons. First, it may be difficult to distinguish reparation proper from "manic" or "mock reparation," with which it shares superficial similarities. "Reparation proper," or what the Kleinian analyst Hanna Segal calls "non-manic" reparation, "is based on the recognition of psychic reality, the experiencing of the pain that this reality causes and the taking of appropriate action to relieve it in phantasy and reality." In other words, nonmanic reparation is characterized by sadness and regret at being a source of harm. Mock reparation, on the other hand, is a defense that aims at avoiding the guilt associated with harm or destructive emotions. Telltale signs of mock reparation include not acknowledging having harmed the damaged object/person and continuing to perceive that damaged person as "inferior" and "contemptible."[44]

The second potential problem with reparation is that it may take a variety of forms, some of which may be symbolic and have little or nothing to do with repairing harms fantasized or done to others. In a notorious passage in which Klein seems nonchalant about the empirically nonreparative ways that psychic reparation can play out, she imagines an "explorer" who "discover[s]" and occupies a "new country." The explorer activates the "aggressive sexual desires, greed, [and] curiosity" of early psychic life, but in doing so he inevitably stimulates his own guilt at having directed aggression to the mother, on whom life depends, through her surrogate, the sensual world. Although Klein excoriates "ruthless cruelty" against "native populations," she concedes that for western colonizers indigenous people constitute part of the sensual world. In such a case, she acknowledges that colonizers may assuage their guilt and practice reparation by "repopulating the country with people of their own nationality."[45] Thus might reparation bypass the repair of injured parties altogether.

The reparative is not only a central category of relational theory but is also a central category of Christian right compassionate approaches to same-sex sexuality. The conservative Christian version of reparativeness focuses on lesbians and gay men exclusively rather than on the relations that link those who care with the objects of their concern. Reparative therapies aim to repair the damaged gender identities of same-sex-attracted people and to help them (re)construct appropriate gender and sexual relations. To that end, the ex-gay movement sponsors extensive networks of experts, lobbyists, websites, publications, ministries, outpatient therapies, and residential regimens for those who struggle with their sexuality. The postabortion ministries version of reparativeness focuses on repairing individual women's relationship with God as well as encouraging them to perceive their abortion decision and the right to have an abortion in terms that are consistent with antiabortion ideology. Similarly, Christian conservatives sometimes conceptualize virginity as susceptible to being symbolically repaired through celibacy and the maintenance of a personal relationship with Jesus Christ.[46]

The mere etymological similarity between Kleinian reparativeness and Christian right reparativeness seems to exhaust their connection, but there is more to it than this. In fact, a shared moral aspiration animates both Christian right and Kleinian perspectives: the interest in not only *doing good* in the sense of obeying the requirements of a particular moral system, but in *making good*—making whole those who have been damaged. Fundamental to both the Kleinian account of reparation and Christian right compassion campaigns is the desire to undo injury to the other and to restore the other to a state of well-being. However, the principal difference between these two projects is crucial: in Klein's conception of reparation, the other is wounded because of my ruthlessness, my aggression, which I have projected outward from my own fearful and chaotic internal world. In Christian right ideology, by contrast, although I am called to help heal the other, she is wounded through no fault of mine. Indeed, my willingness to reach out to her is a sign of my own relative condition of salvation or spiritual maturity.

The biblical parable of the Good Samaritan and its contemporary applications help to represent this difference of perspectives. As it is narrated in the book of Luke, Jesus tells the story of a man waylaid by thieves who rob and beat him. A priest and a Levite who see the injured man pass him by without lending assistance, but a Samaritan who just as easily could have ignored the victim's suffering comes to his aid.[47] The parable is incited by a question about eternal life, but the conversation between Jesus and a lawyer in the crowd quickly moves to a more personal level: the commandment in Leviticus to love one's neighbor as oneself that has long fascinated theologians from Augustine to the present. Who is a neighbor in the Gospel story? A neighbor is a person in need and someone who might even hail from an enemy group—hence, the importance to the Jewish audience Jesus addresses of the fact that the rescuer is a Samaritan whom his listeners might not expect to render assistance.

But the story of the Good Samaritan is intriguing today for another reason: the parable functions as a common contemporary vehicle of exhortation to encourage Christian believers to show compassion for those who in many quarters remain some of the most despised of neighbors—people suffering from same-sex desire and women who have a shameful abortion in their past.[48] Here is one version of this deployment of the story, which I take from an email I received from the prolife project 40 Days for Life under the signature of its national campaign director, David Bereit: "Dear Cindy, Today's devotional is a reflection on Christ's parable of the Good Samaritan. In many ways, the women—and men—who have experienced abortion are a lot like the victim who was left by the side of the road. They've been hurt—and had their money taken—by those who cared nothing for them or their well being . . . or for what happened to them after the deed was done. Can you and I be Good Samaritans to a brother or sister in need?" In the same email, Fr. Frank Pavone, director of Priests for Life and a purveyor of abomination rhetoric on abortion, added a murder-inflected "reflection" on Bereit's message: "Here Jesus commands us to show mercy to the victims of the culture of violence and death." A final prayer in Bereit's compassionate voice follows: "Father, we are moved by the lesson of the Good Samaritan, who allowed compassion to influence him more than fear. Give us the same heart."[49]

The parable is frequently invoked in the context of struggles over same-sex sexuality and abortion, so it is worthwhile to consider more closely how it has been repurposed in these compassion campaigns. Here, the conservative Christian stands in the place of the Samaritan, who comes across a wounded person in need of assistance. Instead of indulging in the disgust or revulsion that this particular kind of wounded person might reasonably elicit, the believer stops to help, informing the injured person of God's laws regarding gender, sexuality, and reproduction, and using resources provided by ex-gay and postabortion ministries to respond to the person's psychological and spiritual needs. In this version of the story, neither the innocence and virtue of the Samaritan/Christian nor the woundedness of the stranger is ever in doubt. Having come along after the fact, the Samaritan/Christian certainly had no part in the attack that brought the stranger to her injured condition. Indeed, those who employ the "Good Samaritan" in this compassionate way will not need to spell out the implication that many of the stranger's grave injuries are either self-inflicted or are a result of the victim's collusion! When the victim is a postabortive woman, she either actively solicited the procedure or, at the very least, submitted to it; when the victim is a same-sex-attracted person, he is likely to have engaged in same-sex relations or to have by some other means reinforced in himself that reprobate form of desire before seeking help. The Samaritan arrives on the scene in time to ascertain the victim's repentant mind and to pick up the pieces after a terrible attack that the victim, in part, has perpetrated on herself.

The elasticity of this parable, and its ability to tolerate diverse interpretations of compassion, is striking. A liberal evangelical version of the story places homosexuals in the position of the Samaritan, encouraging Christians to consider the ways in which members of this ill-regarded group have violated negative stereotypes held of them by practicing loving kindness to those in need.[50] Clearly, the parable of the Good Samaritan continues to be popular because it is a simple tale of victimization and good works. The story highlights the triumph of moral action in a violent and fallen world and invites identification with the generous Samaritan.

However, recent retellings in the context of ex-gay and postabortion ministries remind us that there is greater depth and complexity to the story, including both individual and group dimensions of morality, which I return to below. In order to study the morality of groups and the psychology of group identity, Kleinian and other relational social theorists frequently shift the focus of inquiry from the individual to the large group level of analysis.[51] In this way, theorists analyze the dynamics of group identification that influence even those who will never meet most other members of their cultural, ethnic, national, or other "imaginary community."[52] Taking into account factors such as the psychology of "groupishness," the role and importance of leaders in groups, the value for group members of epistemological ignorance, and the benefits and costs of group membership helps to clarify the ways in which organized compassion can be analyzed not only as a function of individual caring but also as a group phenomenon.

Bad Group!

As different as their conceptions are, both the Christian right and its critics hold an implicit understanding of what makes groups good or bad. For Christian conservatives, bad groups such as those made up of unregenerate queers and liberals or progressives who support women's reproductive rights, proselytize wickedness, and create a collective moral hazard. These groups must be defeated culturally, legally, and politically, and conservative Christians are called by God to accomplish these tasks. For progressive critics of the Christian right, the movement is itself a bad group that threatens outsiders with moral sanctimony backed by threats of punishment. It is reductive to talk about bad groups, as though to suggest, much too dichotomously, that while some groups are good others are bad by some agreed-upon standard.[53] For most psychoanalytic theorists of groups the very process of identification with groups always raises the specter of anxiety, idealization, and aggression. Even if all groups aren't bad, all group identifications have the potential to be transformed into enmity against others—inside the group and without—and, as a result, the threatening quality of groups and group identifications is a common thread in the literature of psychoanalytic social thought.

Psychoanalytic theorizing about groups began with Wilfred Bion, one of the most creative and esoteric of Klein's "students" and the founder of the Tavistock Model of Group Relations. Influenced by Klein's clinical work on defenses, Bion worked extensively with small therapeutic groups. However, Bion's usefulness as a social theorist begins with the insight that all human beings demonstrate psychodynamic effects of what he called "groupishness," that "no individual, however isolated in time and space, can be regarded as outside a group or lacking in active manifestations of group psychology." For Bion, it is not necessary for group members to sit in a circle for their group psychodynamics to be in evidence and to come under study. "It is quite common for someone to ask when the group begins. Now from one point of view the perfectly simple answer is that the group begins at 10:30, or whatever the hour is that has been appointed for the meeting, but a shift of point of view, admittedly of some magnitude, on my part, means that I am viewing group phenomena that do not 'begin'; the matters with which I am concerned continue, and evolve, but they do not 'begin.'"[54] "*The* group" may begin at 10:30, but manifestations of group psychology are latent, and often effectuated, in us all, group creatures and members that we are.

The implications of this insight have proved extremely productive for relational social theorists. Not only individuals, but also groups can operate in a paranoid-schizoid mode whose prominent features are hatred, aggression, persecution, vengefulness, and/or idealization. Indeed, Elliott Jaques opens his classic article on the psychodynamics of groups with the observation: "It has often been noted that many social phenomena show a strikingly close correspondence with psychotic processes in individuals.[55] The unconscious dimensions of group dynamics are usually not immediately salient to observers, but scholars of intergroup relations often find in these conflicts the "violent projections" that are symptoms of the "expulsion of disowned, bad parts of the self," or in this case, of the group.[56] The work of Vamik Volkan and his colleagues has been foundational to this psychoanalytic study of intergroup relations. In *The Need to Have Enemies and Allies*, Volkan uses psychodynamic and child-development sources to construct a developmental account of group identity. For him, subjects use unconscious defenses and social resources to transform strangers into enemies. Central to this process are ideologies and social practices that provide individuals with group-sanctioned "suitable targets of externalization—in short, enemies and the symbolic and material objects associated with enemies."[57]

Group leaders and ideologies help members transmute the raw material of individual developmental processes, and the anxieties and defenses that attend them, into identification with the leader and/or the group. Ideology, including ideas about difference, denigration, and superiority, is crucial to the process. Indeed, it may be that idealization—not necessarily aggression—is the most reliable marker of a group's paranoid-schizoid character because groups may "suppress" aggression.[58] But it is not uncommon for groups to demonstrate both simultaneously; group members may be both idealizing toward their own group and aggressive toward members of other groups and the symbolic and material appurtenances of those groups. More complicated still are the ways groups may conceal aggression, for example, by redefining aggressive impulses and acts as patriotic, as defensive, as mandated by God, as a civilizing burden, or even as compassionate.

For relational social theorists, the dynamics of leadership and followership are central to the acts and psychic processes of groups. Leaders may be formal or informal, but however they attain their position of influence they exercise powerful effects on their group as figures of identification, as ideologists, and as "conductors" of group members' fears, fantasies, and defenses.[59] Directly or indirectly, it is leaders who identify threats and enemies and either stoke or allay group members' fears.[60] Another, more psychoanalytic, way of saying the same thing is that leaders, and the groups, institutions, and belief systems over which they preside, have an important role to play in "holding" or "containing" persecutory and depressive anxieties that are both individual and group-related in origin. Leaders perform a positive holding function when they provide a repository for the frightening unconscious feelings and conflicts of members and return these feelings and conflicts to group members in a form that can be tolerated.[61] The alternative to being "held" in this way is that group members may experience themselves as "precipitated into outer space or at least into a cold, harsh, and unfriendly outside world—in part the creation of [their] own projections and so created in [their] own hostile image—where [they] will be left to perish."[62] Fearing the devastating effects of their own fears and projections, groups are primed to turn to suitable targets of externalization on which to vent their fear, rage, and contempt.

If group members commonly use the group itself and its leaders as containers for anxieties and conflicts, they also use the group to defend themselves against forms of knowledge that implicate them both as individuals and as group members. Charles W. Mills posits an "epistemology of ignorance" to explain sociologically the "racial contract" that operates as a foundation of the unacknowledged white supremacist order of European colonialism. This "inverted epistemology" consists of "a particular pattern of localized and global cognitive dysfunctions (which are psychologically and socially functional), producing the ironic outcome that whites will in general be unable to understand the world they themselves have made."[63] For Mills the construction and maintenance of the racial contract depends on this systematic unconscious ignorance.

With its system of "misunderstanding, misrepresentation, evasion, and self-deception,"[64] Mills' sociological concept of self-interested ignorance finds psychoanalytic parallels in collective denial. Processes of denial and even projection can be key elements in the maintenance of group ideologies as affect is deployed against "links between ideas and feelings, links between words and meanings, between the concrete and the metaphorical, between the [group's] past and future."[65] The point of such vigorous denial is to defend against guilt, dependence, or vulnerability by *not knowing*.[66] Denial helps group members "evade or modify reality."[67] This revision of reality sets the stage for a "severe arrest of development" and the diminution of curiosity about the outside world and our relationsip to it.[68] Much like Mills' epistemology of ignorance, the not-knowing that Bion and other group theorists describe is active—even if unconsciously so—rather than passive. It is a form of protection for group members and one of the benefits of belonging to a group.

A rich motif of psychoanalytic literature on groups is the high cost group members incur for belonging. Psychoanalytic theorists and clinicians explain that group identifications offer many benefits of membership.

Besides being able to share in forms of denial common to the group, these include fusion with the group as a shelter from anxiety, inclusion in the group's interpretation of reality, and also participation in the "warmth of human relationships" that Hannah Arendt associates with pariah peoples.[69] It should be noted that, however valuable this "great privilege," it is not the exclusive province of pariah groups in the strictest sense, since groups often establish their identity and ideology by assuming the mantle of victimization. In the US context, consider Christian conservatives, who weather such insults as an annual "war on Christmas" but who also understand their inability to exercise unchallenged dominion over American culture and government as a condition of abjection.[70]

Group membership carries with it undeniable benefits for individuals. But in exchange for the benefits of group identifications come their inevitable costs. Relational psychoanalysts describe groups and organizations as "projection systems" that incite feelings of being "stupid, helpless, and afraid" of the "mysterious, powerful 'group' " and that "impoverish and distort experience of the self and the perceived world."[71] Especially in large diffuse groups, projection systems erode cognitive complexity as members project those ideas and parts of the self that are inconsistent with the group's narrative. These processes also suggest ways in which groups tend to diminish individual identity: "By definition to 'belong' to the group means to involve, hence to 'give up,' part of the self to the group."[72] Inconsistent beliefs, ideas, feelings, and internal representations that remain place group members at odds with the group and liable to be ejected, hence C. Fred Alford's claim that "the gravest threat to the member's safety stems from the group itself, its willingness to sacrifice the nonconformist."[73]

In large groups the most difficult task that confronts leaders and those who identify with the group as members is "humanizing the group."[74] For this process to occur, a group's leaders and members must be reparative in the sense of being willing "to compose and maintain ambivalent accounts of both the identities they share and those they do not."[75] In interpersonal relations this ambivalence is an achievement, but theorists argue that it is even more difficult to achieve and maintain in circumstances that mobilize group identity for many reasons: because the cohesiveness of group identity is stabilized through projections onto other groups; because other groups are "endowed and littered with parts outcast from the self";[76] and because the possibility of reality-testing declines in the context of the relative isolation that constitutes diffuse social groups.[77] Even when it is achieved, such ambivalence can be reversed, and the boundaries between groups turned into battle lines, by leaders and ideologies that retract reparative imagery and substitute idealization and belligerence.[78]

From a group perspective, the parable of the Good Samaritan is a story about both individual *and* group morality. Crucial to the parable is the understanding of Jews and Samaritans as enemy groups, a fact that underlies the assumption that the Samaritan should be the last man to treat the injured Jew as his neighbor. That the Samaritan recognizes and tends the injured man seems to be a tribute to his ability to overcome group enmity and a lesson for all about care and responsibility. However, as interesting as what we do learn about these characters in the brief narrative is what we don't learn about them. If the Good Samaritan is a tale of the perennial contrast between individual and group morality, it would be illuminating to know if the Samaritan stops and helps the injured Jew as a reparative gesture, that is, because of personal or collective guilt he harbors about his own relations to Jews and Jewishness or because he is being presented as an outlier in his group—personally innocent of the malevolent grip of group identity and collective enmity. If the former, he is a Kleinian subject. If the latter, his uniqueness would seem to vitiate the point of the parable, which turns on individual responsibility even—perhaps especially—in the face of group difference and enmity.

Compassion campaigns illustrate in their operations general features of group life in addition to those that are specific to the configurations of Christian right groups and politics. In compassion ideology and projects, adherents secure and protect the compassion they expend on the repentant by focusing their righteous wrath on the unrepentant. These degenerates, not the penitents, become the most immediate and threatening outgroup for compassionate Christians. Under these circumstances, abomination ideology provides the script for dealing with those who threaten fragile penitents with the lure of sexual or reproductive freedom.

Being Reparative

Given that the source of most bias against lesbians, gay men, bisexuals, and transgender people is some version of traditional religious belief, it is tempting to draw the conclusion that Christian right compassion is a façade for hatred and the will to cause harm.[79] Even so, I am troubled by this conviction and the politics and rhetoric to which it ineluctably leads. What many on the pro-LGBTQ side of current morality debates take as the definitive evidence of the conscious and deliberate duplicity of compassion campaigns is the fact that the roads of abomination and compassion projects lead to the same destination: antigay and antiabortion rights politics and policies. If the politics generated by such different kinds of projects are the same, critics reason, it must be the case that purveyors of abomination and compassion are engaged in a fundamentally similar enterprise with fundamentally similar motivations. On this understanding, compassion ideology and politics is *more* insidious than abomination ideology because of the ways in which actors may use a compassionate guise to hide their motivations and the harmful effects of their interventions. However intuitively accurate this imputation of duplicity to the compassion side of the movement seems, relational psychoanalytic theory offers a way of complicating it.

In Klein's account of the developmental trajectory in which the process of reparation is nested, both individuals and groups may occupy different positions that operate as orientations toward aggression, identification, projection, guilt, despair, and the urge to make good. However, as Kleinian social theorists have demonstrated, groups—which is to say, individuals operating psychodynamically as group members—are more likely to exhibit the modes of feeling and action associated with the paranoid-schizoid position than they are to exhibit the reparation that for Klein is a feature of the depressive position. Thus, Kleinian social theory would consider abomination discourse and politics unsurprising and would analyze the circumstances under which alternative forms of politics would either arise or become more likely.

With regard to the Christian right's sexuality politics, much of the efficacy and versatility of the movement stems from its ability to tolerate and incorporate diverse modes of worship and theological beliefs. Likewise, the movement derives strength from its ability to tolerate and incorporate different systems of motivation and action as long as these systems converge in a set of common political goals. The abomination rhetoric of the Christian right makes gross distinctions between its objects, identifying objects of dread, disgust, and moral antipathy who are also purveyors of wickedness and death, and psychologically segregating them firmly from a fantasized "moral majority" of the American population or a cadre of born again believers. By contrast, compassionate ideology makes finer distinctions, splitting the groups that inspire disgust and moral antipathy into repentant and unrepentant categories and concentrating the attention of Christian conservatives who operate in this arena on those who deserve compassion. Indeed, the leadership, ideology, and activism of the movement summon into being objects of desert—the repentant same-sex attracted and postabortive—that are often invisible in the sectors of the Christian right that champion abomination perspectives on abortion and homosexuality.

A common refrain of compassion campaigns is that as a group, Christian conservatives have been unloving toward same-sex-attracted people and women who have had an abortion. And compassionate Christian conservatives call their fellow believers to account for this deficit of compassion. At meetings and rallies, proponents of Christian conservative compassion apologize to same-sex-attracted women and men and to women who have kept their abortion a secret for the failure of Christians to follow the example of Jesus even as they urge them to adopt the ideology and politics of the movement. At the 2012 Love Won Out conference, Mike Goeke spoke to the audience of strugglers' sense of being unloved and shunned because "the body of Christ has made them feel that way"; Angela Yuan, the mother of a struggler, criticized Christians for expressing "truth [about same-sex sexuality] at the expense of compassion"; and Joe Dallas criticized Christians for their implicit message to same-sex-attracted people: "God loves you although you're unusually disgusting."[80] As compassionate Christians testify to the need for other Christians to embrace strugglers and postabortive women, these groups of penitents are called upon to profess their own belief and to buttress Christian right ideology.

When critics of the Christian right identify compassion campaigns with dissimulation or with outright fraud, they are right in believing that compassion campaigns have a puzzling relationship with morality, at least as liberals and progressives understand it. However, evaluating Christian right compassion through a Kleinian lens suggests that it conforms neither to, on the one hand, paranoid-schizoid group dynamics, and the talion morality that is a likely result, nor with depressive group dynamics and reparative morality. Existing somewhere between these poles, neither patently hating nor unambiguously guilty and loving, compassionate ideology and practices may be best conceptualized with reference to the bundle of characteristics Kleinians refer to as manic or mock reparation.

Alford corrects a common misconception that identifies the difference between reparation and mock reparation as that between, on the one hand, acting reparatively in the real world toward harmed objects and, on the other, engaging in symbolic acts or in reparative gestures that are not directed toward harmed objects. Instead, he argues that Klein's grammar of morality attends to the motives of ostensibly reparative acts and what level of denial lies behind them. "Real" reparation may miss its ideal object or consist primarily in sublimations that repair symbolically rather than in reality.[81] Mock reparation is more a matter of the subject who acts and how that subject perceives the recipient of the acts than it is a matter of how the object/person is actually treated. Certain themes consistently emerge in articulations of mock reparation, including that subjects deny that harm has been inflicted, deny guilt and responsibility for harm, and "direct the reparative wishes . . . to objects to which [they] feel superior." As Emili Steuerman notes, in mock reparation, "there is a frantic wish to make things right," but that wish is stymied by the subject's own anxieties.[82] The tasks of the depressive position—coming to full awareness of our vulnerability and dependency, our desire to harm, and ways in which we and those with whom we identify have actually committed harm—arouse powerful defenses that may obstruct depressive knowledge and the possibility of reparation proper.

As an illustration of these theoretical ideas, consider the case of Peggy and Tony Campolo and their divergence of views on same-sex sexuality. Like Joel Hunter, Tony Campolo is often described as a moderate Christian academic and evangelist, though one who holds conservative beliefs about homosexuality and abortion. He has been criticized by some Christian conservatives, including in the ex-gay movement, because he does not believe that it is possible for exclusively same-sex-attracted people to change the direction of their sexual desires and become heterosexual. Tony has explained his position on sexual transformation by reference to the knowledge he has acquired as a sociologist, and his position is less at odds with some in the movement than it has been in the past. Like many leaders of Exodus today, Tony does not believe that same-sex sexual relations and relationships are consistent with the Word of God, and he speaks for the need to minister compassionately to same-sex-attracted people. Tony's wife, Peggy Campolo, also identifies as an evangelical Christian but takes a very different perspective on same-sex sexuality. Peggy accuses her fellow Christians of ill will toward lesbians and gay men, and she speaks out in favor of monogamous same-sex relationships and same-sex marriage.

Peggy and Tony Campolo have spoken publicly about their differences, and one widely circulated talk bears a title that nods to the Good Samaritan and to Augustine's concerns with establishing common humanity: "Is the Homosexual My Neighbor?" In this dialogue the Campolos lay out their diverse views on same-sex sexuality. Although Tony does not believe in sexual conversion, he provides biblical proof texts for his belief that God disapproves of homosexuality, and he warns that it is "arrogant" to discard "an interpretation of scripture [Romans 1:26–32] that has been around for more than 19 hundred years." In her turn, Peggy disputes Tony's interpretation of scripture and testifies that although she is a "straight, heterosexual lady" with no gay children, God has called her to "love and speak out for my gay brothers and lesbian sisters."

Peggy's personal testimony begins in high school with the mockery directed at her gay friend Tom, whom she was afraid to defend publicly. Later, she and her husband vacation in Provincetown, Massachusetts, and she feels "sadness and shame" at the welcome and acceptance she experiences from gay men and lesbians there and the hostility she knows they face in other spaces. The event that emboldens her to become an advocate for gay people and same-sex intimacy is a car ride with other conservative Christians who expatiate on "the homosexual problem." When the ride ends, Peggy is "left with [her] guilt" and a promise to herself not to be "silent anymore": "For me that day a rooster crowed for the third time. I had not only betrayed my friend, I had betrayed my God too." Tony too has a guilty story; in high school Tony and other boys taunt and assault "Roger" for being gay. Tony is not present the day five boys corner "Roger" in a shower and urinate on him, after which "Roger" goes home and commits suicide. However, Tony identifies himself as responsible for "actually [being] part of those who hurt, who contributed to the death of a young man."

Both of the Campolos clarify in their public dialogue that they aim to make reparation for what they describe as a failure of love and compassion on the part of Christian believers—and the body of believers, the Church—toward homosexuals. But the forms this reparation takes are meaningfully different. Peggy narrates her silent complicity with antigay attitudes and the emotional labor she engages in to overcome her reservations about speaking out on behalf of queers. Her spiritual journey brings her to a progay theology and social ideology that puts her at uncomfortable odds with other conservative believers and with her husband. Tony, on the other hand, confesses his responsibility in the suicide of his classmate but articulates his guilt as a vehicle for persuading other Christian conservatives to love homosexuals properly, which is to say to support them in giving up same-sex intimacy. As Tony puts it, "I am not preaching approval. I am preaching acceptance because I contend that if there is going to be any change of behavior, it is always in the context of love."[83]

Even as he counsels celibacy rather than sexual conversion to gay people, Tony Campolo speaks for the compassionate wing of the Christian right. In a relatively unusual move, he links his personal responsibility for antigay harm to the need to cultivate the right kind of compassion toward same-sex-attracted people. This compassion blends biblical instruction that same-sex sexuality is a violation of God's plan for sexuality with support for abstaining from same-sex intimacy. In what follows I imagine a "Kleinian" version of his testimony that emphasizes guilt, compassion, and reparation:

> When I was in high school my friends and I were so disgusted by the presence of a gay peer that we tormented him until he killed himself. I feel guilty about my role in his death. To make up for it, today I pour out my compassion for gay people, instructing them to forgo love and sexual intimacy for the rest of their lives because that's what God tells me to do. I also encourage other Christians to overcome their disgust and to love gay people in the same way I do. Those who experience this way of being loved as hurtful remain in the grip of sin, but I trust that God will work in their lives through me. In this way I make reparation for my act of harm and serve God's will.

By contrast, Peggy Campolo distances herself from the ideology of compassion generated in compassion crusades and places God's authority behind her apostasy on the "homosexual problem." Her testimony can also be rendered in a way that focuses attention on Kleinian categories of guilt, compassion, and reparation:

> Since I was in high school I've seen gay people treated badly by straight people, many of them Christians like myself, for no other reason than that they were gay. Even though I haven't personally tormented gay people I feel guilty, both because those who have inflicted the harm are members of groups to which I also belong and because for so long I didn't contest these injuries forcefully enough. For me, compassion means doing all I can to end these injustices and to recognize gay people as fellow human beings who are created for love and intimacy.

Reflecting on his and Peggy's testimony about same-sex sexuality, Tony notes that his "own stories [of guilt and responsibility] are very much like hers." But Tony's gloss on the testimonies does not disguise the ways in which they are not alike—the ways in which their stories create two quite distinct moral, political, and psychological narratives. Tony assuages his actual guilt in the matter of "Roger" by reiterating the biblical authority for the moral inferiority of same-sex love and relations, implicitly indicting "Roger" at the same time that he pleads for compassion from fellow Christians. Peggy's narrative, on the other hand, is one in which "the pain of guilt, loss and concern is turned into constructive effort of an altruistic kind."[84] What is clear in Peggy's testimony is that she does not regard her "gay brothers and lesbian sisters" as morally wayward, inferior and in need of spiritual instruction, but as people like herself. Indeed, rather than disavowing the connection, she reinforces it by speaking of the time before she allied herself with lesbians and gay men as her own "time in a closet."

As believers, both the Campolos believe it is imperative that they seek and find biblical grounds for their respective moral understandings. Their testimony is striking, both for its candor and for the stark disagreement between husband and wife that is rarely aired in Christian conservative spaces. As compassionate Christians, Tony and Peggy Campolo illustrate quite different meanings, uses, and effects of compassion in contemporary moral politics. Peggy Campolo frames her "crusade for homosexual justice" as an imperative that arises from her own guilt. Having been called by God, as she believes she has been, to engage in this crusade, she interprets the scripture on sexuality in a way that serves her desire to defend reparatively the well-being, rights, and personhood of queer people. By contrast, Tony extends his compassion and wish to make things right to those whose—by his own admission—immutable desire for intimacy can only fall short of the law he must uphold. I think the distinction Klein makes between reparation and mock reparation can help us to make sense of these different psychic and interpersonal paths.

Can "Compassion" Harm?

In this book I have argued that Christian right compassion ought to be taken seriously by students of American politics, religion, and sexuality. I have also argued that not all compassion is the same. That is to say, even if compassion campaigns enact some version of compassion there remains much to be said about the form that compassion takes, how its proper objects are distinguished, and its effects, both for those objects and for American society and political life. The compassion campaigns of the Christian right movement draw a bright line of ideology and pedagogy between those who are legitimate objects of compassion and those who are best understood as residing in the domain of law, public policy, and social marginalization. Those whose beliefs and behavior place them in the latter category are, by and large, conceptualized as fit objects for the other side of the Christian right movement, the side that is most comfortable with abomination rhetoric, stigma, and punishment.

As valuable as compassion is to the Christian right, it does not extend to those who refuse to renounce their same-sex attractions, to women who steadfastly support the legal right to abortion, and to women who refuse the opportunity to repudiate their own exercise of that right. And the form that compassion takes for those who are within its ambit can be analyzed using not only Christian theology, but also social theory, didactic popular literature, and psychoanalytic theory.

Melanie Klein's thought provides a template for interpreting the rhetorical and political infrastructure of Christian right compassion campaigns. The most obvious way in which this is so lies in Klein's accounts of positions (and the defenses that characterize them) and the possibility of reparation, both of which are complicated in fruitful ways by factoring in a relational psychology of groups that can address the collective features of social groups. Klein's moral theory rests on the psychodynamics of reparation. Although she sometimes summed it up as "put[ting] ourselves in the place of other people,"[85] the process is more difficult than this suggests and more easily derailed. It is also a particular challenge for individuals in their self-understandings as members of groups for the very reason that psychoanalytic theorists are so pessimistic about groups: because group identifications tend to incite and encourage idealization and forms of projection and denial that are particularly antithetical to the realization of responsibility for doing harm.[86]

By their very design, the Christian right's compassion campaigns forestall particular kinds of identifications and depressive guilt on the part of those who understand themselves as called to care for homosexuals and postabortive women. The Christian conservative version of compassion relies on an irreparable split between virtue and evil that is also the hallmark of the more familiar punitive arm of the Christian right movement. This split inhibits a reparative orientation toward social/sexual outgroups while reinforcing idealization of the Christian conservative community and its ideology. What distinguishes compassion from abomination projects is the explicit salvaging of a particular group of repentant outcasts from the diffuse condemnation associated with abomination ideology and believers.

One result of this ingroup/outgroup split is the ex-gay and postabortion ministries phenomenon of feeling sorry for themselves—extending compassion toward those who affirm their commitment to, and belief in, the antigay and antiabortion tenets of the Christian right movement. Postabortive men or women; struggling same-sex-attracted men or women; or friends or family members of any of these: compassion campaigns embrace these suffering, struggling, and sometimes guilty, souls as part of the Godly and idealized group. Far from undermining the denunciation of sin and sinners of the Christian right movement as a whole, this move defines and strengthens the boundary between the deserving and the undeserving and confirms the importance of identification with the group as a condition for sharing in its benefits and protection.

Another result of the split accomplished by compassion campaigns is the flourishing of a morality that superficially resembles what Klein describes as reparative morality. However, unlike the moral orientation Klein describes, compassion campaigns actively work to prevent adherents from connecting harm to postabortive women and the same-sex-attracted to the ideology and public policies they espouse and to the interpersonal interactions in which they have participated. Compassion campaigns' ostensibly reparative morality takes in people damaged by the culture wars, nurtures them on antiabortion and antigay ideology, and then provides them with a restorative membership in the body of believers. But to accomplish this mission compassionate Christian conservatives have to deny the harm that is inflicted on women who seek and have had an abortion and on queer people; they must deny their own guilt and responsibility for that harm, and they must hold toward these objects a perspective of sexual and spiritual superiority.

Given the biblical injunctions against same-sex sexuality found in the books of Leviticus and Romans, it might be hard to imagine Christian believers accepting queers as moral equals or acknowledging any responsibility for harm doing toward them. But, in fact, there is a wide disparity today between, on the one hand, mainline Protestants and liberal Catholics and, on the other hand, traditionalist conservative Christians (Protestants and Catholics, as well as Mormons and others) on this issue. In the face of intrachurch and intradenominational conflict on the issue of sexuality, many moderate and liberal Christian churches across denominations acknowledge harms caused by antigay social sentiment and legal discrimination, and many attest to their position on sexuality by designating themselves as "welcoming," "affirming," or "reconciling" to LGBTQ people and not just to those who repent and embrace a new identity of "holiness."[87] Many of these churches and believers no doubt see their welcoming stance as one way to "stand on the side of love."[88] From a Kleinian perspective, their ideology is reparative.

By contrast, in ex-gay ministries, conservative discourse may acknowledge the existence of some harms to gay people while conceptualizing these harms as the fruits of gay identity and behavior rather than as oppression. If, for example, gay people suffer social stigma and political exclusion, these losses and deprivations are, in a common phrase, "natural consequences" of the embrace of queer identity. The same conclusion would be drawn about the "chronic psychological strain" that researchers find is associated with minority stress under conditions of stigmatization and adverse public policies.[89] For Christian conservatives, these harms follow inexorably from a violation of Natural Law and not from illiberal state policies or the acts of fellow citizens. In all cases, the antidote to harm and stigma is the compassion of ex-gay or postabortion ministries. Christian conservatives reproach theological and political moderates for a tolerance that abides evil and ignores the spiritual needs of those who suffer. Compassion campaigns serve these suffering people by bringing them to Jesus in love. But they also serve believers, providing a way for them to collaborate in administering love and compassion rather than to be implicated in administering harm.

In her ethnographic study of two midwestern United Methodist churches, one theologically liberal and the other theologically conservative, Dawne Moon notes the quite different orientations of the churches to the idea of "gay pain." Moon's liberal church—which embraces members with a wide variety of beliefs on the subject of homosexuality—sponsors conversations on social harms and the effects of prejudice on gay people.[90] Moon thoughtfully critiques the rhetoric of gay pain, pointing out the ways in which an emphasis on feelings can, and often does, depoliticize the identities and claims of stigmatized group members. Moon demonstrates how, in the hands of ex-gay actors and representatives of "Transforming" church ideology, the movement may sometimes discursively distinguish ordinary—repentant or potentially repentant—gay people from gay *activists*, thus crafting a less inclusive category of "activist" that does the work of rescuing recruits from the calumny associated with the term. In addition, the movement redescribes political "militancy" as a function of childhood and adolescent distress with gender nonnormativity and same-sex desire. In this way queers who are fed up with discriminatory public policies and stigmatizing public rhetoric are constructed as hurt children who lash out at Christian believers "standing in the gap" on their behalf.

Moon accurately represents how Christian right compassion functions to position queers as people in need of healing and repair, contingent as always on their repentance and willingness to embrace abstinence and antigay beliefs. Like many feminist/antiracist theorists, she worries about the possible effects of marginalized subjects being reduced to their suffering and victimization. This is a legitimate concern. At the same time, however, it is important to interrogate compassionate ideology to understand how it is deployed to deny the existence, scope, and consequences of group-based harm doing. Group psychoanalysis can be very useful in conceptualizing these effects, often in ways that can be empirically observed.

If Klein is right, or if her work provides a fruitful template for thinking about the relationship of guilt and responsibility to the possibility of less conflictual social relations, then publicizing "gay pain" and the effects of abortion stigma may be more useful than Moon thinks.[91] For Kleinians, a key component of reparative relations between groups is the ability of group members to acknowledge the commission of harm, and for this to be possible it is necessary to make the pain suffered by members of stigmatized groups publicly legible. This is the reasoning behind truth commissions that have been convened in the aftermath of periods of deadly civil strife.

James L. Gibson carried out an empirical investigation of the Truth and Reconciliation Commission (TRC) that operated in South Africa for several years after the end of apartheid. Both victims and perpetrators were invited to testify before the Commission, and perpetrators who testified without reservation received amnesty for their acts. Among other consequences, these public testimonies confronted white South Africans with evidence of the "atrocities" committed by their government and of whites' "guilt and blame for the benefits they enjoyed under apartheid." They also confronted black South Africans with evidence of harmful acts committed by blacks against other blacks and against whites. Because perpetrators who cooperated with the TRC were not punished, the Commission had to overcome the accurate perception that it did not serve the ends of retributive justice. It did so by providing some monetary compensation for victims of the Apartheid regime, but Gibson found that monetary reparations were not the paramount consideration for South Africans in evaluating the justice and efficacy of the TRC. More important was that the Commission provided venues in which personal testimonies of harm could be heard and that it created a space for confessions of wrongdoing and sincere apologies on the part of perpetrators.[92]

Focusing on African American girls and women in US history and cultural texts, Rebecca Wanzo takes up a complementary set of questions about suffering and the legibility of different forms of suffering. Wanzo theoretically and empirically examines the processes by which the sympathetic affect that is "a necessary prerequisite to social and political action" may be mobilized on behalf of those who suffer. She finds that not all victims of harm possess the "affective agency" to make their suffering legible and to use their testimonies of harm to "produce institutional effects." Indeed, far from being random and unpredictable, affective agency reflects raced and gendered hierarchies that precede suffering individuals into the "social problems marketplace." Wanzo vindicates the sentimentality on which social responsiveness to harm is so often predicated by disputing the inherent conservatism of sentimental affect and rhetoric. Sentimental narratives may not be the only vehicle for delivering testimony of harm, but they may be "politically effective" even when they are not sufficient to deliver progressive forms of political change.[93]

This is not to suggest that testimonies and evidence of group-based harm are always dispositive and persuasive even to those who do not share directly in responsibility for harm. Psychologists Michael A. Milburn and Sheree D. Conrad argue that ideologies organize and support different forms of denial, such that "conservatives have a tendency to deny the evidence of others' suffering."[94] If this finding is accurate, Christian conservatives are predisposed to disclaim evidence of harm and to resist any identification with those who inhabit the ignominious side of culture war debates on sexual morality as well as being primed for this position by Christian right culture.

Compassionate Warriors

In part, the softened rhetoric and compassionate interventions of the Christian right are politically strategic, as critics suspect. It's just that they are not only political strategy geared to influencing mainstream attitudes toward Christian conservatives. Besides being aimed at a nonbelieving public outside the boundaries of Christian conservatism, compassion is crafted for believers themselves. Christian right compassion affirms and reinforces the virtues, boundaries, and political goals of the traditionalist Christian right movement *for believers*. It vindicates and reassures believers that they embody and represent the love of God and that they are compassionate—rather than ruthless and merciless—warriors in what has been defined for them as an ultimate cause. It may elicit authentic feelings of "cosuffering" with those who are in pain because of same-sex attraction or because of their choice to have an abortion. It inspires and binds to the community those who come to rely on ex-gay and postabortion ministries for their own sexual and spiritual healing.

Before there was widespread compassion for same-sex-attracted strugglers and women who have had an abortion there was a nascent Christian conservative ideology of compassion that called—and continues to call—that compassion into existence. Whether transmitted from the pulpit, through networks of believers, or through public media, such discourse is psychologically, as well as politically, salient. The calling of Christian believers to mimic the compassion of Jesus effects a significant reversal. It encourages people who have been defined by others as brimming with hatred and *ressentiment*; as pious, narrow minded, and intolerant; and as puritans who fear and loathe bodies and sexuality redefine themselves as people who extend a hand of help and blessing to the stranger, the social leper, the least among us. Thus do compassion campaigns provide a grammar of idealization that bolsters defenses against charges of harm. The tough love of compassion is no less than the scourging, but finally healing, love of God himself.

Compassion campaigns are vehicles for refining and disseminating compassion pedagogy at the same time that they serve the target groups of same-sex-attracted strugglers and postabortive women. The combination and coexistence of Christian right abomination and compassion created, and continues to create, the broken and repentant consumers who will come to need its products just as it inspires believers to a compassion with particular content and contours. To conceptualize the relationships among ideology, pedagogy, compassionate identity, and repentant identity in this way is not to deny that compassion animates these antigay and antiabortion campaigns. Rather, it is to try to map the complexity of the process and to enhance critics' understanding of the intertwined psychological and political dimensions of the Christian right movement.

For many years I have been drawn to Klein's work and to the work of social theorists in the relational tradition who have used her as a resource. I find her arguments about the complex set of processes that constitute human subjects fascinating—not comforting, but compelling and even disturbing in their implications. In particular, Klein's accounts of what the philosopher David Hume called "disagreeable passions"—for Klein, envy, greed, guilt, and hatred—provide a rich template and narrative of human development and relationality.[95] Perhaps Klein is a harder sell with those who experience human selfhood and sociality as benevolent, or always potentially so, than she is with those of us who are less sanguine on these matters. Nor is she or others who work in the Kleinian tradition likely to be convincing to scholars whose interest is the deconstruction of language and radical skepticism about the possibility of representing phenomena that lurk behind language. These thinkers will go elsewhere for inspiration, and the psychoanalytic traditions are diverse enough to provide them alternatives.

As important as empiricism is, there is much in psychoanalytic thinking about human selfhood and mental processes that cannot be verified or that can only find indirect support or disconfirmation, for example through psychological research. That being the case, why give so much weight to relational psychoanalytic accounts of mind and identity? One compelling response to this question is that Klein and her intellectual heirs offer "an account of human nature" with "profound social and political implications."[96] Historically, some other such accounts have seized the imaginations of groups, have been configured into governing or oppositional ideologies, and have dominated the imaginations of nations or eras. By comparison, Klein's account of human nature is relatively obscure. However, Klein's theory has inspired compelling analyses of the psychic turbulence of selfhood, the complexity of intimate relations, the dynamics of group leadership and membership, and the conscious and unconscious dimensions of interpersonal and collective life. A relational psychoanalytic account of compassion invites thoughtful examination precisely because it speaks to the dangerous aspects of self and relationality that always threaten to disrupt and undermine its possibility.

Afterword

Compassion, Where Is Thy Victory?

Whence Compassion?

Many philosophers have found in the human capacity for compassion the source of morality itself. Of course, this genealogy of morality is disputed. Those for whom morality is derived from scripture or from some form of revelation from an often inscrutable God do not, either necessarily or empirically, reject the value of compassion for morality, but they do make God the source and arbiter of compassion. To do otherwise, they believe, is to rob compassion of the compass it needs to function properly rather than as a vehicle and apology for situational sinfulness. Theirs is one way of resolving the problem of, for example, extending tolerance and compassion to all on equal terms: to Eichmann and to his victims alike.

At the same time, drawing the boundary of compassion as the Christian right does and consigning those on the far side of it—be they queers or women who have chosen an abortion unapologetically—to stigma, exclusion, and sometimes, formal modes of punishment seems baffling and hypocritical to those outside the movement. For example, writing in *The New Republic* on culture warriors he sardonically calls "anti-gay-marriage intellectuals," Jonathan Chait seems surprised to note that those who oppose same-sex marriage most vociferously seem willing to "place zero weight upon the preferences of gays" when formulating and defending their policy prescriptions.[1] Chait admits that he has come late to these proceedings, but of course this refusal to weigh the well-being and interests of those who engage in same-sex relationships is nothing new. What is relatively new is the insistence that such policy positions are motivated by, and reflect, Christian love and compassion rather than, say, God's wrath toward unregenerate sinners. It is this turn that invites fresh scrutiny of the beliefs, motives, strategies, and justifications of antigay and antiabortion activism.

The bifurcation of its antigay and antiabortion movements into compassionate initiatives geared to helping those who struggle with sexual sin and other initiatives aimed at revoking rights and stigmatizing particular kinds of desires, behavior, and subjects advances the political agenda of the Christian right. But the bifurcation also has other meanings and effects. I believe that the existence of compassionate sectors of the antigay and antiabortion movements satisfies the desires of many Christian conservatives to intervene personally with suffering others and to spread the Gospel of Jesus in a way they understand as caring rather than punitive. Compassion campaigns take as their task the loving repair of the culture wars' wounded. But first the wounded must capitulate on a number of fronts; they must acknowledge the rectitude of cultural war, embrace the (Christian) right side of the contest, profess their own sinfulness and culpability, construct a new identity that reflects the morality politics of the movement, and vow to manage that identity in a way that's consistent with Christian conservative ideology. Finally, they must commit themselves to espousing and pursuing political goals that are consistent with the ideology that infuses the process of spiritual conviction and conversion.

My project in this book has been to use the resources offered by a set of theorists to explore the worldview of Christian right compassion, its social meanings, and its implications. In this project, Hannah Arendt's critique of politicized compassion, Ayn Rand's enunciation of a discriminating model of compassion, and Melanie Klein's articulation of modes of reparation advance students of the movement beyond the perceptions and conclusions of the Christian right's use of compassion that circulate in everyday political discourse. Christian right compassion campaigns are not just exercises in duplicity and hypocrisy; they do not merely cloak hatred for particular groups; and they are not only media-genic ways of negotiating the movement's reputation for puritanical sexuality. When it comes to compassion, there often is more to the Christian right than meets the eye. And mainstream theorists who take love, empathy, compassion, and their relationship to political life as their subject matter can help elucidate the complexities that are easily obscured in political struggle.

Afterword

A Last Word on Theory

All scholars make choices of theoretical systems to use in analyzing texts and social or political phenomena. These choices are not self-evident, although once they are made they can seem natural to authors and readers alike. Justifications for theoretical choices can be both general and specific. At the general level, theoretical systems foster and foreclose particular modes of inquiry. For example, queer theory has become a dominant paradigm in women's studies as well as in many humanities disciplines and some social science subfields. It's possible to imagine a queer-theoretical version of this analysis of Christian right compassion that would employ a different vocabulary, cite different theorists, and probably, arrive at some different conclusions. There is much to be said for a system of critique that is constructed to root out hidden binaries and normative hierarchies and expose circuits of power, and such a critique would no doubt deliver valuable perspectives on, for example, Christian right compassion. At the same time, all theoretical systems are better suited to some intellectual enterprises than others. I agree with Janice McLaughlin, Mark Casey, and Diane Richardson that religious fundamentalism is one subject that should not be explored solely through the lens of queer theory's commitment to "contingency, ambiguity and transgression"; such an analysis is unlikely to yield a comprehensive conception of a fundamentalist world-view.[2]

At a more specific level, I believe there are perspectives on a phenomenon such as compassion on the Christian right that come from examining how it articulates with particular bodies of thought: in this case, democratic political theory, popular ideology, and psychoanalysis. Such an analysis can simultaneously trace genealogies of influence, problematics of political citizenship, payoffs of ideological affinity, and modes of ethical orientation toward groups of citizens whose identities situate them in particular kinds of historically conditioned relations with others. Finally, I believe that the task of political theory is unavoidably normative and, thus, that political theorizing is a conversation between different visions of normativity. Although many theorists in the academy today reject normative prescriptiveness, I find the idea that a commitment to nonnormativity will somehow clear the way for a world that is more just, free, and humane misguided. The three principal theorists I rely on here for guidance fiercely held normative visions of what constitutes "the good" for humans, individually and in our shared existence. Their clarity lays the foundation for agreement, disagreement, and other hybrid forms of response.

With regard to the choices I have made in this book, Hannah Arendt, who understood herself to operate intellectually outside the political traditions of her day, is not just a theorist of totalitarianism and a proponent of classical democratic practices. Ayn Rand is not just a proponent of extreme libertarianism and an avatar of selfishness. And Melanie Klein is not just a legatee of Freudian object relations and an idiosyncratic investigator of the infant mind. All three of these theorists produced rich texts and rich theoretical systems that have enabled scholars to apply their concepts, insights, and connections to the investigation of problems in our time. Although Rand is most often put to work in the context of ideological questions about the scope of state power and the superiority of the free market, Arendt and Klein have continued to be popular theorists whose expositors work and rework their ideas to cast new light on a vast array of contemporary questions.

Disputes about modes of compassion in American life and politics certainly can be a matter for abstract theorizing, but they are not merely academic. In 2009, as President Barack Obama spoke about, and prepared for, his first nomination to the Supreme Court, he galvanized conservatives by suggesting that one qualification for a position as justice should be empathy, and he refused to retract the view when political opponents decried it as code for liberal judicial activism. Dahlia Lithwick's commentary on Obama's "empathy" is instructive. Returning to Obama's book, *The Audacity of Hope: Thoughts on Reclaiming the American Dream*, for clues about how he interprets the moral mandate, Lithwick notes, "Webster's definition of empathy as 'the experiencing as one's own the feelings of another.' Obama . . . described empathy as a 'a call to stand in somebody else's shoes and see through their eyes.' To Obama, empathy chiefly means applying a principle his mother taught him: asking, 'How would that make you feel?' before acting."[3] Criticizing conservative opponents of the administration for their wholesale repudiation of empathy as a placeholder for "intellectual weakness, judicial immodesty, favoritism, bias, and grandiosity," Lithwick does not explore the subtle but important distinctions between Obama's and his mother's definitions of empathy, but Hannah Arendt does.

In spite of her profound skepticism about the political work that can and should be done by compassion, Arendt assays into what we might call broadly a psychology of compassion. The enlarged mentality she championed demands that moral actors imagine themselves in specific and concrete positions that are not their own in order to reason better as political actors. While she explicitly declines empathy—feeling *with* the other or assuming one is doing so—as a foundation of response to the suffering and predicaments of the other, she offers representative thinking supplemented by as much information as the thinker can receive as an alternative. For Arendt, the human heart is opaque and, thus, unreliable as a guide for public action and judgment. We are not all Eichmann—a man she regarded, rightly or wrongly, as having disciplined his compassion into submission with a terrible set of linguistic and intellectual tactics—but we are all capable of deceiving ourselves about the sources and implications of our feelings.[4] And when we deceive ourselves, substituting ignorance, identity, ideology, or interest for judgment, we are capable of great destructiveness.

For Arendt, the dangers of public, mass compassion are so great that the circumference of compassion itself must shrink to intimate proportions, erecting a firewall that protects both intimacy and politics. Under questioning from interviewer Günter Gaus in 1964, Arendt expanded on her famous refusal in the post-*Eichmann* letter to Gershom Scholem to profess a love for the Jewish people. In that interview, Gaus asked her if human beings don't "need commitment to a group, a commitment that can then to a certain extent be called love." Arendt responded to this assertion with an emphatic "No" and went on to briefly differentiate identity groups from interest groups. With regard to the former, she noted that "in the first place, belonging to a group is a natural condition. You belong to some sort of group when you are born, always." Later, she returned to the question of preference for one's own group and extolled the pursuit of truths that are always threatened, not only by interests of the powerful, but also by love for the group: "If someone is not capable of this impartiality because he pretends to love his people so much that he pays flattering homage to them all the time—well, then there's nothing to be done. I do not believe that people like that are patriots."[5]

So far I have largely side-stepped the question Arendt raises about the pernicious consequences of compassion as a motivation for political action. On the one hand, I am uncomfortable valorizing a politics in which compassionate motives have no place; how would it be possible to excise them even if we wanted to? On the other hand, I have come to be persuaded by many of Arendt's anxieties about compassionate politics: the ways in which compassion can be constructed and manipulated for partisan ends; the ease with which compassion can be used to authorize and sanctify those ends; and the need to acknowledge and contend with the intended and unintended consequences these compassionate interventions leave in their wake. Far from being an incontestable foundation for political action, compassion ought to compel tough scrutiny whenever it is applied, not only from its foes but also from its friends.

It doesn't settle the question, but Tamsin Bradley's study of compassionate activism by Christian nongovernmental organizations suggests some implications of compassionate intervention that might unsettle defenders of compassion. Setting out to assess the success of compassionate interventions on target populations in the developing world, Bradley finds that the compassion of workers in these faith-based NGOs is "linked to the gift of the spirit and the obligation to follow the example set by Christ." The result is that these workers are positively distinguished from other development actors by their "long term commitment and high levels of motivation." On the negative side of the ledger, Bradley found that members of faith-based groups who engage in compassionate interventions tend to construct a "permanent picture of the suffering other" that is relatively impervious to empirical information. And because members assume that the motivation of compassion means that the impact of their labor on target populations will be positive, they don't see the need to document the actual consequences for those they help. After all, Jesus did not "stand back and assess the effectiveness of his interventions."[6] These conclusions would not be out of place as a summary of antigay and antiabortion compassion campaigns: high commitment, identification with the love of Christ, imperviousness to empirical information, and indifference to harmful consequences.

Compared to Arendt's "muscular scepticism" about empathy and compassion, in her work Ayn Rand was strikingly naïve about feelings. In her fiction she insisted on a taxonomy of human character that was more or less transparent, at least to the discerning (objectivist) observer. Human beings would, she believed, exhibit those traits that were consistent with the quality of their character, such that feelings, motives, and actions would reflect, to the self and others, where one stood in the hierarchy of moral being. Any deviation from this consistency signaled repression as she understood the concept or a more serious psychological problem that might well exile the hapless sufferer outside the charmed circle defined by Rand's "sense of life."[7] As in totalitarian ideologies that Rand repudiated outright, she consistently produced fictitious equations between spiritual, moral, and physical characteristics that linked beauty and physical competence with superior morality and emotions.[8] As a psychologist who once used his vocation to inculcate and torment fellow objectivists with

Rand's philosophy, Rand's protégé, Nathaniel Branden, has taken pains to renounce the psychology entailed by objectivism:

> [Rand] used to say to me, "*I don't know anything about psychology, Nathaniel.*" I wish I had taken her more seriously. She was right; she knew next to nothing about psychology. What neither of us understood, however, was how disastrous an omission that is in a philosopher in general and a moralist in particular. The most devastating single omission in her system and the one that causes most of the trouble for her followers is the absence of any real appreciation of human psychology and, more specifically, of developmental psychology, of how human beings evolve and become what they are and of how they can change.[9]

Although Rand insisted that she drew her characters from the real world, she also confirmed that she sought to portray human beings as she believed they ought to be, writing, for example, that "the motive and purpose of [her] writing was *the projection of an ideal man*" and that she asked herself, "what kind of men do I want to see in real life—and why?"[10] In real life Rand pressured her acolytes, persuading, harassing, and sometimes coercing, them into proper modes of response that would make them worthy of the heroic identity she could confer on them. Her followers' adherence to her commands confirmed the rectitude and, ironically, the naturalness, of their responses.[11]

Rand created a world in which, at least for those whose identifications are properly aligned, there is nothing to feel sorry for and no malign consequences to be undone. As this suggests, for Rand reparation is unlikely and unnecessary. The good and innocent may suffer for a season at the hands of the wicked and guilty, but ultimately good triumphs over evil, the good are vindicated, and the wicked are punished by receiving the fruits of their own deeds and motives. Rand is preoccupied with evil; her bad characters are studies in envy, greed, and hatred, including contemptuous self-hatred. But far from becoming anxious and depressed by their capacity for destructiveness, they revel in it, at least until they arrive at their narrative moment of reckoning. The good, however, exemplify competence and serenity, even in moments that would try lesser beings. They have no need of reparation because they don't harbor destructive impulses toward their fellows; indeed, except on the occasions when they are forced to think of them, they don't. If anything, the good are perplexed by the malice of villains and by the vast scope of the villains' malignant designs on virtue.

Unlike both Arendt and Klein, Rand is a thinker to be contended with in the realm of popular ideas. One example of her popularity is that when the Modern Library polled readers in 1998 to determine their favorite works of fiction, Rand scored four works in the top thirty selections, including *Atlas Shrugged* in first place and *The Fountainhead* in second.[12] Rand's earlier novels, *Anthem* and *We the Living*, came in at numbers seven and eight, respectively. *The Fountainhead* and *Atlas Shrugged* have sold millions of copies since their publication, but they are only two of many vehicles for the dissemination of Rand's ideas. In addition to novels and nonfiction writing, her ideas and her philosophy, objectivism, have been spread by institutes and centers dedicated to their exegesis and popularization, college and university objectivist clubs, training seminars, newsletters, biographies, websites, blogs, films, and occasional endorsements by celebrities. No parallel anti-Rand intellectual infrastructure exists, though objectivists might cite humanities disciplines as nurturing a tacit antiobjectivist ethos.[13]

By any estimation Rand has enjoyed a huge following and has influenced American political ideology profoundly.[14] In her hilarious essay "Psyching Out Ayn Rand," Barbara Grizzuti Harrison notes that "she is not adorable. But she can't be shrugged off."[15] Jennifer Burns' more sober assessment in her study of Rand's philosophy is that "for over a half a century Rand has been the ultimate gateway drug to life on the right."[16] But Rand has also enjoyed a renaissance as a result of both corporate philanthropy and populist hard right conservatism. In the realm of corporate philanthropy, consider this: since the 1990s, BB&T has been quietly carrying out a plan to interject Rand and "Rand studies" into college and university curricula.[17] In other venues, Rand serves as a vehicle of protest against the policy positions of the Obama administration and the Democratic Party. Conservative commentators briefly rehearse the broad plot outlines of *Atlas Shrugged* for viewers/readers in the context of denouncing impending socialism and/or the collapse of the US economic system.

Depicting Rand as prescient in foreseeing a time when freedom-loving producers would withdraw their intelligence and labor from the incipient socialist system and flee to safe harbor in Colorado, Randians use the blogosphere, as well as more conventional media, to discuss the pros and cons of dropping out and leaving the rest of the nation to fend for itself. In an article for the *Village Voice* entitled, "Rightbloggers Say: Go Galt! We'll Catch Up with You Later!" Roy Edroso jokes that the

Obama presidency has caused right-wing bloggers to go "full metal Randroid," threatening to "go Galt" and deprive the expropriating state of its resources.[18] On the left, some have responded to the tumult by *inviting* bankers, hedge fund managers, and CEOs of failed or failing corporations to resign or by suggesting that lower-earning adherents to Rand's philosophy are not, in fact, capable of "going Galt" because they lack the financial wherewithal to fulfill the role assigned to them in Rand's vision.[19]

The renewed attention to Rand in the context and aftermath of a global recession is not difficult to understand. Rand's novels, particularly *Atlas Shrugged*, furnish partisans of free markets who see socialism/totalitarianism in liberal political parties and Keynesian economic measures with a detailed ideological script for the resolution of the crisis. *Atlas's* apocalyptic hopefulness may raise fears of corrupt politicians mouthing platitudes of peace and prosperity, but it also no doubt reassures many that economic collapse is reversible. In these respects the appeal of Rand's ideas is intellectual, but it is also, as Gary Weiss notes, "subtle, almost subliminal." One of Weiss's interviewees, Christian tea party organizer Mark Meckler, testifies not only that Rand "is more widely read" in the movement than any other author but also that Rand's "ideas go into our heads and our hearts" and that her "philosophy lives as a part of who we are."[20] It's a remarkable testimony to the influence of a novelist who has been dead for over thirty years.

As leaders of intellectual movements, both Rand and Klein cultivated cult followings and, thus, encouraged conformist groupishness in those around them. Both excommunicated followers who did not toe the lines of personal and intellectual fealty to the leader. Both did their best to create closed systems of thought whose principle tenets would not be disputed by admirers and expositors. In Rand's case, many "lay" followers continue to vie with each other to enunciate and align themselves with the authentic core beliefs of objectivism. Ironically, Rand's legacy had begun to slip from her control by the end of her lifetime, and her ideas have now been incorporated idiosyncratically into various political philosophies, especially on the American right.[21] While it is true that those who devote themselves to analysis of Randian texts often have been easily distinguished from one another as either critics of Rand's oeuvre or as close readers and sympathetic rearticulators of Rand's metaphysics, epistemology, ethics, politics, or psychology, even that state of affairs appears to be changing.[22]

Melanie Klein also made vigorous efforts to control her associates, analysands, admirers, and others in the British School of psychoanalysis, but she fared less well than Rand at this enterprise. Instead of fixing her intellectual legacy once and for all, Klein ended up initiating an open system of ideas. Her contemporaries and later clinicians dissented from some of her specific claims and clinical interpretations, reshaping her work as she famously had reshaped Freud's. Feminists and other social theorists would read in her work implications that she did not foresee and have treated her ideas with less respect for their integrity than she demanded of those in her circle. In perhaps the gravest blow to a dedicated clinician who treated individual patients, her work has been metaphorized and has had many of the empirically questionable elements—such as, for example, the always dubious Freudian notion of a "death instinct"—virtually excised. In contrast to Julia Kristeva, who characterizes Klein as "worshiped to the point of dogmatic fanaticism by her disciples—and held in utter contempt by her detractors,"[23] I find the contemporary scholarly project of Klein studies to be less an exercise in hagiography than it is a vigorous project of dissection, dissension, expansion, skepticism, and even empirical testing. In scholarship on Klein there is little to be gained from excavating and clinging doggedly to the sage's own ideas and much to be gained from testing the reasonableness of new ones.

As a psychoanalytic theorist and clinician, Melanie Klein expended more of her thinking on human psychology and on the subject of feelings than either Arendt or Rand. Her work was dedicated to revealing and articulating the "mosaic of turbulence" that she believed constituted the "infant's mind" and, in meaningful ways, the mind itself.[24] Klein's innovation in the study of feelings and their role in the making of the self was to use the clinical material at her disposal and her talent for theoretical system building to put disagreeable passions and defenses against them at them at the center of her model of mind. Unlike Arendt, she studied the intimate and largely left it to her followers to interpret the social and political implications of her ideas. Her legacy is a protean tradition that excavates complexity, concealment—including feelings and motivations the self keeps hidden from itself—and ambivalence.

Despite differences in their theoretical styles and objects of analysis, both Arendt and Klein took up problems of harm doing that consistently bedevil individuals, groups, and states. In her analysis of Eichmann, Arendt takes the problem of evil to be thoughtlessness, the failure to think what one is doing, a theme she returned to in her writing until the end of her life.[25] In Elisabeth Young-Bruehl's reading, thoughtlessness is for Arendt the "necessary condition for evildoing." However, Young-Bruehl also suggests it is not that "thinking *per se*" that keeps us from committing evil but rather that thinking is "the necessary condition for judging," and judging is the faculty that employs the enlarged mentality in its functioning.[26] Comparing Arendt and Klein directly, Alford concludes that in spite of her rich attention to the subject of evil and harm, Arendt doesn't understand evil as well as Klein does because she takes "the phenomenon to be explained as though it were itself the explanation." If Klein and those, like Bion, who followed her are right, thoughtlessness—the refusal to "think what we are doing"—as an explanation of harm doing is misleading because it doesn't sufficiently take account of unconscious forms of malevolent desire and the active urge to deny and falsify knowledge of what we are doing and what we have done.[27]

Clearly Arendt and Klein would not agree on every question. What Arendt and Klein have in common is not that they provided the same answers to similar questions but that as thinkers they point in the direction of a more chastened than sanguine conception of human motivations and relationships. Here, summing up Klein's thought, is Robert M. Young:

> According to Klein, our minds are always in one or the other of two positions. One involves extreme splits, brittle guilt, blaming, hating, scapegoating, paranoia and the tendency to aggression and fighting, whether verbal or physical. The other involves granting that life is not just extremes but consists of things all mixed up, some good, some bad: the middle ground. In this frame of mind guilt is not punitive but reparative. One is not in a manic state but a rather subdued, depressive (not to say depressed) one. Miracles don't happen. Hard graft is one's lot. You have to sit on your extreme feelings and live and let live.[28]

It's not a particularly sophisticated ethic: hard graft; live and let live. And yet this ethic does set a high standard for human conduct, especially in the face of group interests in idealizing our own, stigmatizing difference, compelling obedience or subordination, and defeating foes.

Feeling(s) and Knowing

As important as political beliefs, acts, and institutions are, the domain of the political can only be cordoned off from the psychological by sacrificing valuable forms of knowledge about political ideology and action. For example, empirical research in political psychology continues to generate fascinating insights into the influence of context, emotions, and group affiliation on political ideas and motivations. Much of this research is chastening to optimism about democracy, or at least to progressive visions of deliberative democracy, though it makes sense of continuing ideological and political strife over such compelling issues as queer citizenship and reproductive choice/justice.

As psychologists Jonathan Haidt and Jesse Graham note, literature on left-right/liberal-conservative differences in moral intuitions and policy usually privileges particular moral foundations that derive from attention to two moral foundations: "harm/welfare/care and justice/rights/fairness." These two are associated with the political left in the United States and Europe. However, liberals and progressives don't recognize or use three other moral foundations that can be identified exclusively with conservatives: "unconditional loyalty to one's group [ingroup/loyalty], respect for one's superiors [authority/respect], and the avoidance of carnal pleasures [purity/sanctity]." Haidt and Graham argue that even though the last three are foundations that liberals do not incorporate into their moral repertoires, they have long been domains of moral understanding and expression.[29]

Like many who wade into culture wars debates, Haidt and Graham counsel scholars who work in these nettlesome precincts "to understand, respect, and work with the moral concerns of people with whom they disagree." But of course such counsel is easier given than followed in the political realm, especially when those on the left and right turn to the issues on which they most disagree. Indeed, issues such as abortion, same-sex sexuality (including state recognition of same-sex partnerships and families), immigration, and even contraception and taxation activate in conservatives the very anxieties about purity and sanctity that those on the political left tend to believe have no place in political discourse.[30] By the terms of these debates over same-sex sexuality and abortion, those who countenance abortion and refuse to denigrate same-sex sexuality and relationships are not just *liberals*, but "*dirty liberals*."[31] That is, in the framework of conservative thought, they fail to properly link threats of contamination—to the body as well as to the body politic—to the appropriate sanctions and policy positions that should follow from those threats.

In thinking through the tenacious opposition to same-sex sexuality, queer identity, and reproductive rights in the United States, it is difficult to avoid the salience and political significance of disgust, including the way in which disgust works to fortify boundaries between goodness and badness. Psychologist Susan B. Miller concludes that heterosexual disgust with homosexuals and same-sex sexuality is stimulated by a "last-ditch effort to establish an essential difference between oneself and the disgustingly animal."[32] A thorough account of the implications of disgust for democratic life is found in the writings of philosopher Martha Nussbaum, who has written not one, but two, books about the problem of disgust in our collective legal, social, and political lives: *Hiding from Humanity: Disgust, Shame, and the Law* and the more recent *From Disgust to Humanity: Sexual Orientation and Constitutional Law*.[33]

While stigma toward same-sex sexuality—including moral panic and the "homosexual-provocation" defense for criminal behavior—is a significant theme in *Hiding from Humanity*, in *From Disgust to Humanity* Nussbaum focuses exclusively on the intersection of same-sex sexuality and the law, an intersection in which disgust has played a central role. In response, Nussbaum's colleague, legal scholar Mary Anne Case, published a thoughtful critique of Nussbaum's argument. Case, who points out that she shares with Nussbaum an LGBTQ rights agenda, expresses skepticism about Nussbaum's exacting call for "love" of homosexuals from those who oppose lesbian and gay rights and equality.[34] I share Case's skepticism of Nussbaum's call for a "politics of humanity" that requires not only respect but "something closer to love."[35] Nussbaum's own example of a moral journey from disgust to a politics of humanity is the decline of disgust and contagion-based white racism against African Americans in the United States. While Nussbaum alludes briefly to racism as a motivation for some voters who opposed Barack Obama for president in 2008, she sets the near elimination of such racism in a future in which American children "who grow up modeling themselves on Sasha and Malia Obama" finally complete the moral and psychological project of a politics of humanity.[36] Clearly, white racism has declined substantially, both as a foundation for public policy and in the attitudes of white Americans from *Brown* to the present. Even so, such a hopeful note cannot help but be at odds with recent mobilizations of racism that coincided with the 2008 presidential election and the publication of *From Disgust to Humanity*.[37]

Whatever its objects in particular sociopolitical contexts, disgust correlates strongly with conservative political attitudes and continues to be a durable foundation and justification for moral and political judgment. It is also clear from the psychological literature on disgust that disgust responses, and their political corollaries, can be manipulated in a variety of ways in experimental conditions, including by exposing research subjects to unpleasant odors and by asking research subjects to recall a disgusting experience.³⁸ But such manipulations are not confined to the laboratory. Christian right elites also manipulate the conditions of disgust for activists and followers, deploying "feeling rules" that "instigate the 'emotion work' required to elicit" responses consonant with the aims of the movement.³⁹ In political contexts of the antiabortion and antigay movements, elites and activists use abortion descriptions and imagery and descriptions and imagery associated with the threat of homosexuality to prime believers for disgust. The struggle between proabortion rights and antiabortion activists provides many examples of the use of such images, including graphic images of aborted fetuses, to provoke disgust and outrage among prolife supporters.⁴⁰

Compared to other unpleasant emotions, disgust also is relatively stable and resilient. Indeed, although it can be intensified by priming, and may decline over time—for example, in response to exposure to disgust-inducing stimuli—there is no reliable method to eliminate disgust reactions.⁴¹ Nevertheless, some social conservatives clearly worry that the disgust reactions that undergird political opposition to *the proper objects of disgust* can wane and believe that conservatives have an interest in shoring up the disgust that operates as a "natural" foundation of conservative sexuality politics. This anxiety is evident in texts, speeches, sermons, and other forms of discourse about abortion and same-sex sexuality that originate within the Christian right and emanates from outside the compassionate sector of the movement as well as from within.

Christian conservatives who do not subscribe to compassion campaigns often are anxious to recuperate and sustain the boundary between "repellent people" and "normals." These actors may reject compassion altogether and excoriate both progay opponents and conservative allies who fall for the finer distinction between the repentant and the unrepentant. In his work, antigay psychologist Paul Cameron has long ignored this distinction that is so central to compassion campaigns in favor of a more totalizing characterization of all those who experience same-sex desire. For example, in an essay entitled "Homosexuals Disruptive from the 'Get-Go,'" Cameron argues that young people with same-sex attractions are more rebellious, dangerous to others, and "sleazy" than their heterosexual peers.⁴² Naturally manipulative and psychopathic, adult gays "provoke attacks against themselves and then count these 'attacks' as injustices they ha[ve] suffered." Far from recommending compassionate interventions with the same-sex attracted, Cameron defends "discrimination against those with homosexual inclinations," both for their own good and for the good of society.⁴³

As prominent as Cameron has been in the social and political effort to uphold the stigma and legal jeopardy associated with same-sex sexuality, it's telling that he and his Family Research Institute now have become marginal actors in debates over LGBT issues. As Cameron himself no doubt understands, much of this loss of standing is due to his uncompromising refusal to express his beliefs and policy goals in terms that are more appropriate for mainstream public consumption: compassion for same-sex-attracted people and a firm democratic defense of majoritarianism, choice, and rights when that is suited to defending Christian right understandings of traditional values and religious freedom. In terms of messaging, it is fruitful to compare Cameron and his Family Research Institute, founded in 1982, to the National Organization for Marriage (NOM), founded in 2007.[44]

A Christian right organization with explicitly political rather than therapeutic goals, NOM doesn't engage in compassionate rhetoric and projects aimed at LGBT people. But it does engage in pedagogy with its supporters to instruct them in the proper modes of public discourse that then coexist with abomination rhetoric—of the sort purveyed by Cameron—inside the Christian conservative movement. NOM accomplishes this task by providing "Marriage Talking Points" of the sort that have been vetted by elites across the movement. According to the "Talking Points," the single most effective message is:

> "*Gays and Lesbians have a right to live as they choose, they don't have the right to redefine marriage for all of us.*"
> This allows people to express support for tolerance while opposing gay marriage. Some modify it to 'People have a right to live as they choose, they don't have the right to redefine marriage for all of us.'[45]

Clearly, NOM supporters remain free to understand same-sex-attracted people as sleazy and repellent as long as they don't express those sentiments in public dialogue outside the boundaries of the movement.

However, the Christian right today is not just comprised of groups, projects, institutions, and discourses that engage in explicitly political interventions for which some version of "democratic" rhetoric is necessary and sufficient. Compassionate ministries are likely to provoke a special kind of anxiety among Christian conservatives because, unlike political projects, therapeutic projects bring Christian conservatives into close contact with subjects stigmatized by sins related to the body and sexuality. This unavoidable fraternization accounts for the determination I have heard in the movement to keep compassion from interfering with moral condemnation.

Do compassion crusades such as ex-gay and postabortion ministries risk undermining disgust as a "natural" and unambiguous response to abortion and same-sex sexuality? There is no clear-cut answer to this question in the empirical literature on disgust, but there are suggestive clues. While *disgust* is associated with "revulsion and desires for social distance"—what Gary D. Sherman and Jonathan Haidt refer to as the "value of cutting off relationships"—*compassion* is associated with social engagement and even the moderation of punitive impulses toward its objects.[46] Given the complexities inherent in compassionate ministries, perhaps it makes sense to scrutinize these compassion campaigns both as authorizing antigay and antiabortion politics by making these politics less hateful and, thus, more palatable *and* as sowing the seeds of their own destruction by mitigating and eroding moral condemnation. Even if this latter possibility is accurate, the personal, social, and political effects of Christian compassion will remain with us for the foreseeable future.

In this book, I've made certain appeals to empiricism: there are a variety of Christian right projects in the areas of sexuality and reproductive rights that fruitfully can be understood as connected to each other by a common ideology. When it produces and disseminates this ideology, the movement engages in pedagogy with Christian conservative followers, carefully instructing them in the acts, views, and even the emotional orientations that God requires of them. The common terms of the ideology, and the pedagogy that undergirds it, can be discerned in the movement's diverse literatures, media, and venues. Questions of meaning and effects are different matters, and articulating these requires both faithful representation of the Christian right movement, its ideology and practices, and the use of literatures and practices of interpretation.

In its compassion crusades, the Christian right enforces a continuity between affect, ideology, and action (or activism). In this regime of compassion, the appropriate affect ought to produce the appropriate ideology and action. Leaders reinforce this identity between feeling and action to secure the inevitability of the particular responses, support, participation, and activist innovations that shore up the political agenda of the Christian right movement. To feel—or to understand the need to feel—compassion for women who have killed their own child through abortion and for women or men who violate God's design for the precious gift of sexuality is, for Christian conservative followers, to already know what must be done. In the course of receiving the Word of God on the subjects of abortion and same-sex sexuality, Christian conservatives are interpellated as political subjects who support political interventions that are already defined as loving and compassionate.[47] Certainly, these subjects can dissent, and some do, but dissent is difficult and carries a high cost. Most don't dissent.

In the end, and in spite of their many differences, the arguments of Hannah Arendt and Melanie Klein disrupt inflexible and seemingly inexorable equations between affect and action and call into question the inevitability of links among affective, moral, pedagogical, and political meanings. What the work of Arendt and Klein suggests is that even compassion genuinely felt and lovingly enacted, and not merely simulated for the benefit of reputation or political gain, is no guarantee of virtue and no hedge against harm. This is a sobering lesson, and one from which citizens across the political spectrum can benefit as we traverse our own favored political paths.

Notes

Introduction

1. Alan Cooperman, "Second New Leader Resigns from the Christian Coalition," *Washington Post*, November 29, 2006 A13.

2. As might be expected for a socially and politically diverse group, there is no agreement on nomenclature. In this book I will use "LGBT" or "LGBTQ" to refer to those who identify as lesbian, gay, bisexual, transgender or queer, and "gay" or "lesbian" to be more specific from time to time. Given the preoccupation of the Christian right with same-sex sexuality and gay/lesbian identity, it remains accurate to refer to that movement as "antigay."

3. As Sarah Posner points out, pastors in the "Word of Faith" movement who propound a "prosperity gospel" also adhere to conservative positions on same-sex sexuality and abortion. See Sarah Posner, *God's Profits: Faith, Fraud, and the Republican Crusade for Values Voters* (Sausalito, CA: Polipoint, 2007).

4. For an account of softening rhetoric that focuses on the Christian right, see Ann Burlein, *Lift High the Cross: Where White Supremacy and the Christian Right Converge* (Durham: Duke University Press, 2002).

5. See Melani McAlister, "Evangelical Internationalism" (*Under Fire*, no date) http://underfire.eyebeam.org/?q=node/509 (accessed June 17, 2011); Bruce Pilbeam, "The Tragedy of Compassionate Conservatism," *Journal of American Studies* 44, no. 2 (2010): 251–68; For Berlet, see "Mobilizing Resentment," a talk delivered for and recorded by *Alternative Radio* on June 10, 2003, and available for download at http://www.alternativeradio.org/products/berc003.

6. George Lakoff, *Moral Politics: What Conservatives Know that Liberals Don't* (Chicago: University of Chicago Press, 1996). Lakoff analyzes "two models of Christianity" in chapter 14. A 2002 edition of the book bears the subtitle, *What Liberals and Conservatives Think*.

7. David C. Barker and James D. Tinnick III, "Competing Visions of Parental Roles and Ideological Constraint," *American Political Science Review* 100, no. 3 (2006): 249–63.

8. Lakoff analyzes "two models of Christianity" in chapter 14.

9. See, e.g., Dana Rose Carney, John Jost, Samuel Gosling, and Jeff Potter, "The Secret Lives of Liberals and Conservatives: Personality Profiles, Interaction Styles, and the Things They Leave Behind," *Political Psychology* 29, no. 6 (2008): 807–40. See also John Jost, "The End of the End of Ideology," *American Psychologist* 61, no. 7 (2006): 651–70.

10. See Jacob B. Hirsch, Colin G. DeYoung, Xiaowen Xu, and Jordan B. Peterson, "Compassionate Liberals and Polite Conservatives: Associations of Agreeableness with Political Ideology and Moral Values," *Personality and Social Psychology Bulletins* 36, no. 5 (2010): 655–64.

11. See Cynthia Burack and Jyl J. Josephson. "Origin Stories: Same-Sex Sexuality and Christian Right Politics," *Culture and Religion* 6, no. 3 (2005): 369–92.

12. For descriptions of these organizations and differences, see John C. Green, "Antigay: Varieties of Opposition to Gay Rights," in *The Politics of Gay Rights*, ed. Craig A. Rimmerman, Kenneth D. Wald, and Clyde Wilcox, 129–30 (Chicago: University of Chicago Press, 2000).

13. Aristotle, *The Nicomachean Ethics*; Jean Jacques Rousseau, *Discourse on the Origin of Inequality*, translated by Donald A. Cress (Indianapolis: Hackett, 1992); Susan Sontag, *Regarding the Pain of Others* (New York: Farrar, Straus, and Giroux, 2002).

14. I draw on Martha C. Nussbaum's reading of compassion in Aristotle's *Rhetoric*; see Nussbaum, *Upheavals of Thought: The Intelligence of Emotions* (Cambridge: Cambridge University Press, 2001), 306–07.

15. Lauren Berlant, "Introduction: Compassion (and Withholding)" in *Compassion: The Culture and Politics of an Emotion* (New York: Routledge, 2004), 4, 7.

16. Ibid., 4.

17. Marvin Olasky, *The Tragedy of American Compassion* (Washington, DC: Regnery, 1992).

18. See Charles Murray, *Losing Ground: American Social Policy 1950–1980* (New York: Basic Books, 1986); Richard J. Herrnstein and Charles Murray, *The Bell Curve: Intelligence and Class Structure in American Life* (New York: Free Press, 1994).

19. George W. Bush, "Fact Sheet: Compassionate Conservatism," (*The White House*, April 30, 2002) http://www.whitehouse.gov/news/releases/2002/04/20020430.html (accessed September 18, 2006).

20. Pilbeam, "The Tragedy of Compassionate Conservatism," 262–63.

21. For several quotes from President Bush in support of Crisis Pregnancy Centers and programs see Henry Waxman, "False and Misleading Health Information Provided by Federally Funded Pregnancy Resource Centers" (*United States House of Representatives Committee on Government Reform, Special Investigations Division*, July, 2006) http://www.prochoice.org/about_abortion/facts/cpc.html (accessed December 15, 2011).

22. Pilbeam, "The Tragedy of Compassionate Conservatism," 265–68.

23. Star Parker, CURE homepage, (*Center for Urban Renewal and Education*, no date) http://www.urbancure.org/ (accessed August 11, 2011).

24. For analyses of these conservative appropriations see, respectively, Angela D. Dillard, *Guess Who's Coming to Dinner Now? Multicultural Conservatism in America* (New York: New York University Press, 2001); Anna Marie Smith, *New Right Discourse on Race and Sexuality: Britain, 1968–1990* (Cambridge University Press, 1994); Doris E. Buss and Didi Herman, *Globalizing Family Values: The Christian Right in International Politics* (Minneapolis: Minnesota University Press, 2003).

25. Buss and Herman, *Globalizing Family Values*, 114–15.

26. Daniel Patrick Moynihan, *Miles to Go: A Personal History of Social Policy* (Cambridge, MA: Harvard University Press, 1996).

27. Linda Kintz, *Between Jesus and the Market: The Emotions That Matter in Right-Wing America* (Duke University Press, 1997), 25.

28. It is not common, but on occasion Christian right leaders talk openly about this tension in the Republican Party to activists. One example was a talk by Gary Bauer at the Family Research Council Action Values Voter Summit, held in Washington, DC in 2006. Author's notes, September 22, 2006.

29. ConservativeHome's Dictionary, "Condom (or Russian Roulette) Compassion" (*ConservativeHome*, August 9, 2005) http://conservativehome.blogs.com/dictionary/2005/08/condom_or_russi.html (accessed November 30, 2007).

30. Ibid., "Compassionate Conservatism" (*ConservativeHome*, August 9, 2005) http://conservativehome.blogs.com/dictionary/2005/08/compassionate_c.html (accessed November 30, 2007).

31. Michael Gerson, "Rick Santorum and the Return of Compassionate Conservatism" (*Washington Post*, January 5, 2012) http://www.washingtonpost.com/opinions/rick-santorum-and-the-return-of-compassionate-conservatism/2012/01/04/gIQATYRfdP_story.html (accessed January 5, 2012).

32. Francis Schaeffer, *Plan for Action: An Action Alternative Handbook for "Whatever Happened to the Human Race?"* (New York: Flemming H. Revell, 1980).

33. Patricia Baird-Windle and Eleanor J. Bader, *Targets of Hatred: Anti-Abortion Terrorism* (New York: Palgrave, 2001).

34. On sexual shaming, see Jyl Josephson, "The Politics of Sexual Shaming: Religion and Abstinence-Only Sex Education in TANF-Linked Policymaking" (paper presented at the annual meeting of the American Political Science Association, September 1–4, 2005, Washington, DC).

35. Henry A. Waxman, "False and Misleading Health Information Provided by Federally Funded Pregnancy Resource Centers" (*United States House of Representatives Committee on Government Reform*, July 2006) http://www.chsourcebook.com/articles/waxman2.pdf (accessed March 2, 2010).

36. Cynthia Burack, *Sin, Sex, and Democracy: Antigay Rhetoric and the Christian Right* (Albany: State University of New York Press, 2008).

37. Carol J. C. Maxwell, *Pro-Life Activists in America: Meaning, Motivation, and Direct Action* (Cambridge: Cambridge University Press, 2002), 132.

38. Ibid., 1.

39. Ann Coulter, "Ann Coulter calls John Edwards a faggot" (*YouTube*, March 2, 2007) http://www.youtube.com/watch?v=GB3X4iz8jTU (accessed February 21, 2009).

40. Exodus International, "Worldwide Network of Former Homosexuals Denounces Coulter Comments" (*Exodus International*, 2007) http://exodus.to/content/view/688/37/ (accessed March 26, 2007).

41. Joe Dallas, "How Should We Respond? An Exhortation to the Church on Loving the Homosexual," *Love Won Out* Series (Colorado Springs: Focus on the Family, 2008), 6.

42. The phrase is found in Surina Khan, "Calculated Compassion: How the Ex-Gay Movement Serves the Right's Attack on Democracy" (*Public Eye*, 1998), http://www.publiceye.org/equality/x-gay/X-Gay.htm (accessed November 6, 2001). The paper indicts the strategic hypocrisy of the Christian right *movement* rather than its individual members, but critics use the notion of a compassionate mask to describe the movement and its individual members.

43. Ervin Staub, *The Psychology of Good and Evil: Why Children, Adults, and Groups Help and Harm Others* (Cambridge: Cambridge University Press, 2003).

44. Robert Wuthnow, *Acts of Compassion: Caring for Others and Helping Ourselves* (Princeton, NJ: Princeton University Press, 1991), 45.

45. Tim Montgomerie, "Whatever Happened to Compassionate Conservatism?" (*Centre for Social Justice*, November 1, 2004) http://www.centreforsocialjustice.org.uk/client/downloads/pubCompCon.pdf (accessed July 29, 2010).

46. Julie Ingersoll, *Evangelical Christian Women: War Stories in the Gender Battles* (New York: New York University Press, 2003), 41–42. The Evangelical and Ecumenical Women's Caucus was known as the Evangelical Women's Caucus when it adopted the resolution in 1986.

47. The phrase is from Kintz, *Between Jesus and the Market*.

48. Rob Stein, "The Politics of Yuck," (*Washington Post*, June 8, 2009) http://www.washingtonpost.com/wp-dyn/content/article/2009/06/07/AR2009060702166_pf.html (accessed June 8, 2009).

49. Andrew Holleran, *Grief* (New York: Hyperion, 2006), 76. Emphasis in the original.

50. For additional theoretical reflections on the multiple meanings of disgust as aversion and attraction, see William Ian Miller, *The Anatomy of Disgust* (Cambridge, MA: Harvard University Press, 1998); Jonathan Dollimore, "Sexual Disgust," in *Homosexuality and Psychoanalysis*, ed. Tim Dean and Christopher Lane (Chicago: University of Chicago Press, 2001), 367–86.

51. Susan B. Miller, *Disgust: The Gatekeeper Emotion* (Hilldale, NJ: Analytic Press, 2004), 4, 6, 17.

52. Miller discusses disgust as a group phenomenon in Chapter 9, "Group Identities and Hostility Across Borders: Affairs of Ethnicities, Classes, and

Sects." See Miller, *Disgust*, 153–69; Simone Schnall, Jonathan Haidt, Gerald L. Clore, and Alexander H. Jordan, "Disgust as Embodied Moral Judgment," (*NIH National Institutes of Health*, 2008) http://www.ncbi.nlm.nih.gov/pmc/articles/PMC2562923/pdf/nihms-40182.pdf (accessed January 6, 2012).

53. Miller, *Disgust*, 4, 12, 13.

54. Lauren Berlant and Michael Warner, "Sex in Public," *Critical Inquiry* 24 (1998): 548.

55. See Gregory M. Herek, "The Context of Anti-Gay Violence: Notes on Cultural and Psychological Heterosexism," *Journal of Interpersonal Violence* 5, no. 3 (1990): 316–33.

56. George Weinberg, *Society and the Healthy Homosexual: How to Get the Most out of Being Gay* (New York: St. Martin's, 1972).

57. See Jennifer Terry, "Anxious Slippages between 'Us' and 'Them': A Brief History of the Scientific Search for Homosexual Bodies," in *Deviant Bodies: Critical Perspectives on Difference in Science and Popular Culture*, ed. Jennifer Terry and Jacqueline Urla (Bloomington: Indiana University Press, 1995).

58. Martha Nussbaum, *Hiding from Humanity: Disgust, Shame, and the Law* (Princeton, NJ: Princeton University Press, 2004), 13.

59. Ange-Marie Hancock, *The Politics of Disgust: The Public Identity of the Welfare Queen* (New York: New York University Press, 2004).

60. University of Arkansas, "Disgust, not Fear, Drives Homophobia, Say UA Psychologists" (*News Releases*, June 8, 2002) http://advancement.uark.edu/news/2002/ JUN02/Homophobia.html (accessed September 10, 2002).

61. Yoel Inbar, David A. Pizarro, Joshua Knobe, and Paul Bloom, "Disgust Sensitivity Predicts Intuitive Disapproval of Gays," *Emotion* 9, no. 3 (2009): 435.

62. Ibid., "Conservatives Are More Easily Disgusted than Liberals," *Cognition and Emotion* 23, no. 4 (2008): 720. Although no correlation was detected between disgust sensitivity and many other conservative policy positions, the researchers did find that disgust-sensitive individuals are more likely than the nonsensitive to support tax cuts.

63. Timothy J. Dailey, "The Slippery Slope of Same-Sex Marriage," *Family Research Council* (Washington, DC: Family Research Council, 2004). Emphasis in the original.

64. Brian Keith Williams, *Ministering Graciously to the Gay and Lesbian Community: Pouring in the Oil and the Wine* (Shippensburg, PA: Destiny Image, 2005).

65. See Andrea Smith, "Beyond Pro-Choice Versus Pro-Life: Women of Color and Reproductive Justice," *NWSA Journal* 17, no. 1 (2005): 119–40.

Chapter 1

1. See Kenji Yoshino, *Covering: The Hidden Assault on Our Civil Rights* (New York: Random House, 2006).

2. In 1973 psychologist Robert L. Spitzer was instrumental in the effort to have same-sex sexual orientation removed from the DSM. However, in 2003 he published an article in which he concluded that some motivated individuals could change their sexual orientation. For the text of that article ("Can Some Gay Men and Lesbians Change Their Sexual Orientation? 200 Participants Reporting a Change from Homosexual to Heterosexual Orientation") and a variety of responses to it, see Jack Drescher and Kenneth J. Zucker, eds. *Ex-Gay Research: Analyzing the Spitzer Study and Its Relation to Science, Religion, Politics, and Culture* (New York: Harrington Park, 2006). In 2012 Spitzer retracted the conclusions in his 2003 article in public statements.

3. For progay readings of this history see Hannah Lerman, *Pigeonholing Women's Misery: A History and Critical Analysis of the Psychodiagnosis of Women in the Twentieth Century* (New York: Basic Books, 1996), and Wayne Besen, *Anything but Straight: Unmasking the Scandals and Lies Behind the Ex-Gay Myth* (New York: Harrington Park, 2003); for an antigay reading of the history see Jeffrey B. Satinover, "The 'Trojan Couch': How the Mental Health Associations Misrepresent Science" (NARTH, no date). http://www.narth.com/docs/TheTrojanCouchSatinover.pdf (accessed April 3, 2008).

4. See Report of the American Psychological Association Task Force on Appropriate Therapeutic Responses to Sexual Orientation (*American Psychological Association*, August 5, 2009) http://www.apa.org/pi/lgbc/publications/therapeutic-response.pdf (accessed August 7, 2009).

5. Jack Drescher, "I'm Your Handyman: A History of Reparative Therapies," in *Sexual Conversion Therapy: Ethical, Clinical and Research Perspectives*, ed. Ariel Shidlo, Michael Schroeder, and Jack Drescher (New York: Haworth Medical, 2001). See also Thomas Dominici and Ronnie Lesser, editors, *Disorienting Sexuality: Psychoanalytic Reappraisals of Sexual Identities* (New York and London: Routledge, 1995).

6. The subject of natural gender differentiation and complementarity pervades virtually all ex-gay literature, but see Elizabeth R. Moberly, *Psychogenesis: The Early Development of Gender Identity* (London: Routledge and Kegan Paul, 1983); Joseph Nicolosi and Linda Ames Nicolosi, *A Parent's Guide to Preventing Homosexuality* (Downer's Grove, IL: InterVarsity Press, 2002); and Anne Paulk, *Restoring Sexual Identity: Hope for Women Who Struggle with Same-Sex Attraction* (Eugene, OR: Harvest House, 2003).

7. At the 2008 Exodus International Freedom Conference, the "Mistress of Ceremony," Christine Sneeringer, engaged in this kind of banter with the audience. Although campy humor is usually proscribed in ex-gay contexts, Sneeringer's feminine attire was played for laughs for the same-sex attracted/struggling men in order to emphasize her evolution from androgynous lesbian to ex-lesbian femme. Given the ubiquity of drag performance in the queer community this call and response seemed to me more a function of gay men's responses to feminine drag than appropriate heterosexual male lust for a feminine object.

8. National Association for Research and Therapy of Homosexuality, "Mission Statement" (*NARTH*, March 10, 2008) http://www.narth.com/menus/mission.html (accessed April 3, 2009).

9. Gerard J. M. van den Aardweg, "'Science' Games Lesbian Psychologists Play" (*NARTH*, September 11, 2006) http://www.narth.com/docs/sciencegames.html (accessed September 12, 2006).

10. Michael Barkun, *A Culture of Conspiracy: Apocalyptic Vision in Contemporary America* (Berkeley: University of California Press, 2003), 26–27.

11. See, for example, Tim LaHaye, *The Unhappy Gays: What Everyone Should Know about Homosexuality* (Wheaton, IL: Tyndale House, 1978), and Michael Saia, *Counseling the Homosexual: A Compassionate and Biblical Guide for Pastors and Counselors as well as Non-Professionals and Families* (Minneapolis: Bethany House, 1988).

12. See Marlin Maddoux and Christopher Corbett, *Answers to the Gay Deception* (Dallas: International Christian Media, 1994) and Jeffrey Satinover, M.D., *Homosexuality and the Politics of Truth* (Grand Rapids: Baker Book House, 1996).

13. Janelle Hallman, MA, http://janellehallman.com/biography.php (accessed September 12, 2006). Hallman is an author and a frequent contributor to the "NARTH Bulletin."

14. David Pruden, (*NARTH*, July 25, 2011) "Presidential Politics Places NARTH Issues on Front Page!" http://narth.com/2011/07/presidential-politics-places-narth-issues-on-front-page/ (accessed August 9, 2011).

15. Jean Hardisty, *Mobilizing Resentment: Conservative Resurgence from the John Birch Society to the Promise Keepers* (Boston: Beacon, 1999), 116.

16. Didi Herman, *The Antigay Agenda: Orthodox Vision and the Christian Right* (Chicago: University of Chicago Press), 50.

17. Love in Action moved to Memphis, Tennessee, in the 1990s, and the California ministry that had been Love in Action was rechristened New Hope.

18. For this history, see Tanya Erzen, *Straight to Jesus: Sexual and Christian Conversions in the Ex-Gay Movement* (Berkeley: University of California Press, 2006), 22–37.

19. See, for example, Michael Saia, *Counseling the Homosexual: A Compassionate and Biblical Guide for Pastors and Counselors as well as Non-Professionals and Families* (Minneapolis: Bethany House, 1988).

20. Paulk, *Restoring Sexual Identity*.

21. Christian right literature on homosexuality often employs the shorthand abbreviations "SSA women" and "SSA men."

22. At one time, John J. Smid's article, "Exploring the Homosexual Myth," was available online. Smid discusses the idea of the "homosexual myth" in this interview: Patricia Pair and John J. Smid, "Love in Action's Rev. John J. Smid Talks Openly (Ex-Gay Watch, July 12, 2005). http://www.exgaywatch.com/wp/2005/07/love-in-actions/ (accessed May 6, 2013).

23. Tanya Erzen, *Straight to Jesus*, 218–21.

24. Stephanie Simon, "Approaching Agreement in Debate over Homosexuality" (*Los Angeles Times*, June 18, 2007) http://articles.latimes.com/2007/jun/18/nation/na-exgay18 (accessed June 20, 2007).

25. John Paulk has been a controversial figure in the movement. On Paulk's indiscretion in a Washington DC gay bar in 2000 see Wayne R. Besen, *Anything but Straight: Unmasking the Scandals and Lies behind the Ex-Gay Myth* (Binghamton, NY: Harrington Park, 2003). As of 2013, Paulk has come out as a gay man.

26. Cynthia Burack and Jyl J. Josephson, "A Report from 'Love Won Out: Addressing, Understanding, and Preventing Homosexuality'" (*National Gay and Lesbian Task Force Policy Institute*, 2005). http://www.thetaskforce.org/downloads/reports/reports/LoveWonOut.pdf (accessed May 5, 2005).

27. Anita Worthen and Bob Davies, *Someone I Love Is Gay: How Family and Friends Can Respond* (Downers Grove, IL: InterVarsity, 1996).

28. Erzen, *Straight to Jesus*, 157.

29. Burack, *Sin, Sex, and Democracy*, 85–86. After many years as an ex-gay expert and speaker at Focus on the Family, Fryrear left in 2010 to take a position as the women's shepherd at Heights Church in Prescott, Arizona.

30. Exodus International, http://www.exodus-international.org/ (accessed March 24, 2009).

31. The term "problems in living" was coined by the radical psychiatrist Thomas Szasz as an alternative to the category and diagnosis of "mental illness." See Thomas Szasz, *The Myth of Mental Illness: Foundations of a Theory of Personal Conduct* (New York: Harper, 1984/1960).

32. Donald Woods Winnicott, *The Maturational Processes and the Facilitating Environment: Studies in the Theory of Emotional Development* (London: Karmac Books, 1965). In her recent memoir, Alison Bechdel makes extensive use of the latter formulation and other key Winnicottian terms to explore her relationship with her mother. See Alison Bechdel, *Are You My Mother?* (Boston: Houghton Mifflin Harcourt, 2012).

33. For psychological literature on shame and guilt see Helen B. Lewis, *Shame and Guilt in Neurosis* (New York: International Universities Press, 1971). Theses specifically antigay renderings of true/false selves and shame versus guilt were discussed by speakers at the 2008 Exodus International Conference, July 15–20, 2008 (Author's notes).

34. Robert L., "Spiritual Warfare: Defeating Guilt and Shame" (*Great Bible Study*, 2008) http://www.greatbiblestudy.com/sws_guilt_shame.php (accessed September 6, 2012). Emphasis in the original.

35. Randy Alcom, "Guilt, God, and Self-Esteem" (*Eternal Perspective Ministries*, January 28, 2010) http://www.epm.org/resources/2010/Jan/28/guilt-god-and-self-esteem/ (accessed September 6, 2012).

36. Terry Norris, "The Direction of Guilt" (*LifeCHANGE: A Center for Christian Counseling and Spiritual Development*, September 17, 2009) http://

lifechangesavannah.com/counselors-corner/the-direction-of-guilt/ (accessed September 6, 2012).

37. Timothy S. Lane, "How Do I Deal with My Guilt?" (FamilyLife Christian Counseling and Educational Foundation, 2012) http://www.familylife.com/articles/topics/life-issues/challenges/mental-and-emotional-issues/how-do-i-deal-with-my-guilt (accessed September 6, 2012). The subtitle of the article is "You can devise all kinds of ways to try to get rid of your guilty feelings. But your guilt is not just a feeling or a personal problem."

38. Patricia Jones M.A., "What Is Guilt?" (*Dove Christian Counseling Center*, 2012) http://www.dovechristiancounseling.com/GuiltIssues.html (accessed September 6, 2012).

39. Kent Philpott, *The Third Sex? Six Homosexuals Tell Their Stories* (London: Good Reading, 1975).

40. Besen, *Anything but Straight*, 55.

41. "Our Stories" (PFOX, 2012) http://pfox.org/stories.html (accessed January 6, 2012); "Ex-Gay Testimonies (*YouTube*, no date) http://www.youtube.com/playlist?list=PL951E417EBE9BD0E4 (accessed January 6, 2012).

42. Michele Bachmann, "References," (*Janet Boynes Ministries*, 2010) http://www.janetboynesministries.com/about/2.asp (accessed December 13, 2011).

43. My partner and I were married in Washington, DC in March 2010 when the effort to prevent same-sex marriage failed.

44. Janet Boynes, *Called Out: A Former Lesbian's Discovery of Freedom* (Lake Mary, FL: Creation House, 2008), 16.

45. Ibid., 82, 86.

46. Ibid., 87–88. Emphasis added.

47. Ibid., 91, 90.

48. Ibid., 164–65. Emphasis in the original.

49. Angela D. Dillard, *Guess Who's Coming to Dinner Now? Multicultural Conservatism in America* (New York: New York University Press, 2001), 48–64.

50. Boynes, *Called Out*, 167.

51. Dillard, *Guess Who's Coming to Dinner* Now?, 137–70. Dillard notes that the "tactic of effecting a greater unification, a multiracial *Religious* Right, at the expense of gay [sic] and lesbians has been successful in the past and shows no signs of abating" (176).

52. Nancy Heche, *The Truth Comes Out: The Story of My Heart's Transformation* (Ventura, California: Regal Books, 2006), 26.

53. Ibid., 165.

54. Joe Dallas and Nancy Heche, *The Complete Christian Guide to Understanding Homosexuality: A Biblical and Compassionate Response to Same-Sex Attraction* (Eugene, Oregon: Harvest House, 2010). Contributors to the volume are regular speakers at exgay events.

55. Erzen, *Straight to Jesus*, 101, 100.

56. Love Won Out is an ex-gay ministry founded by Focus on the Family; launched in 1998, the brand was sold to Exodus International in 2009.

57. Michel Foucault, *Discipline and Punish: The Birth of the Prison* (New York: Vintage Books, 1979), 203.

58. Hedgebuilders, "Security" (Hedgebuilders.com, no date) http://www.hedge.org/ (accessed June 9, 2009).

59. CovenantEyes, "Fight Internet Temptation" (*CovenantEyes*, 2009) http://www.covenanteyes.com/ (accessed June, 10, 2009).

60. At the 2012 Love Won Out conference sponsored by Exodus, Alan Chambers emphasized his ongoing struggle against same-sex desire by sharing with the audience that he continues to use content-blocking software on his personal computer because he is a "man of integrity" who recognizes the potential for temptation. Cynthia Burack, field notes, Love Won Out conference, Mechanicsburg, Pennsylvania, September 22, 2012.

61. For identification of same-sex sexual desire with addiction see Paulk, *Restoring Sexual Identity*. For a critique that calls attention to the high percentages of people with addiction problems identified as strugglers in ex-gay movement literature, see Besen, *Anything but Straight*, 40–43. For an examination of the close relationship between ex-gay ministries and the twelve-step movement see Erzen, *Straight to Jesus*, 162–65.

62. Barbara Ehrenreich, *Bright-Sided: How the Relentless Promotion of Positive Thinking Has Undermined America* (New York: Henry Holt, 2009), 90.

63. See, e.g., Mark A. Yarhouse, Erica S. N. Tan, and Lisa M. Pawlowski, "Sexual Identity Development and Synthesis among LGB-Identified and LGB Dis-Identified Persons," *Journal of Theology and Psychology* 33, no. 1 (2005): 3–6. For an extensive conversation regarding dilemmas in studying heterosexual conversion see Jack Drescher and Kenneth J. Zucker, eds., *Ex-Gay Research: Analyzing the Spitzer Study and Its Relation to Science, Religion, Politics, and Culture* (Binghamton, NY: Haworth 2006).

64. Exodus International, "How Should the Church Respond?" (*Exodus International*, 2005) http://exodus.to/content/view/124/34/ (accessed June 17, 2009). For a discussion of differences between responses of church networks, see Jyl J. Josephson and Cynthia Burack, "Inside, Out, and In-Between: Sexual Minorities, the Christian Right, and the Evangelical Lutheran Church in America," in *Religion, Politics, and American Identity: New Directions, New Controversies*, ed. David S. Gutterman and Andrew R. Murphy (Lanham, MD: Lexington Books, 2006).

65. Exodus International produces a brochure for pastors and congregations entitled, "Exodus Church Network. Exodus International: Grace and Truth for a World Impacted by Homosexuality" (*Exodus International*, 2007).

66. Jim Sidanius and Felicia Pratto, *Social Dominance: An Intergroup Theory of Social Hierarchy and Oppression* (Cambridge: Cambridge University Press, 2001), 103, 106.

67. Ibid., 104–05.

68. Lambert Dolphin, "Masturbation and the Bible" (*Lambert Dolphin's Library*, 2007) http://www.ldolphin.org/Mast.shtml (accessed June 16, 2009). In addition to providing the biblical case against masturbation, Exodus organizers try to help strugglers remain pure by, for example, conducting a roommate matching service at the conference. Presumably organizers hope that randomly assigning strangers as roommates will diminish the risk of sexual behavior at meetings.

69. Angelia R. Wilson, field notes, 2008 Exodus International Freedom Conference, Asheville, North Carolina, July 17, 2008.

70. See Worthy Creations on the web at http://www.worthycreations.org/. This statement explains the organization's mission: "Founded in 1986, Worthy Creations is an interdenominational Christian ministry dedicated to helping men and women find freedom from homosexuality and sexual brokenness. We operate locally in South Florida and are a part of the worldwide network of Exodus International."

71. The PEW Forum on Religion and Public Life, "Religious Beliefs Underpin Opposition to Homosexuality" (PEW Research Center, November 18, 2003) http://www.pewforum.org/uploadedfiles/Topics/Issues/Gay_Marriage_and_Homosexuality/religion-homosexuality.pdf (accessed December 1, 2003).

72. I say "relative" consistency because the Catholic ministry to people with same-sex attraction emphasizes abstinence rather than change to heterosexuality. See "Courage: A Roman Catholic Apostolate" (Courage Apostolate, 2012) http://couragerc.net/ (accessed December 20, 2012).

73. Warren Throckmorton, "Transcripts of Catholic University Presentations" (*Warren Throckmorton*, May 2, 2007) http://wthrockmorton.com/2007/05/02/transcripts-of-catholic-university-presentations/ (accessed December 21, 2012).

74. For an example of this research, see Ivanka Savic and Per Lindström, "PET and MRI Show Differences and Cerebral Asymmetry and Functional Connectivity between Homo- and Heterosexual Subjects (*Proceedings of the National Academy of Sciences*, February 27, 2008) http://www.pnas.org/content/early/2008/06/13/0801566105.full.pdf+html (accessed December 12, 2010).

75. Cynthia Burack, field notes, Exodus International Freedom Conference, Asheville, North Carolina, July 19, 2008.

76. William R. Rice, Urban Friberg, and Sergey Gavrilets, "Homosexuality as a Consequence of Epigenetically Canalized Sexual Development" *The Quarterly Review of Biology* 87, no. 4 (2012): 343–68. I thank Andrea Lawson for bringing this new research to my attention.

77. Erik Eckholm, "Rift Forms in Movement as Belief in Gay 'Cure' is Announced" (New York Times, July 6, 2012) http://www.nytimes.com/2012/07/07/us/a-leaders-renunciation-of-ex-gay-tenets-causes-a-schism.html?pagewanted=all&_r=0 (accessed August 12, 2012).

78. Jeff Schapiro, "Exodus International Rejects Reparative Therapy for Gays (*The Christian Post*, June 29, 2012) http://www.christianpost.com/news/exodus-

international-rejects-reparative-therapy-for-gays-77413/ (accessed December 21, 2012).

79. The Church of Jesus Christ of Latter Day Saints, "Love One Another: A Discussion on Same-Sex Attraction" (2012) http://www.mormonsandgays.org/ (accessed December 25, 2012).

80. Robert A. J. Gagnon, "Time for a Change of Leadership at Exodus?" (*Robert Gagnon*, June 30, 2012) http://www.robgagnon.net/articles/homosexAlan-ChambersAtlanticInterview.pdf (accessed December 21, 2012).

81. Cynthia Burack, field notes, *Love Won Out*, Mechanicsburg, Pennsylvania, September 22, 2012.

82. Ibid.

83. Julie Rodgers, "Making Room: A Shift toward Compassion" (*Exodus International*, November 15, 2012) http://exodusinternational.org/2012/11/making-room-a-shift-toward-compassion/ (accessed December 3, 2012). Emphasis in the original.

84. Warren Throckmorton, "A Look inside the Restored Hope Network" (*Warren Throckmorton*, August 3, 2012) http://wthrockmorton.com/2012/08/03/a-look-inside-the-restored-hope-network/ (September 20, 2012).

85. For the more common delineation of this choice between paradigms, see The Dan Gilgoff, "Amid Bachmann Controversy, Many Christians Cool to Conversation Therapy for Gays" (*CNN Belief Blog*, July 18, 2011) http://religion.blogs.cnn.com/2011/07/18/amid-bachmann-controversy-many-christians-cool-to-conversion-therapy-for-gays/ (accessed December 22, 2012).

Chapter 2

1. See, e.g., Christopher Mooney, ed., *The Public Clash of Private Values: The Politics of Morality Policy* (Chatham, NJ: Chatham House, 2001).

2. Pew Research Forum for the People and the Press, "A Slight but Steady Majority Favors Keeping Abortion Legal: But Most Also Favor Restrictions" (Pew, September 16, 2006) http://pewforum.org/docs/?DocID=350 (Accessed March 6, 2009). A later poll shows declining support for abortion throughout 2008, especially among men: Pew Research Forum for the People and the Press, "Public Takes Conservative Turn on Gun Control, Abortion" (Pew, April 30, 2009) http://pewresearch.org/pubs/1212/abortion-gun-control-opinion-gender-gap (accessed May 4, 2009).

3. Pew Research Forum for the People and the Press, "Support for Abortion Slips" (Pew, October 1, 2009) http://pewresearch.org/pubs/1361/support-for-abortion-slips (accessed October 1, 2009).

4. Randall Balmer, *Thy Kingdom Come. How the Religious Right Distorts the Faith and Threatens America: An Evangelical's Lament* (New York: Basic Books, 2006) 11–17.

5. Ibid., 15.

6. State and local governments quickly began to promulgate laws restricting abortions after *Roe*, and these laws and ordinances led to many court cases in the 1970s. See Barbara Hinkson Craig and David M. O'Brien, *Abortion and American Politics* (Chatham, NJ: Chatham House, 1993).

7. On women's demand for abortion and the consequences of criminalization see Laura R. Woliver, *The Political Geographies of Pregnancy* (Urbana: University of Illinois Press, 2002), 84–92.

8. Operation Rescue, "About Us" (2008) http://www.operationrescue.org/archives/history-of-operation-rescue/ (March 19, 2009). In 1999, under the leadership of Flip Benham, Operation Rescue expanded its mandate and became Operation Save America. Today two separate organizations operate, one as Operation Rescue and the other as Operation Rescue/Operation Save America.

9. Mark Allen Steiner, *The Rhetoric of Operation Rescue: Projecting the Pro-Life Message* (New York: TandT Clark, 2006), 75, 84–88.

10. Ibid., 99, 96.

11. Angelia R. Wilson, *Below the Belt: Sexuality, Religion, and the American South* (London: Cassell, 2000), 104–05.

12. Ibid., 108, 106.

13. Personal communication with Angelia R. Wilson, September 1, 2007. Christian conservative leader Al Mohler rejects abortion, but he received a great deal of attention with his suggestion that pregnant Christian women should be willing to consider medical treatment to avoid bearing a homosexual child. See, for example, Albert Mohler, "Is Your Baby Gay? What If You Could Know? What If You Could Do Something About It?" (*AlbertMohler.com*, March 2, 2007) http://www.albertmohler.com/blog_read.php?id=891 (accessed October 3, 2009).

14. Many episodes of violent protest are documented in Patricia Baird-Windle and Eleanor J. Bader, *Targets of Hatred: Anti-Abortion Terrorism* (New York: Palgrave, 2001).

15. Carol Mason, *Killing for Life: The Apocalyptic Narrative of Pro-Life Politics* (Ithaca, NY: Cornell University Press, 2002).

16. See Alesha E. Doan, *Opposition and Intimidation: The Abortion Wars and Strategies of Political Harassment* (Ann Arbor: University of Michigan Press, 2007), especially chapter 5: "Does Harassment Pay Off? Assessing the Success of Anti-Abortion Tactics."

17. Mason, *Killing for Life*, 9–10. Mason argues that the contemporary apocalyptic construction of abortion is a product of the displacement of a military imaginary from the Vietnam War to domestic US culture. On the continuing issue of abortion foes who consider abortion to constitute a murder but who resist applying criminal charges to women to seek abortion, see William Saletan, "Punitive Dissonance: Abortion, the Death Penalty, and Selective Prosecution" (*Slate*, September 20, 2010) http://www.slate.com/id/2267933/ (accessed September 25, 2011).

18. Howard J. Osofsky and Joy D. Osofsky, eds., *The Abortion Experience: Psychological and Medical Impact* (New York: Harper and Row, 1973). Another

resource from the same period is Roberta Kalmar, ed., *Abortion: The Emotional Implications* (Dubuque, IA: Kendall/Hunt, 1977).

19. Koop's letter to President Reagan can be found in many sources. See "The Koop 'Non-Report' " (Priests for Life, no date) http://www.priestsforlife.org/postabortion/89-01-09koop.htm (accessed March 6, 2009).

20. Peter L. Allen, *The Wages of Sin: Sex and Disease, Past and Present* (Chicago: University of Chicago Press, 2000), 129–33.

21. Warren E. Leary, "Koop Challenged on Abortion Data" (January 15, 1989) http://query.nytimes.com/gst/fullpage.html?res=950DE1DB153CF936A25752C0A96F948260&sec=health&spon=&pagewanted=all (accessed March 19, 2009).

22. Ibid., "Koop Says Abortion Report Couldn't Survive Challenge" (New York Times, March 17, 1989). http://query.nytimes.com/gst/fullpage.html?sec=health&res=950DEEDF1F3CF934A25750C0A96F948260 (accessed March 17, 2009).

23. David C. Reardon, *Aborted Women: Silent No More* (Springfield, IL, 1987), back cover text.

24. On WEBA, see Sara Diamond, *Spirtual Warfare: The Politics of the Christian Right* (Cambridge, MA: South End, 1989), 97–98.

25. Reardon, *Aborted Women*, 131–32.

26. Ibid., 314. As recent PEW survey data show, women and men are virtually equally likely to support a right to abortion, but women are more likely than men to believe that abortion should be legal in all circumstances. See Pew Research Forum for the People and the Press, "A Slight but Steady Majority Favors Keeping Abortion Legal."

27. The quote is from David C. Reardon, *The Jericho Plan: Breaking Down Walls Which Prevent Post-Abortion Healing* (Springfield, IL, 1996), chapter 1: Focusing on Women. The chapter is available from The Elliot Institute (2000) at http://www.afterabortion.org/jericho/CHAP1.htm (accessed October 3, 2009). Surgeon General Koop is one of these critics. In an interview with the Christian reconstructionist organization, the Rutherford Institute, Koop worried about "contaminat[ing] the morality of your stand" by focusing on the woman rather than on the life of the fetus. See Reardon, *Making Abortion Rare*, 1–3.

28. Francis J. Beckwith, "Taking Abortion Seriously: A Philosophical Critique of the New Anti-Abortion Rhetorical Shift," *Ethics and Medicine* 17, no. 3 (2001): 162.

29. Barkun, *A Culture of Conspiracy*, 23.

30. Some sources, such as the National Right to Life Educational Trust Fund, list other symptoms, including avoidance of children, child abuse, other aggressive behavior, sleep difficulties, sexual dysfunction, difficulty recalling the abortion, and others.

31. American Psychological Association, "APA Research Review Finds No Evidence of 'Post-Abortion Syndrome' but Research Studies on Psychological Effects of Abortion Inconclusive," Press release, January 18, 1989.

32. In 2006 the APA pulled its 2004 "Briefing Paper on the Impact of Abortion on Women" from its website.

33. David M. Fergusson, L. John Horwood, and Elizabeth M. Ridder, "Abortion in Young Women and Subsequent Mental Health," *Journal of Child Psychology and Psychiatry* 47, no. 1 (2006): 16, 22.

34. American Psychological Association, "Report of the APA Task Force on Mental Health and Abortion" (APA Task Force, August 13, 2008) http://www.apa.org/releases/abortion-report.pdf (September 10, 2008). Emphasis in the original.

35. Abortion Facts, "Abortion Information You Can Use: Post Abortion Syndrome" (2006) http://www.abortionfacts.com/PAS/PAS.asp (accessed March 18, 2009).

36. Anuradha Kumar, Keila Hessini, and Ellen M. H. Mitchell, "Conceptualising Abortion Stigma," *Culture, Health, and Sexuality* 11 (2009): 628, 625, 633.

37. For the former, see Brenda Major and Richard H. Gramzow, "Abortion as Stigma: Cognitive and Emotional Implications of Concealment," *Journal of Perspectives Social Psychology* 77, no. 4 (1999): 735–45. For the latter, see Alison Norris, Danielle Bessett, Julia R. Steinberg, Megan L. Kavanaugh, Silvia De Zordo, and Davida Becker, "Abortion Stigma: A Reconceptualization of Constituents, Causes, and Consequences," *Women's Health Issues* 21, no. 3 (2011): 849–54.

38. Liz Welch, "The Serious Health Decision These Women Are Ready to Talk About: Eight Women Share Their Abortion Stories" (*Glamour*, February 10, 2009) http://www.glamour.com/sex-love-life/2009/02/eight-women-share-their-abortion-stories?currentPage=8 (accessed April 1, 2009); Steven Ertelt, "*Glamour* Magazine Stories Point to Need for More Post-Abortion Help for Women (LifeNews.com, February 11, 2009) http://www.lifenews.com/nat4832.html (accessed April 1, 2009).

39. For the Exhale homepage see, Exhale: An After-Abortion Counseling Talkline (*Exhale*, 2009) http://www.4exhale.org/index.php (accessed April 1, 2009). Quotes in this passage are found on the website under "Home," "Who We Are," and "After-Abortion Resources."

40. Henry Waxman, "False and Misleading Health Information Provided by Federally Funded Pregnancy Resource Centers" (*United States House of Representatives Committee on Government Reform, Special Investigations Division*, July, 2006) http://www.prochoice.org/about_abortion/facts/cpc.html (accessed December 15, 2011).

41. See Terry Ianora, *Crisis Pregnancy Centers: The Birth of a Grassroots Movement* (Bloomington, IN: AuthorHouse, 2009). Ianora does not provide a true history of crisis pregnancy centers, but she does offer some useful information from inside the movement on Birthright and First Way centers, and some regional information on CPCs in the Eugene, Oregon area.

42. Kristin Harrison, "Crisis Pregnancy Centers" (*National Abortion Federation*, 2006) http://www.prochoice.org/about_abortion/facts/cpc.html (accessed December 15, 2011).

43. Ellen Curro, *Caring Enough to Help: Counseling at a Crisis Pregnancy Center* (Grand Rapids, MI: Baker Book House, 1990), 18–19.

44. Ianora, *Crisis Pregnancy Centers*, xv.

45. Vitoria Lin and Cynthia Dailard, "Crisis Pregnancy Centers Seek to Increase Political Clout, Secure Government Subsidy" (*Guttmacher Institute*, May, 2002) http://www.guttmacher.org/pubs/tgr/05/2/gr050204.html (accessed December 16, 2011). Governor Jeb Bush supported the "Choose Life" license plates when they debuted in Florida in 1999.

46. A key resource is Kristin Luker, *Abortion and the Politics of Motherhood* (Berkeley: University of California Press, 1984). For her study Luker interviewed "key" prolife and prochoice activists, with both women and men in each of these categories. For a study of women workers on the prochoice side of the issue see Carol Joffe, *The Regulation of Sexuality: Experiences of Family Planning Workers* (Philadelphia: Temple University Press, 1986).

47. Silent No More Awareness can be found on the web at http://www.silentnomoreawareness.org/.

48. Carol J. C. Maxwell, *Pro-Life Activists in America: Meaning Motivation, and Direct Action* (Cambridge: Cambridge University Press, 2002), 214–22.

49. Curro, *Caring Enough to Help*, 12, 34–35, 57, 135, 127.

50. Ianora, *Crisis Pregnancy Centers*, 98.

51. Heritage House Victory Won, "Promotional > Silent No More" (*Heritage House*, 2003) http://www.hh76.com/pro_life_products.asp?sitc_id=2&group_id=74 (accessed March 17, 2009).

52. Cynthia Burack, field notes, March for Life, Washington, DC, January 22, 2008. The incorporation of men into postabortion ministries has been documented by Sarah Blustain, "The Mourning After" (*The Nation*, February 4, 2008) http://www.thenation.com/doc/20080204/blustain (accessed Janurary 18, 2008).

53. Faye D. Ginsburg, *Contested Lives: The Abortion Debate in an American Community* (Berkeley: University of California Press, 1989), 143–45.

54. Burack, field notes, March for Life, January 22, 2008.

55. Project Rachel, "In Their Own Words" (*Project Rachel*, 2000) http://www.hopeafterabortion.com/hope.cfm?sel=C18L (accessed March 17, 2009).

56. Unlike ads placed in the metrorail system by the exgay organization, Parents and Friends of Ex-Gays (PFOX) in 2002–2003, entitled "I Chose to Change," the Rachel ads excited little controversy.

57. The Justice Foundation was originally the Texas Justice Foundation.

58. In August 2008, the Justice Foundation, a conservative legal organization, put out a press release touting the successful reliance of courts on postabortive women's testimony. See the Justice Foundation, "U.S. Supreme Court Is Right: 'Abortion does Cause Severe Depression and Loss of Esteem' Says 100 American Scientists, Medical and Mental Health Professionals" (*Justice Foundation*, August 2008) http://64456.netministry.com/images/OO-APAPRESSRELEASE.pdf (June 20, 2009).

59. Carole Joffe, *Dispatches from the Abortion Wars: The Costs of Fanaticism to Doctors, Patients, and the Rest of Us* (Boston: Beacon, 2009), xv.

60. Pat Robertson, "Pat Robertson Quotes" (*Brainy Quotes*, 2006) http://www.brainyquote.com/quotes/authors/p/pat_robertson.html (accessed December 1, 2006).

61. Flip Benham explained to Angelia Wilson that this is "why the homosexual community is always around the abortion mill." Wilson, *Below the Belt*, 112.

62. Douglas S. Wood, "Who Is 'Jane Roe'? Anonymous No More, Norma McCorvey No Longer Supports Abortion Rights (CNN, June 18, 2003) http://www.cnn.com/2003/LAW/01/21/mccorvey.interview/ (accessed March 18, 2009). See also Norma McCorvey and Gary Thomas, *Won by Love: Norma McCorvey, Jane Roe of Roe V. Wade, Speaks Out for the Unborn as She Shares Her New Conviction for Life* (Nashville, TN: Thomas Nelson, 1998).

63. Prolife activist Lila Rose founded the antiabortion organization Live Action, which has engaged in videotaped undercover actions against Planned Parenthood to demonstrate the organization's racism and willingness to flout legal requirements for reporting statutory rape.

64. Dorothy Roberts, *Killing the Black Body: Race, Reproduction, and the Meaning of Liberty* (New York: Pantheon Books, 1997), 98–103.

65. Curro, *Caring Enough to Help*, 55.

66. "In Brief: Facts on Induced Abortion in the United States" (*Guttmacher Institute*, July, 2008) http://www.guttmacher.org/pubs/fb_induced_abortion.html (accessed April 11, 2009).

67. Joffe, *Dispatches from the Abortion Wars*, 107–08.

68. For example, at the 2008 Values Voter Summit in Washington, DC, Lila Rose noted that African American women "submit" to more than 30 percent of all abortions and that this reality constitutes "the black genocide of abortion." African American proponents of abortion rights counter this rhetoric of black genocide; see Loretta Ross, "Re-Enslaving African American Women" (*On the Issues*, November 24, 2008) http://www.ontheissuesmagazine.com/2008fall/cafe2/article/22 (accessed March 5, 2010).

69. See Nancy Wadsworth, "Bridging Racial Change: Political Orientations in the Multiracial Church Building Movement," *Religion and Politics* 3, no. 3 (2010): 439–68; *Ambivalent Miracles: Evangelicals and the Politics of Racial Healing* (Charlottesville: University of Virginia Press, 2013). The racial reconciliation efforts associated with compassion campaigns constitute a small part of the evangelical racial change projects Wadsworth analyzes that have had a variety of political effects.

70. Sara Diamond, "Cultural Projects in Christian Right Mobilization," in *Unraveling the Right: The New Conservatism in American Thought and Politics*, Amy Ansell (Boulder, CO: Westview, 2003), 51. For a study of racism in adoption politics after WWII see Rickie Solinger, *Wake Up Little Susie: Single Pregnancy and Race before Roe v. Wade* (New York: Routledge, 1994).

71. Alan Chambers, "I Questioned Homosexuality" (*Exodus International*, no date) http://www.bewareofthegod.com/wp-images/Exodus_ad.pdf (accessed May 1, 2006).

72. For responses to many Christian conservative positions on same-sex sexuality and marriage see R. Claire Snyder, *Gay Marriage and Democracy: Equality for All* (Lanham, MD: Rowman and Littlefield, 2006).

73. Erving Goffman, *Stigma: Notes on the Management of Spoiled Identity* (New York: Simon and Schuster, 1986), 4–5. Goffman is conscientious about skepticism toward the term "normals."

74. See A. Lee Beckstead, "Cures versus Choices: Agendas in Sexual Reorientation Therapy," in *Sexual Conversion Therapy: Ethical, Clinical and Research Perspectives*, ed. Ariel Shidlo, Michael Schroeder, and Jack Drescher, 87–115 (New York: Haworth Medical, 2001).

75. On Christian right opposition to measures against anti-LGBTQ bullying in schools, see Jyl J. Josephson, "The Missing Children: Safe Schools for Some," in *Fundamental Differences: Feminists Talk Back to Social Conservatives*, ed. Cynthia Burack and Jyl J. Josephson, (Lanham, MD: Rowman and Littlefield, 2003), 173–87.

76. Tanya Erzen, *Straight to Jesus*, 18.

77. Deborah Nelson, "Suffering and Thinking: The Scandal of Tone," in *Eichmann in Jerusalem*," in *Compassion: The Culture and Politics of an Emotion*, ed. Lauren Berlant (New York: Routledge, 2004), 234.

Chapter 3

1. Young-Bruehl, *Hannah Arendt*, 56. The phrase is taken from a 1936 letter from Arendt to Blücher, whom she married in 1940.

2. The book was originally published in English as *Rahel Varnhagen: The Life of a Jewess*. It is now published as Hannah Arendt, *The Life of a Jewish Woman* (San Diego: Harvest Books, 1974).

3. See, for example Angela Dillard, *Guess Who's Coming to Dinner Now? Multicultural Conservatism in America* (New York: New York University Press, 2002).

4. Morris Kaplan, *Sexual Justice: Democratic Citizenship and the Politics of Desire* (New York: Routledge, 1997), 159. For another application of Arendt's analysis of Jewish to same-sex identity, see Larry Kramer, *Report from the Holocaust: The Story of an AIDS Activist* (New York: St. Martin's, 1994).

5. Hannah Arendt, "Reflections on Little Rock," *Dissent* 6, no. 1 (1959): 45–56. Critical essays published with "Reflections" were by David Spitz and Melvin Tumin. Ralph Ellison was among those who responded to Arendt's argument later. For an analysis of Ellison's critique of Arendt and her response, see Ralph Posnock, "Ralph Ellison, Hannah Arendt, and the Meaning of Politics," in *The Cambridge Companion to Ralph Ellison*, ed. Ross Posnock (Cambridge: Cambridge University Press, 2005), 201–14. See also Hannah Arendt, "Reply to My Critics," *Dissent* 6, no. 2 (1962).

6. Andrew Sullivan, *Virtually Normal: An Argument about Homosexuality* (New York: Vintage, 1996).

7. Steven Maloney, "Abortion Escorts and Participatory Behavior" (paper presented at the annual meeting of the Western Political Science Association, Albuquerque, New Mexico, March 17, 2006); Steven Maloney, "Abortion Escorts and 'Reflections on Little Rock': Justifying the Power of the Political Act" (unpublished manuscript).

8. Jennifer Ring, *The Political Consequences of Thinking: Gender and Judaism in the Work of Hannah Arendt* (Albany: State University of New York Press, 1997).

9. George Kateb, *Hannah Arendt: Politics, Conscience, Evil* (Totowa, NJ: Rowman and Allanheld, 1984), 89. See the discussion of Arendt's relationship with the Judeo-Christian tradition in Margaret Canovan, *A Reinterpretation of her Political Thought* (Cambridge: Cambridge University Press, 1994), 176–81.

10. Hannah Arendt, *On Revolution* (New York: Penguin Books, 1990). The quote is from back matter to the 1990 edition.

11. Ibid., 85.

12. Ibid., 70–72.

13. Kateb, *Hannah Arendt*, 93.

14. Kathleen B. Jones, *Compassionate Authority: Democracy and the Representation of Women* (New York: Routledge, 1993), 170.

15. Arendt, *On Revolution*, 83.

16. Margaret Canovan, *Hannah Arendt*, 194.

17. Ibid., 190, 197.

18. Herman Melville, *Billy Budd, Sailor and Other Stories* (New York: Bantam, 1984), 5; Hannah Arendt, *On Revolution*, 84.

19. Canovan, *Hannah Arendt*, 176.

20. Shiraz Dossa, *The Public Realm and the Public Self: The Political Theory of Hannah Arendt* (Ontario, Canada: Wilfred Laurier University Press, 1989), 116–18.

21. Norma Claire Moruzzi, *Speaking through the Mask: Hannah Arendt and the Politics of Social Identity* (Ithaca, NY: Cornell University Press, 2000), 31.

22. For an analysis of the limits of literary critique for political argument, see Simon Stow, *Republic of Readers? The Literary Turn in Political Thought and Analysis* (Albany: State University of New York Press, 2008).

23. Compare Daryl Michael Scott's warning that "again and again, contempt has proven to be the flip side of pity." Scott specifically addresses the political consequences of social science images of damage to the black psyche: Daryl Michael Scott, *Contempt and Pity: Social Policy and the Image of the Damaged Black Psyche, 1880 to 1996* (Chapel Hill: University of North Carolina Press, 1997), xviii.

24. Hannah Arendt, *On Violence* (San Diego: Harcourt Brace Jovanovich, 1970), 63–65.

25. Jones, *Compassionate Authority*, 171.

26. In her own terms, Arendt was a spectator in this case, as she was using the faculty of judgment to construct meaning from past political action. For this distinction between actor and spectator, see Arendt, *The Human Condition*, 192, and Arendt, *Lectures on Kant's Political Philosophy*, ed. Ronald Beiner (Chicago: University of Chicago Press, 1982).

27. Hannah Arendt, "A Daughter of Our People," 392–93. Leon Wieseltier concurs in a pithy formulation describing responses to the first anniversary of the September 11 attacks: "The American heart is the bouncer at the door of the American mind." See Wieseltier, "Washington Diarist: A Year Later" (August 27, 2002) http://www.tnr.com/doc.mhtml?i=20020902&s=diarist090202 (accessed August 8, 2007).

28. Hannah Arendt, *Eichmann in Jerusalem: A Report on the Banality of Evil* (New York: Penguin, 1977), 106. In this passage, Arendt describes Himmler, not Eichmann.

29. Jack Drescher, "I'm Your Handyman: A History of Reparative Therapies," in *Sexual Conversion Therapy: Ethical, Clinical and Research Perspectives*, ed. Ariel Shidlo, Michael Schroeder, and Jack Drescher (New York: Haworth Medical, 2001).

30. See Arendt, *Lectures on Kant's Political Philosophy*, 42–44, and Hannah Arendt, "Truth and Politics," in *Between Past and Future* (New York: Penguin, 1977). Many contemporary theorists have found the concept of the imagination going visiting to be fruitful. See, for example, Lisa Jane Disch, *Hannah Arendt and the Limits of Philosophy* (Ithaca, NY: Cornell University Press, 1994) and David S. Gutterman, *Prophetic Politics: Christian Social Movements and American Democracy* (Ithaca, NY: Cornell University Press, 2005).

31. Martha Nussbaum, "Exactly and Responsibly: A Defense of Ethical Criticism," *Philosophy and Literature* 22, no. 2 (1998): 351–52. In taking up the "empathetic torturer" problem Nussbaum is responding to a point raised by Richard Posner.

32. Tamsin Bradley, "Does Compassion Bring Results? A Critical Perspective on Faith and Development," *Culture and Religion* 6, no. 3 (2005): 348.

33. Ronald Beiner, "Hannah Arendt on Judging," in *Lectures on Kant's Political Philosophy*, ed. Ronald Beiner, Hannah Arendt (Chicago: University of Chicago Press, 1982), 107–08. The passage in which the example of the "specific slum dwelling" is embedded is quoted from an unpublished lecture by Arendt.

34. Arendt, *On Revolution*, 73.

35. Ibid., 74.

36. Cynthia Burack, field notes, 2007 Values Voter Summit, Washington, DC, October 19–21, 2007. See also Jim Wallis, *God's Politics: Why the Right Gets It Wrong, and the Left Doesn't Get It* (New York: HarperCollins, 2006).

37. See Arendt, *On Revolution*, 68–69.

38. See Tanya Erzen, *Straight to Jesus: Sexual and Christian Conversions in the Ex-Gay Movement* (Berkeley: University of California Press, 2006), 109–11. Erzen points out that some people in ex-gay ministries have never experienced a same-sex sexual relationship. Such individuals rely on other ex-gays and on movement literature for their knowledge of gay community and sexuality.

39. See John Stuart Mill, *Utilitarianism* (Indianapolis: Hackett, 2001). See also Joseph Hamburger, *John Stuart Mill on Liberty and Control* (Princeton, NJ: Princeton University Press, 1999), ch. 8. Hamburger argues that Mill supported

more of the kind of social disapprobation expressed through "distaste, contempt and shaming" than is usually identified with him. This is so particularly when those shamed pursue "lower pleasures" and exhibit a "miserable individuality."

40. Antigay "researcher" Paul Cameron has specialized in these characterizations, but he is only one of the more visible spokespersons. See, for example, Cameron, *The Gay 90s: What the Empirical Evidence Reveals about Homosexuality* (Franklin, TN: Adroit, 1993).

41. See Linda Kintz, *Between Jesus and the Market: The Emotions That Matter in Right-Wing America* (Durham, NC: Duke University Press, 1997).

42. Steve Chapman, "George W.'s Heart Attack" (*Slate*, February 8, 2001), http://www.slate.com/id/1 00424/ (accessed July 13, 2001).

43. Nelson, "Suffering and Thinking," 241.

44. Kateb, *Hannah Arendt*, 91, 94.

45. Hannah Arendt, *The Human Condition* (Chicago: University of Chicago Press, 1958).

46. Ibid., "On Humanity in Dark Times: Thoughts about Lessing," in *Men in Dark Times* (New York: Harcourt, Brace and World, 1968), 13, 16–17. The subject of the essay is the German humanist Gotthold Ephraim Lessing.

47. The speaker was Laura Leigh Stanlake in a session for women entitled "With Our Hearts Open and Our Walls Down." Cynthia Burack, field notes, 2008 Exodus International Freedom Conference, Asheville, North Carolina, July 15–20.

48. Michelle Wolkomir, "Giving It Up to God: Negotiating Femininity in Support Groups for Wives of Ex-Gay Christian Men," *Gender and Society* 18, no. 6 (2004): 744.

49. Shiba, "Hannah Arendt on Love and the Political," 529–30. Shiba borrows some language from George B. Caird.

50. This quote, versions of which are routinely recited by Christian right leaders, is from ex-lesbian Joanna Highly in Mishara Canino-Hussung and Bill Hussung, *Chasing the Devil: Inside the Ex-Gay Movement*, Coqui Zen Entertainment, 2008.

51. Although contraception is not generally explicitly treated on the same terms as abortion in the prolife movement, ingroup rhetoric sometimes equates the two. One example is this comment from the Reverend Ben Sheldon, Presbyterians for Life: "God's intention is that we multiply and fill the earth. One of the most pernicious lies that sociologists have foisted off on the public is that the earth is becoming overpopulated. What kind of sadistic god would create the earth and human creatures on it, only to have them literally reproduce themselves into oblivion. . . . The spread of the contraception mentality that has so permeated our culture is, undoubtedly, a factor in the ready acceptance of abortion" (40 Days for Life, "Day 27: Abortion Facilities Impacted," email message, March 23, 2009).

52. See, for example, Diane Richardson, "Constructing Sexual Citizenship: Theorizing Sexual Rights," *Critical Social Policy* 20, no. 1 (2000): 105–35; Cynthia Burack and Angelia R. Wilson, "Constructing Christian Right Enemies and Allies: US, UK and Eastern Europe," in *Remoralizing Britain? Political, Ethical*

and Theological Perspectives on New Labour, ed. Peter Manley Scott, Christopher R. Baker, and Elaine L. Graham (London: Continuum, 2009), 136–55; Jyl J. Josephson, "Sexual Citizenship, Sexual Regulation, and Identity Politics" (paper presented at the annual meeting of the Western Political Science Association, San Diego, California, March 20, 2008).

53. Arendt, *The Human Condition,* 7–8.

54. This is not to say that Arendt's own account of plurality is immune to criticism. For a critique that focuses on Arendt's tendency to equate socioeconomic equality with threats to plurality, see James Bohman, "The Moral Costs of Political Pluralism: The Dilemmas of Difference and Equality in Arendt's 'Reflections on Little Rock,' " in *Hannah Arendt: Twenty Years Later,* ed. Larry May and Jerome Kohn (Cambridge, MA: MIT Press, 1996), 53–80.

55. Bonnie Honig, "Toward an Agonistic Feminism: Hannah Arendt and the Politics of Identity," in *Feminist Interpretations of Hannah Arendt,* ed. Bonnie Honig (University Park: Pennsylvania State University Press, 1995), 149.

56. Jennifer Ring, "The Pariah as Hero: Hannah Arendt's Political Actor," *Political Theory* 19, no. 3 (1991): 433–52; Arendt, *The Human Condition,* 179–81.

57. See Susan Bickford, "In the Presence of Others: Arendt and Anzaldúa on the Paradox of Public Appearance," in *Feminist Interpretations of Hannah Arendt,* ed. Bonnie Honig (University Park: Pennsylvania State University Press, 1995).

58. See Hannah Arendt, *The Jewish Writings,* ed. Jerome Kohn and Ron H. Feldman (New York: Schocken, 2007).

59. Arendt has perplexed some readers with the traditional conception of gender and difference she revealed in brief comments on the subject. Calling herself "rather old-fashioned," she notes that "a woman [who] gives orders" might find it difficult to "remain feminine." For her part, however, she points out that she had always "done what [she] liked to do." See, " 'What Remains? The Language Remains': A Conversation with Günter Gaus," in *Essays in Understanding 1930–1954: Uncollected and Unpublished Works by Hannah Arendt,* ed. Jerome Kohn (New York: Harcourt Brace, 1994), 2–3.

60. Hannah Arendt, " 'What Remains?' " 11–12. For a similar later statement on the same theme see Arendt, "On Humanity in Dark Times: Thoughts on Lessing," 17: "I cannot gloss over the fact that for many years I considered the only adequate reply to the question, Who are you? To be: A Jew. That answer alone took into account the reality of persecution."

61. Margaret Betz Hull, *The Hidden Philosophy of Hannah Arendt* (New York: Routledge, 2002), 137.

62. Hanna Fenichel Pitkin, *The Attack of the Blob: Hannah Arendt's Concept of the Social* (Chicago: University of Chicago Press, 1998), 158.

63. Some change in these representations seems to be occurring, and Exodus International has lead the way, no doubt to the chagrin of those who disapprove of what may be taken as signs of approval of LGBTQ identification.

64. Scott Barclay, "The Strange Absence of Gays in the Same-Sex Marriage Movement" (paper presented at the annual meeting of the Western Political Science Association, Las Vegas, Nevada, March 8, 2007).

65. Laura R. Olson and Wendy Cadge, "Talking about Homosexuality: The Views of Mainline Protestant Clergy" *Journal for the Scientific Study of Religion* 41, no. 1 (2002): 153.

66. Disch, *Hannah Arendt and the Limits of Philosophy*, 156; Hannah Arendt, "Truth and Politics," 241.

67. Iris Marion Young, "Asymmetrical Reciprocity: On Moral Respect, Wonder, and Enlarged Thought," in *Intersecting Voices: Dilemmas of Gender, Political Philosophy, and Policy* (Princeton, NJ: Princeton University Press, 1997), 59.

68. Gutterman, *Prophetic Politics*, 37–40, 125.

69. One recent text that encourages Christian right political activism has been distributed free at some Christian conservative meetings: Neil Mammen, *Jesus Was Is Involved in Politics! Why Aren't You? Why Isn't Your Church?* (Create Space Independent Publishing Platform, 2012).

70. Groups that report not knowing anybody who is gay at higher rates than other Americans include men, conservative Republicans, noncollege graduates, and older and rural Americans. For survey data that include these demographic categories, see PEW Research Center, "Four-in-Ten Americans Have Close Friends or Relatives Who Are Gay" (*PEW*, May 23, 2007) http://pewresearch.org/pubs/485/friends-who-are-gay (accessed July 29, 2007).

71. See, for example, Bob Altemeyer, "Changes in Attitudes toward Homosexuals," *Journal of Homosexuality* 42, no. 2 (2001). See also Altemeyer's recent book that summarizes his career of research on right-wing authoritarianism: Bob Altemeyer, *The Authoritarians* (February 26, 2007) http://members.shaw.ca/jeanaltemeyer/drbob/TheAuthoritarians.pdf (accessed May 15, 2007).

72. Hanna Pitkin, *The Attack of the Blob*, 10–18.

73. Hannah Arendt, *The Origins of Totalitarianism*, 54

74. Honig, "Toward an Agonistic Feminism," 147.

75. Hannah Arendt, *Rahel Varnhagen*, 199–228.

76. The Justice Foundation, "About the Justice Foundation" (*Justice Foundation*, 2009) http://www.txjf.org/pages.asp?pageid=22827 (accessed June 20, 2009). Although the organization does not describe itself as a Christian conservative organization, it is understood as a Christian conservative alternative to the American Civil Liberties Union by Christian conservatives. Its website is constructed and maintained by NetMinistry: Complete Website Solutions for Churches, Christian Ministries, and Businesses.

77. The Justice Foundation, "Home" (Justice Foundation, 2009) http://www.txjf.org/ (accessed June 20, 2009).

78. Operation Outcry is found on the web at http://www.operationoutcry.org/.

79. Operation Outcry, "Faces of Abortion: A Unique Must-See TV Show" (2009) http://www.operationoutcry.org/pages.asp?pageid=27773 (accessed March 19, 2009).

80. See Alesha E. Doan, *Opposition and Intimidation: The Abortion Wars and Strategies of Political Harassment* (Ann Arbor: University of Michigan Press, 2007), 182.

81. For a report on the Summit that contains some of this information, see Sean Cahill and Cynthia Burack, "Internal Enemy: Gays as the Domestic al-Qaeda: A Report from the Family Research Council's Values Voter Summit, September 22-24, 2006" (*The National Gay and Lesbian Task Force*, October 27, 2006) http://www.thetaskforce.org/downloads/Internal_enemy_ValuesVoter.pdf (accessed November 1, 2006). Other information is from Burack, field notes, 2006 Values Voter Summit, Washington, DC, September 22-24, 2006.

82. The biblical story of the woman taken in adultery is related in John 8: 1-11.

83. Hannah Arendt, *Love and Saint Augustine*, ed. Joanna Vecchiarelli Scott and Judith Chelius Stark (Chicago: University of Chicago Press, 1996), 102.

84. This question is raised in the parable of the Good Samaritan related in Luke 10:25-37. See the more extensive discussion of this parable in chapter 5.

85. Joanna Vecchiarelli Scott, "Hannah Arendt Twenty Years Later: A German Jewess in the Age of Totalitarianism," *New German Critique* 86 (2002): 38.

86. Quoted in Arendt, *Love and Saint Augustine*, 43.

87. Augustine, *Basic Writings of Saint Augustine: Volume 2* (New York: Random House, 1948), 246. The passage in question is found in *The City of God*, book 14, chapter 6.

88. For an example, see Sermon 114 in Saint Augustine, *Essential Sermons*, ed. Boniface Ramsey (New York: New City Press, 2007), 192-95.

89. Arendt, *The Human Condition*, 238.

90. The other mode of redemption is promising. See Theresa Calvet de Magalhães, "The Frailty of Action. Forgiving and Promising: The Redemption of Action through the Potentialities of Action Itself in Arendt" (Hannah Arendt. net, no date) http://hannaharendt.net/research/Calvet.html (accessed December 30, 2009).

91. Arendt, *The Human Condition*, 237.

92. Arendt, *Rahel Varnhagen*, 81; Julia Kristeva, *Hannah Arendt*, translated by Ross Guberman (New York: Columbia University Press, 2001), 49.

93. Shiraz Dossa, "Hannah Arendt on Billy Budd and Robiespierre: The Public Realm and the Private Self," *Philosophy and Social Criticism* 9 (1982): 315.

94. Ayn Rand, "The Age of Envy," in *Return of the Primitive: The Anti-Industrial Revolution* (New York: Meridian, 1999), 132.

95. C. Fred Alford, *Psychology and the Natural Law of Reparation* (Cambridge: Cambridge University Press, 2006), 98.

96. Ayn Rand Institute, "Essentials of Objectivism" (*Ayn Rand Institute*, 2009) http://www.aynrand.org/site/PageServer?pagename=objectivism_essentials (accessed July 3, 2009).

Chapter 4

1. Tea Party Express, "Mission Statement" (*Tea Party Express*, 2011) http://www.teapartyexpress.org/mission (accessed March 15, 2012).

2. Don Hazen and Adele M. Stan, *Dangerous Brew: Exposing the Tea Party's Agenda to Take Over America* (San Francisco, CA: AlterNet Books, 2010); Angelia R. Wilson and Cynthia Burack, "'Where Liberty Reigns and God Is Supreme: The Christian Right and the Tea Party Movement," *New Political Science* 34, no. 2 (2012): 172–90. For the distinction between public and hidden transcripts, see James C. Scott, *Domination and the Arts of Resistance* (New Haven: Yale University Press, 1990).

3. Adele Stan, "Tea Party, Meet Religious Right. Everybody, Meet Ayn Rand" (July 24, 2010) http://blogs.alternet.org/speakeasy/2010/07/24/tea-party-meet-religious-right-everybody-meet-ayn-rand/ (accessed September 14, 2010); For data on membership and support of the tea party movement see PEW Research Forum, "The Tea Party, Religion, and Social Issues," (February 23, 2011) http://pewresearch.org/pubs/1903/tea-party-movement-religion-social-issues-conservative-christian (accessed February 24, 2011).

4. Gary Weiss, *Ayn Rand Nation: The Hidden Struggle for America's Soul* (New York: St. Martin's, 2012), 155.

5. As Jennifer Burns explains, Hickman kidnapped, murdered, and mutilated a twelve-year-old girl in 1927. See Burns, *Goddess of the Market: Ayn Rand and the American Right* (Oxford: Oxford University Press, 2009), 43; 25.

6. Harriet Rubin. Ayn Rand's Literature of Capitalism." (*The New York Times*, September 15, 2007) http://www.nytimes.com/2007/09/15/business/15atlas.html?ei=5087%0A&em=&en=c6fc1c1b0f70b13a&ex=1190174400&pagewanted=print (accessed September 17, 2007).

7. William E. Connolly, "The Evangelical-Capitalist Resonance Machine," *Political Theory* 33, no. 6 (2005): 869–86.

8. This description appears on the back cover of editions of *Atlas Shrugged* and in much copy about the novel.

9. Gore Vidal, "Two Immoralists: Orville Prescott and Ayn Rand," in *Rocking the Boat* (Boston: Little, Brown, 1962), 232–34.

10. E. J. Dionne, *Why Americans Hate Politics* (New York: Simon and Schuster, 2004), 264–65.

11. Lisa McGirr, *Suburban Warriors: The Origins of the New American Right* (Princeton, NJ: Princeton University Press, 2001), 152.

12. Ibid., 164–65.

13. Jerome Tucille, *It Usually Begins with Ayn Rand. Twenty-fifth Anniversary Edition* (San Francisco: Fox and Wilkes, 1997), 29, 32; 29.

14. Burns, *Goddess of the Market*, 204.

15. Vidal, "Two Immoralists," 233; Burns, *Goddess of the Market*, 205.

16. Tucille, *It Usually Begins with Ayn Rand*, 4–7.

17. Murray N. Rothbard, "The Sociology of the Ayn Rand Cult" (*LewRockwell.com*, 2003) http://www.lewrockwell.com/rothbard/rothbard23.html (accessed February 26, 2009).

18. For a no doubt dissenting view see Donald L. Luskin and Andrew Greta, *I Am John Galt: Today's Heroic Innovators Building the World and the Villainous Parasites Destroying It* (Hoboken, NJ: John Wiley and Sons, 2011).

19. While writing this book I visited the North Yorkshire town of Whitby, where Bram Stoker set portions of *Dracula*, and then read Stoker's novel. By Rand's logic, the fact that Bram Stoker wrote *Dracula* and that it was published (and continues to be read more than one hundred years after its publication) is proof that such beings as the count exist.

20. Rand, *The Fountainhead*, 93. Arguably, there is a set of middle positions between these two poles of character, but they receive scant attention from Rand. On his website, Nathaniel Branden answers a question about what becomes of Eddie Willers, Dagny Taggart's "right hand man" in *Atlas Shrugged*—in particular, why Rand did not see fit to include him in the exodus to Galt's Gulch. Branden's answer is that, in Rand's view, Willers's position in the category "the best of the average" did not qualify him for entry to this "elite society." See Nathaniel Branden, "Questions and Answers: June 7, 1998" (*The Official Web* Site of Dr. Nathaniel Branden, 1998) http://www.nathanielbranden.com/catalog/pdf/QA-98june7.pdf (May 28, 2009).

21. Anne C. Heller, *Ayn Rand and the World She Made* (New York: Nan A. Talese/Doubleday, 2009), 320–21, 128.

22. Rand made her comments after a speech at Northeastern University in 1971. See Paul Varnell, "Ayn Rand and Homosexuality" (*Independent Gay Forum*, 2003) http://www.indegayforum.org/news/show/27018.html (accessed January 23, 2007).

23. Leonard Peikoff, "An Interview with Leornard Peikoff," in *Essays on Ayn Rand's* The Fountainhead, ed. Robert Mayhew (Lanham, MD: Rowman and Littlefield, 2006), 334.

24. Sciabarra, *Ayn Rand, Homosexuality, and Human Liberation*. For an alternative reading that is critical of Sciabarra, see Reginald Firehammer, *The Hijacking of a Philosophy: Homosexuals vs. Ayn Rand's Objectivism* (Charleston, SC: BookSurge, 2004).

25. Reginald Firehammer, T*he Hijacking of a Philosophy: Homosexuals vs. Ayn Rand's Objectivism* (BookSurge, 2004).

26. Ilana Mercer, "Return to Reason: Ayn Rand, Homosexuality, and Human Liberation" (*WorldNetDaily*, July 9, 2004) http://www.wnd.com/news/article.asp?ARTICLE_ID=39360 (accessed April 10, 2009).

27. See Branden, *The Passion of Ayn Rand*.

28. Heller traces Rand's penchant for cultivating young men and identifying them as "intellectual heirs" in the years before she met Branden. See Heller, *Ayn Rand and the World She Made*, 177–78.

29. Nathaniel Branden, "Was Ayn Rand a Feminist?" in *Feminist Interpretations of Ayn Rand*, ed. Mimi Reisel Gladstein and Chris Matthew Sciabarra (University Park: Pennsylvania State University Press, 1999), 223–30.

30. Ayn Rand, *Atlas Shrugged* (New York: Random House, 1957), 133.

31. Rand's break with Branden occurred after the end of an affair between the two and Branden's announcement of his relationship with another woman. Nathaniel's ex-wife has written an insider account of both the affair and the

subsequent rupture; see Barbara Branden, *The Passion of Ayn Rand* (Garden City, NY: Doubleday, 1986).

32. The scene is found in Ayn Rand, *The Fountainhead* (New York: Penguin, 1993), 215–18; Branden, *The Passion of Ayn Rand*, 134.

33. Wendy McElroy, "Looking through a Paradigm Darkly," in *Feminist Interpretations of Ayn Rand*, ed. Mimi Reisel Gladstein and Chris Matthew Sciabarra (University Park: Pennsylvania State University Press, 1999), 157–71. See also Andrew Bernstein, "Understanding the 'Rape' scene in *The Fountainhead*," in *Essays on Ayn Rand's The Fountainhead*, ed. Robert Mayhew (Lanham, MD: Lexington Books, 2006), 201–08.

34. Mercer, "Return to Reason: Ayn Rand, Homosexuality, and Human Liberation."

35. See, for example, Joseph Nicolosi and Linda Ames Nicolosi, *A Parent's Guide to Preventing Homosexuality* (Downer's Grove, IL: InterVarsity, 2002).

36. Tanya Erzen describes a "femininity workshop" she attended in the course of her research on the ex-gay movement. There, Anne Paulk, an author and spokesperson of the movement, described women as "soft, warm, nurturing" and men as "hard and muscular." Paulk, who was seated in the audience at this event, was held up as a model and described as "radiat[ing] femininity." Erzen, *Straight to Jesus*, 150.

37. Angelia R. Wilson, field notes, session on "True Femininity," 2008 Exodus International Conference. While the essence of femininity is "having the ability to receive," Wilson learned that a cosmetic makeover is always useful as a way to feel more feminine.

38. Beverly LaHaye, *I am a Woman by God's Design* (Old Tappan, NJ: Fleming H. Revell, 1980). See also Tim LaHaye and Beverly LaHaye, *The Act of Marriage: The Beauty of Sexual Love* (Grand Rapids, MI: Zondervan, 1978).

39. Michelle Wolkomir, "Giving It Up to God: Negotiating Femininity in Support Groups for Wives of Ex-Gay Christian Men," 18, no. 6 (2004): 748, 749.

40. Nathaniel Branden, *The Psychology of Self-Esteem: A New Concept of Man's Psychological Nature* (New York: Bantam, 1971).

41. Barbara Branden, "Ayn Rand: The Reluctant Feminist," in *Feminist Interpretations of Ayn Rand*, ed. Mimi Reisel Gladstein and Chris Matthew Sciabarra (University Park: Pennsylvania State University Press, 1999), 31.

42. King James Version.

43. The Christian conservative organization, Promise Keepers has incorporated both of these tiers of servant headship. For an analysis of its uses in politics, see Michael Lindsay, "Sarah Palin: Sending the Signals" (*Beliefnet*, September 10, 2008) http://blog.beliefnet.com/castingstones/2008/09/sarah-palin-sending-the-signal.html (accessed October 3, 2009).

44. Ruth Marcus, "Would Michele Bachmann Be a Submissive President?" (Washington Post, July 19, 2011) http://www.washingtonpost.com/opinions/would-michele-bachmann-be-a-submissive-president/2011/07/19/gIQAOfNfOI_story.html (accessed August 12, 2011).

45. Carolyn Pevy, Christine L. Williams, and Christopher G. Ellison, "Male God Imagery and Female Submission: Lessons from a Southern Baptist Ladies' Bible Class," *Qualitative Sociology* 19, no. 2 (1996): 185.

46. Bryan Register. "Should Ayn Rand Have Been a Feminist?" (*The Atlas Society and Its Objectivist* Center, 2005) http://www.objectivistcenter.org/showcontent.aspx?ct=139&h=53 (accessed February 6, 2007).

47. Susan Love Brown, "Ayn Rand: The Woman Who Would *Not* Be President," in *Feminist Interpretations of Ayn Rand*, ed. Mimi Reisel Gladstein and Chris Matthew Sciabarra (University Park: Pennsylvania State University Press, 1999), 276–77; Ayn Rand, "About a Woman President," in *The Voice of Reason: Essays in Objectivist Thought*, (New York: Plume), 267–70.

48. W. Teed Rockwell. "Altruism, Pity and Compassion: Significant (and Ignored) Differences," *Truth Seeker* 120, no. 2 (1993): 10–15; W. Teed Rockwell. "Altruism, Pity and Compassion: Significant (and Ignored) Differences. Part Two—Compassion," *Truth Seeker* 120, no. 3 (1993): 4–9.

49. Nathaniel Branden, "The Benefits and Hazards of the Philosophy of Ayn Rand: A Personal Statement" (*The Website of Dr. Nathaniel Branden*, 1984) http://www.nathanielbranden.com/articles/catalog_essays/benefits_and_hazards.html (accessed May 27, 2009).

50. Ayn Rand, "Return of the Primitive," 139.

51. Ayn Rand and Alvin Toffler, "Playboy Interview, 1964" (*Playboy*, no date) http://www.ellensplace.net/ar_pboy.html (April 9, 2009).

52. These arguments are found throughout Rand's massive canon. See, for example, Ayn Rand, *For the New Intellectual: The Philosophy of Ayn Rand* (New York: Random House, 1961). In this text, Rand lays out some basics of her worldview in an essay entitled, "For the New Intellectual," and then abstracts passages from her novels to define a variety of terms and to illustrate points.

53. See Dorothy Roberts, *Killing the Black Body: Race, Reproduction, and the Meaning of Liberty* (New York: Pantheon Books, 1997); Mary Fraser and Linda Gordon, "Decoding 'Dependency': Inscriptions of Power in a Keyword of the US Welfare State," in *Reconstructing Political Theory*, Mary Lyndon Shanley and Uma Narayan, eds. (State College: Pennsylvania State University, 1997), 25–47; Gwendolyn Mink, *Welfare's End* (Ithaca, NY: Cornell University Press, 2002).

54. Theda Skocpol and Vanessa Williamson, *The Tea Party and the Remaking of Republican Conservatism* (New York: Oxford University Press, 2012), 72.

55. John Locke, *Second Treatise of Government* (Indianapolis: Hackett, 1980), 21–22.

56. For a collection of documents that bear witness to these beliefs see John David Smith, *Anti-Black Thought, 1863-1925. "The Negro Problem": An Eleven-Volume Anthology of Racist Writings* (New York: Garland, 1993).

57. Rand, *The Fountainhead*, 389.

58. "Anti-Life" is chapter 4 in part 3 of *Atlas Shrugged*.

59. Ayn Rand, *Atlas Shrugged*, 824–28, 842–43.

60. Ibid., 921–22.

61. Ibid., 825.

62. Rand, *The Fountainhead*, 282.

63. Tanya Erzen, *Straight to Jesus: Sexual and Christian Conversions in the Ex-Gay Movement* (Berkeley: University of California Press, 2006).

64. For an analysis of this eschatology and the theme of national punishment invoked by Falwell and Robertson, see Cynthia Burack, *Sin, Sex, and Democracy: Antigay Rhetoric and the Christian Right* (Albany: State University of New York Press, 2008).

65. D. James Kennedy, *Why Was America Attacked? Answers for a Nation at War* (Nashville, TN: Broadman and Holman, 2001).

66. Thomas F. Bertonneau, "Ayn Rand's *Atlas Shrugged*: From Romantic Fallacy to Holocaustic Imagination," *Modern Age: A Quarterly Review* 46, no. 4 (2004): 304.

67. Bertonneau calls the episode the "Winston Tunnel Disaster" because it takes place near Winston Station, Colorado. The disaster occurs in part 2, chapter 7 ("The Moratorium on Brains"), but it is reported in chapter 8 as having taken place in Taggart Tunnel ("All Our Love").

68. Rand, *Atlas Shrugged*, 566.

69. Ibid., 566–68.

70. Bertonneau, "Ayn Rand's *Atlas Shrugged*," 305.

71. Tim LaHaye and Jerry B. Jenkins, *Left Behind*. See also the controversy over the *Left Behind* video game, in which the "forces of the antichrist" are killed by the righteous Tribulation Force. In a rejoinder to critics, LaHaye and Jenkins point out that the game avoids gratuitous violence and that instead of "buckets of blood and flying body parts," victims in the Left Behind game "fall in a puff of smoke." See Jerry Jenkins, "Left Behind Video Game Controversy" (LeftBehind.com, 2007) http://www.leftbehind.com/channelnews.asp?pageid=1322&channelID=17 (accessed February 2, 2007).

72. Whittaker Chambers, "Big Sister Is Watching You" (*National Review Online*, 2005) http://www.nationalreview.com/flashback/flashback200501050715.asp (accessed June 3, 2009).

73. On the psychology of apocalyptic fantasies, see Charles B. Strozier, *Apocalypse: On the Psychology of Fundamentalism in America* (New York: Beacon, 1994).

74. Ayn Rand, "The Age of Envy" in *Return of the Primitive: The Anti-Industrial Revolution* (New York: Penguin, 1999), 149. *Return of the Primitive* is an expanded version of an earlier volume of Rand's essays entitled, *The New Left: The Anti-Industrial Revolution*.

75. Rand, "The Age of Envy," 148–49.

76. Ibid., "Racism," in *The Return of the Primitive: The Anti-Industrial Revolution* (New York: Penguin, 1999), 188.

77. Dinesh D'Souza, *The End of Racism: Principles for a Multiracial Society* (New York: Free Press, 1995), 544–45. More recently, D'Souza has impressed Christian right readers and audiences with his book, *What's So Great about Christianity?* (Washington, DC: Regnery, 2007).

78. See Arlene Stein, *The Stranger Next Door: The Story of a Small Community's Battle over Sex, Faith, and Civil Rights* (Boston: Beacon, 2001) 33-34, 117, 122-23. Arguments that equate gay rights policies with the death of religious freedom in America are commonplace. See, for example, Massachusetts Family Institute. "Family Research Council: Boston to Host National 'Religious Freedom' Simulcast" (Newnet, 2006), http://newne.net/db_public/u14_public/index_EN.php?display=onepage&what=1544 (accessed February 22, 2007).

79. Jacqueline L. Salmon, "Faith Groups Increasingly Lose Gay Rights Fights" (*Washington Post*, April 10, 2009) http://www.washingtonpost.com/wp-dyn/content/article/2009/04/09/AR2009040904063.html?wpisrc=newsletter (accessed April 10, 2009).

80. Rand, "Racism," 182.

81. For an analysis of positional goods, see Fred Hirsch, *Social Limits to Growth* (Cambridge: Harvard University Press, 1976).

82. Rand, "Racism," 186. Emphasis is in the original.

83. Jyl J. Josephson and Cynthia Burack, "Inside, Out, and In-Between: Sexual Minorities, the Christian Right and the Evangelical Lutheran Church in America," in *Religion, Politics, and American Identity: New Directions, New Controversies*, ed. David S. Gutterman and Andrew R. Murphy (Lanham, MD: Lexington Books, 2006), 247-65.

84. Dawne Moon, *God, Sex, and Politics: Homosexuality and Everyday Theologies* (Chicago: University of Chicago Press, 2004).

85. See Romans 1:27, KJV.

86. Heller, *Ayn Rand and the World She Made*, 326-27.

87. Rand, *Atlas Shrugged,*, 922-23.

88. Ibid., 923.

89. WallBuilders, http://www.wallbuilders.com/default.asp (accessed April 10, 2009).

90. See, for example, Mark A. Beliles and Stephen K. McDowell, *America's Providential History: Including Biblical Principles of Education, Government, Politics, Economics, and Family Life* (Charlottesville, VA: Providence Foundation, 1991).

91. Richard Hofstadter, *Anti-Intellectualism in American Life* (New York: Vintage, 1966).

92. Rand, "The Age of Envy," 132.

93. Nathaniel Branden, "The Benefits and Hazards of the Philosophy of Ayn Rand."

94. For the influence of Neitzsche on Rand—an influence she sometimes denied and began to occlude as time went on—see Ronald E. Merrill, *The Ideas of Ayn Rand* (Chicago: Open Court, 1998).

95. See Burack, *Sin, Sex, and Democracy*. For an analysis of conservative Christianity and its relation to pop culture see especially chapter 2, "The Nightmare of Homosexuality," which focuses on Chick tracts; Kristy Maddux, *The Faithful Citizen: Popular Christian Media and Gendered Civic Identities* (Waco:

Baylor University Press, 2010); Heather Hendershot, *Shaking the World for Jesus: Media and Conservative Evangelical Culture* (Chicago: University of Chicago Press, 2004).

96. Stein, *The Stranger Next Door*, 28.

Chapter 5

1. See, for example, Charles W. Socarides, *The Overt Homosexual* (Northvale, NJ: Jason Aronson, 1968) and Elizabeth R. Moberly, *Homosexuality: A New Christian Ethic* (Cambridge: Lutterworth, 2006). For an account of how antigay bias has lingered in the psychoanalytic profession see Arthur H. Lilling, Ph.D. and Richard C. Friedman, M.D., "Bias towards Gay Patients by Psychoanalytic Clinicians: An Empirical Investigation," *Archives of Sexual Behavior*, 24, no. 5 (1995): 563-70.

2. In a critique of prominent profamily conservative, David Blankenhorn, I point out that Blankenhorn conscripts authors such as Anna Freud, John Bowlby, and D. W. Winnicott and their ideas into unlikely support for his ideological agenda. See Cynthia Burack, "Defense Mechanisms: Using Psychoanalysis Conservatively," in *Fundamental Differences: Feminists Talk Back to Social Conservatives*, ed. Cynthia Burack and Jyl J. Josephson (Northvale, NJ: Rowman and Littlefield, 2003), 81-94.

3. Jean Grimshaw, *Philosophy and Feminist Thinking* (Minneapolis: University of Minnesota Press, 1986), 55.

4. Jane Flax, "Political Philosophy and the Patriarchal Unconscious: A Psychoanalytic Perspective on Epistemology and Metaphysics," in *Discovering Reality: Feminist Perspectives on Epistemology, Metaphysics, Methodology, and Philosophy of Science*, ed. Sandra Harding, and Merrill B. Hintikka (New York: Springer, 1983), 250. For a survey of these debates see Cynthia Burack, "A House Divided: Feminism and Object Relations Theory," *Women's Studies International Forum* 15, no. 4 (1992): 499-506.

5. Melanie Klein, "Love, Guilt, and Reparation," in *The Writings of Melanie Klein Volume 1: Love, Guilt and Reparation and Other Works 1921-1945* (New York: Free Press, 1975), 310.

6. Ibid., "A Contribution to the Psychogenesis of Tics," in *The Writings of Melanie Klein Volume 1: Love, Guilt and Reparation and Other Works 1921-1945* (New York: Free Press, 1975), 106-18. For "Felix's" identity, see Julia Kristeva, *Melanie Klein*, translated by Ross Guberman (New York: Columbia University Press, 2001), 45-46; Janet Sayers, *Mothers of Psychoanalysis: Helene Deutsch, Karen Horney, Anna Freud, Melanie Klein* (New York: Norton, 1991), 215-16.

7. Melanie Klein, "Envy and Gratitude," in *The Writings of Melanie Klein Volume III: Envy and Gratitude and Other Works 1946-1963* (New York, Free Press, 1975), 199-201.

8. Noreen O'Connor and Joanna Ryan, *Wild Desires and Mistaken Identities: Lesbianism and Psychoanalysis* (New York: Columbia, 1998), 73-83.

9. Ramón E. Soto-Crespo, "Heterosexuality Terminable or Interminable? Kleinian Fantasies of Reparation and Mourning," in *Homosexuality and Psychoanalysis*, Tim Dean and Christopher Lane (Chicago: University of Chicago Press, 2001), 195.

10. For an excellent volume that surveys antigay attitudes and professional restrictions on lesbians and gay men in the psychoanalytic profession, see Thomas Domenici and Ronnie C. Lesser, eds., *Disorienting Sexuality: Psychoanalytic Reappraisals of Sexual Identities* (New York: Routledge, 1995).

11. Feminists have used relational psychoanalysis to fashion theories to explain the persistence of gendered forms of development. See Dorothy Dinnerstein, *The Mermaid and the Minotaur: Sexual Arrangements and Human Malaise* (New York: Harper and Row, 1976); Nancy J. Chodorow, *The Reproduction of Mothering: Psychoanalysis and the Sociology of Gender* (Berkeley: University of California Press, 1979); Jessica Benjamin, *The Bonds of Love: Psychoanalysis, Feminism, and the Problem of Domination* (New York: Pantheon Books, 1988).

12. There is an extensive Christian conservative literature that explains natural sex roles, authority, and submission, but see James Dobson, *Straight Talk to Men: Recovering the Biblical Meaning of Manhood* (Nashville: Word, 1995); Elisabeth Elliot, *Let Me Be a Woman* (Carol Stream, IL: Tyndale House, 1999).

13. See the discussion of normative masculinity in Tanya Erzen, *Straight to Jesus: Sexual and Christian Conversions in the Ex-Gay Movement* (Berkeley: University of California Press, 2006), 102–14.

14. Melanie Klein, "A Contribution to the Psychogenesis of Manic-Depressive States, 286; C. Fred Alford, *Melanie Klein and Critical Social Theory: An Account of Politics, Art, and Reason Based on Her Psychoanalytic Theory* (New Haven, CT: Yale University Press, 1989), 33.

15. Klein, "A Contribution to the Psychogenesis of Manic-Depressive States," 265.

16. The concept of the "good-enough mother" comes from the work of Donald Winnicott and is specifically associated with his reworking of the depressive position, which he called the "stage of concern." See D. W. Winnicott, *Playing and Reality* (London: Tavistock, 1971); *Through Paediatrics to Psycho-Analysis: Collected Papers* (New York: Routledge, 1992).

17. Melanie Klein, "A Contribution to the Psychogenesis of Manic-Depressive States, in *The Writings of Melanie Klein Volume 1: Love, Guilt and Reparation and Other Works 1921-1945* (New York: Free Press, 1975), 272.

18. See Thomas H. Ogden, *Projective Identification and Psychotherapeutic Technique* (Lanham, Maryland: Jason Aronson, 1977); Elizabeth Bott Spillius, *Melanie Klein Today. Developments in Theory and Practice*. Volume I: *Mainly Theory* (London: Routledge, 1988). The Spillius volume is divided into four parts, and part 2 consists of four papers on the key concept of projective identification.

19. Melanie Klein, "Notes on some schizoid mechanisms," in *The Writings of Melanie Klein Volume III: Envy and Gratitude and Other Works 1946-1963* (New York, Free Press, 1975), 8.

20. Ibid., "On Identification," in *The Writings of Melanie Klein Volume III: Envy and Gratitude and Other Works 1946–1963* (New York: Free Press, 1975), 153.

21. Elizabeth Bott Spillius, "Developments in Kleinian Thought: Overview and Personal View (The Melanie Klein Trust, 1994) http://www.melanie-klein-trust.org.uk/ejb2003.htm (July 13, 2009).

22. Ibid., "Some Developments from the Work of Melanie Klein," *International Journal of Psycho-Analysis* 64 (1983): 321–32.

23. As Klein and others explicated the defenses they corrected, for example, the spatial misconceptions often associated with them and clarified that projective identification is an unconscious fantasy in which a part of the self is disowned and attributed to someone else. For an argument against the use of spatial imagery to illustrate mental processes, see Roy Schaeffer, *A New Language for Psychoanalysis* (New Haven: Yale University Press, 1981).

24. Klein, "Notes on Some Schizoid Mechanisms," 9.

25. R. D. Hinshelwood, *A Dictionary of Kleinian Thought* (London: Free Association Books, 1989), 164. Klein's biographer, Phyllis Grosskurth, emphasizes this theme of projective identification as "putting oneself in another's shoes" in a meeting Klein attended with colleagues in 1958.

26. Klein, "Love, Guilt, and Reparation," 311.

27. George Lakoff, *The Political Mind: A Cognitive Scientist's Guide to Your Brain and Its Politics* (New York: Penguin, 2009), 101.

28. John Zinner and Roger L. Shapiro, "Projective Identification as a Mode of Perception and Behavior in Families of Adolescents," in *Foundations of Object Relations Family Therapy*, Jill Savege Scharff (Northvale, NJ: Jason Aronson, 1989), 109

29. Klein, "Envy and Gratitude," 192.

30. Hannah Arendt, *Between Past and Future: Eight Exercises in Political Thought* (New York: Viking, 1968), 241.

31. Ibid., *Rahel Varnhagen*, xviii.

32. Ibid., *Between Past and Future*, 241.

33. Elisabeth Young-Bruehl, *Hannah Arendt: For Love of the World* (New Haven: Yale University Press, 1982), 314–17. See also Ross Posnock, "Ralph Ellison, Hannah Arendt, and the Meaning of Politics," in *The Cambridge Companion to Ralph Ellison*, ed. Ross Posnock (Cambridge: Cambridge University Press, 2005), 201–02.

34. One good resource for these arguments is Celia Kitzinger and Rachel Perkins, *Changing Our Minds: Lesbian Feminism and Psychology* (New York: New York University Press, 1993).

35. Michael Rustin, "Klein on Human Nature," in *Other Banalities: Melanie Klein Revisited*, ed. Jon Mills (London: Routledge, 2006), 37.

36. Klein does furnish grounds to regard her thought as moralizing and normalizing. For example, "Character is the foundation for all human achievement. The effect of a good character on others lies at the root of healthy social

development." Melanie Klein, "Our Adult World and Its Roots in Infancy," in *The Writings of Melanie Klein Volume III: Envy and Gratitude and Other Works 1946–1963* (New York: Free Press, 1975), 262.

37. Klein, "Love, Guilt and Reparation," 310.

38. Ibid., 65–66. Klein and many other analysts in the relational tradition have used "phantasy" to denote the workings of the unconscious, differentiating between unconscious phantasy and conscious fantasy.

39. Emili Steuerman, *The Bounds of Reason: Habermas, Lyotard, and Melanie Klein on Rationality* (New York: Routledge, 1999), 71.

40. Hinshelwood, *A Dictionary of Kleinian Thought*, 399.

41. Klein, "Love, Guilt and Reparation," 326.

42. Alford, *Melanie Klein and Critical Social Theory*, 42

43. For one example, see John D. Cash, *Identity, Ideology and Conflict: The Structuration of Politics in Northern Ireland* (Cambridge: Cambridge University Press, 1996).

44. Hanna Segal, *Introduction to the Work of Melanie Klein, Second Edition* (New York: Basic Books, 1974), 95–96.

45. Klein, "Love, Guilt, and Reparation," 333–34.

46. The result is often referred to as spiritual or "secondary" virginity.

47. See Luke, 10:25–37.

48. The parable is commonly invoked in ministerial contexts, but see also Brian Keith Williams, *Ministering to the Gay and Lesbian Community: Pouring in the Oil and the Wine* (Shippensburg, PA: Destiny Image, 2005), 17–19.

49. David Bereit and Fr. Frank Pavone, "Day 8: Be a Good Samaritan," email message to 40 Days for Life subscribers, October 1, 2008. In the first Bereit quote the ellipsis is in the original.

50. Letha Dawson Scanzoni and Virginia Ramey Mollenkott, *Is the Homosexual My Neighbor?* revised and updated edition (San Francisco: HarperSanFrancisco, 1994). See especially chapter 3, "The Homosexual as Samaritan." Another example occurred during an interview on British television in 1980 when Prime Minister Margaret Thatcher invoked the parable to redescribe her economic policies as compassionate. When the interviewer pressed her to concede that a policy under discussion would "mean more inequality," Thatcher replied: "Does mean more. . . . yes indeed, if opportunity and talent is unequally distributed, then allowing people to exercise that talent and opportunity means more inequality, but it means you drag up the poor people, because there are the resources to do so. No-one would remember the good Samaritan if he'd only had good intentions; he had money as well." See Margaret Thatcher, "TV Interview for London Weekend Television *Weekend World* (January 6, 1980) "http://www.margaretthatcher.org/speeches/displaydocument.asp?docid=104210 (accessed May 11, 2009).

51. John D. Cash, *Identity, Ideology and Conflict: The Structuration of Politics in Northern Ireland* (Cambridge: Cambridge University Press, 1996), 76.

52. Benedict Anderson, *Imagined Communities: Reflections on the Origin and Spread of Nationalism* (New York: Verso, 1991). Anderson does not use psychoanalysis to reflect on nationalist group identities and their variations.

53. In *Healing Identities* I made something like this distinction between good and bad groups to explore the idea that, even if we remain wary of the malign things groups do, it matters both that some groups and group identifications are less destructive than others and what the sources of those differences might be. See Cynthia Burack, *Healing Identities: Black Feminist Thought and the Politics of Groups* (Ithaca, NY: Cornell University Press, 2004).

54. W. R. Bion, *Experiences in Groups and Other Papers* (London: Routledge, 1989), 88.

55. Elliott Jaques, "Social Systems as Defense against Persecutory and Depressive Anxiety: A Contribution to the Psycho-Analytical Study of Social Processes," in *New Directions in Psychoanalysis* ed. Melanie Klein, Paula Heimann, and R. E. Money-Kyrle (London: Tavistock, 1955), 478–98.

56. Hinshelwood, *A Dictionary of Kleinian Thought*, 162. For an example of this interpretation, see Howard F. Stein, "The Indispensable Enemy and American-Soviet Relations," in *The Psychodynamics of International Relationships. Volume 1: Concepts and Theories*, ed. Vamik Volkan, Demetrios A. Julius, and Joseph V. Montville (Lexington, MA: Lexington Books, 1990), 71–89.

57. Vamik Volkan, *The Need to Have Enemies and Allies: From Clinical Practice to International Relationships* (Northvale, NJ: Jason Aronson, 1988),

58. Alford, *Melanie Klein and Critical Social Theory*, 88.

59. S. H. Foulkes, *Selected Papers of S. H. Foulkes: Psychoanalysis and Group Analysis* (London: Karnac Books, 1990), 292.

60. For an account of the psychosocial tasks of group leaders, see Burack, *Healing Identities*, 71–85.

61. C. Fred Alford, *Group Psychology and Political Theory* (New Haven, CT: Yale University Press, 1994), 59 61. See also D. W. Winnicott, *Holding and Interpretation* (New York: Grove, 1986).

62. Pierre Turquet, "Threats to Identity in the Large Group," in *The Large Group: Dynamics and Therapy*, ed. Lionel Kreeger (Itaska, IL: F. E. Peacock, 1975), 118.

63. Charles W. Mills, *The Racial Contract* (Ithaca, NY: Cornell University Press, 1997), 18.

64. Ibid., 19.

65. Hanna Biran, "'Attacks on Linking' and 'Alpha Function' as Two Opposite Elements in the Dynamics of Organizations," in *Building on Bion: Branches. Contemporary Developments and Applications of Bion's Contributions to Theory and Practices*, ed. Robert Lipgar and Malcolm Pines (London: Jessica Kingsley, 2003), 166. See also W. R. Bion, *Second Thoughts: Selected Papers on Psycho-Analysis* (New York: Jason Aronson, 1984), 102.

66. C. Fred Alford, *Psychology and the Natural Law of Reparation* (Cambridge: Cambridge University Press, 2006), 93.

67. Robert Caper, "Envy, Narcissism and the Destructive Instinct," in *Envy and Gratitude Revisited* ed. Priscilla Roth and Alessandra Lemma (London: Karnac Books, 2008) 42; 40. See also, Michael A. Milburn and Sheree D. Conrad, *The Politics of Denial* (Cambridge: MIT Press, 1996).

68. Bion, *Second Thoughts*, 106–07.

69. Hannah Arendt, "On Humanity in Dark Times: Thoughts about Lessing," in *Men in Dark Times* (New York: Harcourt, Brace and World, 1968), 13.

70. As examples, see John Gibson, *The War on Christmas: How the Liberal Plot to Ban the Sacred Holiday Is Worse Than You Thought* (New York: Sentinel HC, 2005) and David Limbaugh, *Persecution: How Liberals Are Waging War against Christianity* (Washington, DC: Regnery, 2003). The cover of Limbaugh's book features a stalking lion, and the "t" in Persecution is a cross.

71. Main, "Some Psychodynamics of Large Groups," 86, 60, 85.

72. Malcolm Pines, "Overview" in *The Large Group: Dynamics and Therapy*, ed. Lionel Kreeger (Itaska, IL: F. E. Peacock, 1975), 294.

73. C. Fred Alford, *Group Psychology and Political Theory*, 55.

74. Patrick B. De Maré, Robin Piper, Sheila Thompson, *Koinonia: From Hate, through Dialogue, to Culture in the Large Group* (London: Karnac Books, 1991), 25.

75. Burack, *Healing Identities*, 60.

76. Stein, "The Indispensable Enemy and American-Soviet Relations," 73.

77. See Turquet, "Threats to Identity in the Large Group."

78. The skepticism about group boundaries in psychoanalytic social theory is consistent with that found in much feminist thought. Stein notes that "the 'boundary' is . . . a sacred illusion and delusion, often defended to the death to keep the 'good' inside and the 'bad' outside." See Stein, "The Indispensable Enemy and American-Soviet Relations," 73.

79. Pew Forum on Religion and Public Life, "Religious Beliefs Underpin Opposition to Homosexuality" (*Pew Forum*, November 18, 2003) http://pewforum.org/docs/index. php?DocID=37 (accessed July 22, 2005).

80. Cynthia Burack, field notes, Love Won Out conference, Mechanicsburg, Pennsylvania, September 22, 2012.

81. Alford, *Psychology and the Natural Law of Reparation*, 101–03. See also Donald Meltzer, *The Kleinian Development* (London: Karnac Books, 1998), 190.

82. Steuerman, *The Bounds of Reason*, 70. See also Segal, *Introduction to the Work of Melanie Klein*, 84, 95; Alford, *Psychology and the Natural Law of Reparation*, 101.

83. Tony Campolo and Peggy Campolo, "Tony and Peggy Campolo: Is the Homosexual My Neighbor?" (Bridges across the Divide, no date) http://www.bridges-across.org/ba/campolo.htm (accessed October, 2008).

84. R. D. Hinshelwood, *Clinical Klein: From Theory to Practice* (New York: Basic Books, 1004), 84.

85. Klein and Riviere, *Love, Hate, and Reparation*, 66.

86. For a psychoanalytic account of how Christian right social outgroups can function as enemies, see Cynthia Burack, "God, Gays, and Good-Enough Enemies." *Psychoanalysis, Culture, and Society*, 14, no. 1 (2009): 41–48.

87. See Jyl J. Josephson and Cynthia Burack, "Inside, Out, and In-Between: Sexual Minorities, the Christian Right and the Evangelical Lutheran Church in

America," in *Religion, Politics, and American Identity: New Directions, New Controversies*, David S. Gutterman and Andrew R. Murphy (Lanham, MD: Lexington Books, 2006), 247–65.

88. "We stand on the side of love" is a principle espoused by Unitarian Universalist Congregations in Maryland, Washington, DC, and Northern Virginia (no date) http://www.md-dc-va-churches.org/religion-welcoming-all?gclid=CLyIs 5nZ16ICFcdS6wod8SYIzA (accessed July 6, 2010).

89. Ellen Riggle, Jerry D. Thomas, and Sharon S. Rostosky, "The Marriage Debate and Minority Stress," *PS: Political Science and Politics* 38 (2005): 222.

90. Dawne Moon, *God, Sex, and Politics: Homosexuality and Everyday Theologies* (Chicago: University of Chicago Press, 2004). See especially chapter 8: "Gay Pain and Politics."

91. Shane Phelan refers to this move as "credentialing by pain" and, although she reads it as an assimilationist political strategy, she does not reject it outright as she does other assimilationist strategies, noting only that the move is an attempt to "'put a human face' on a social problem. . . . [by] appeal[ing] to the heterosexual reader who thinks of homosexuals as 'them.'" See Phelan, *Sexual Strangers: Gays, Lesbians, and Dilemmas of Citizenship* (Philadelphia, PA: Temple University Press), 284–85.

92. James L. Gibson, *Overcoming Apartheid: Can Truth Reconcile a Divided Nation?* (New York: Russell Sage Foundation, 2004), 159–62, 263–64, 284–855, 337.

93. Rebecca Wanzo, *The Suffering Will Not Be Televised: African American Women and Sentimental Political Storytelling* (Albany: State University of New York Press, 2009), 3, 6, 9. "Social problems marketplace" is a term Wanzo borrows from Joel Best.

94. Michael A. Milburn and Sheree D. Conrad, *The Politics of Denial* (Cambridge: MIT Press, 1996), 8.

95. For a study of feminist appropriations of Klein and of feminist ambivalence toward the disagreeable passions, see Cynthia Burack, *The Problem of the Passions: Feminism, Psychoanalysis, and Social Theory* (New York: New York University Press, 1994).

96. Alford, *Melanie Klein and Critical Social Theory*, 197. Kristeva cites Klein for having inspired a broad scope of "political reflections" from clinical work that did not, in the first instance, focus attention on "modern history and society." See Kristeva, *Melanie Klein*, 231.

Afterword

1. Jonathan Chait, "Miss Guided: Carrie Prejean and Other Anti-Gay-Marriage Intellectuals," *The New Republic* (June 17, 2009) http://www.tnr.com/article/miss-guided-0 (accessed May 31, 2010).

2. Janice McLaughlin, Mark E. Casey, and Diane Richardson, "Introduction: At the Intersections of Feminist and Queer Debates," in *Intersections between*

Feminist and Queer Theory, ed. Diane Richardson, Janice McLaughlin, and Mark E. Casey (New York: Palgrave, 2006), 2.

3. Dahlia Lithwick, "Once More, without Feeling: The GOP's Misguided and Confused Campaign against Judicial Empathy" (*Slate*, May 11, 2009) http://www.slate.com/id/2218103/ (accessed May 11, 2009). Emphasis is in the original.

4. Many critics have disagreed with Arendt's conception of Eichmann; for a recent dissent see Deborah E. Lipstadt, *The Eichmann Trial* (New York: Schoken Books, 2011).

5. Hannah Arendt, "'What Remains? The Language Remains': A Conversation with Günter Gaus," in *The Portable Hannah Arendt, ed.* Peter Baehr (New York: Penguin, 2000), 16, 19.

6. Tamsin Bradley, "Does Compassion Bring Results? A Critical Perspective on Faith and Development," *Culture and Religion* 6, no. 3 (2005): 341, 348, 343, 341.

7. For the central importance of this concept for Rand see Anne C. Heller, *Ayn Rand and the World She Made* (New York: Nan A. Talese/Doubleday, 2009).

8. My favorite example in this area is an obscure textbook used to train members of the Hitler Youth, which employs illustrations with captions explaining the "unity" of physical, mental, and spiritual characteristics of "every human being." See Harwood L. Childs, trans., *The Nazi Primer: Official Handbook for Schooling the Hitler Youth* (New York: Harper and Brothers, 1938), 15.

9. Nathaniel Branden, "The Benefits and Hazards of the Philosophy of Ayn Rand: A Personal Statement" (*The Website of Dr. Nathaniel Branden*, 1984) http://www.nathanielbranden.com/articles/catalog_essays/benefits_and_hazards.html (accessed May 27, 2009). Emphasis in the original.

10. Ayn Rand, "The Goal of My Writing," in *The Romantic Manifesto* (New York: Signet, 1971), 162, 163. Emphasis in the original.

11. A provocative lens for distinguishing Rand from both Arendt and Klein can be found in the distinction between "written" and "unwritten worlds." Both Arendt and Klein set out to describe actually existing realities that are independent of the observer's description of them at the same time that they invite and require theoretical description and redescription. Rand produced a fictional world that is normative, hortatory, and she hoped, irresistible in its persuasive force on readers. For an analysis of the difference between these "worlds," see Simon Stow, *Republic of Readers? The Literary Turn in Political Thought and Analysis* (Albany: State University of New York Press, 2007).

12. Bruce Headlam, "Forget Joyce, Bring on Ayn Rand," (The New York Times, 1998) http://tech2.nytimes.com/mem/technology/techreview.html?_r=1&res=9B01E5DC1738F933A05754C0A96E958260&oref=login (accessed February 2, 2007).

13. Compared to the extensive web presence of objectivist and pro-Rand writing, there is a small anti-Rand presence on the web. See, for example, the blog "Ayn Rand Contra Human Nature," http://aynrandcontrahumannature.blogspot.com/.

14. Linda Kintz does not mention Rand in her genealogy of right-wing thought, but this is an odd omission. Kintz stresses the theme of victimization that runs through entrepreneurial and "frontier ideology" and the belief that entrepreneurs receive little in comparison to their contributions to human welfare. Both are favorite themes of Rand's in fiction and nonfiction. See Linda Kintz, *Between Jesus and the Market: The Emotions that Matter in Right-Wing America* (Durham, NC: Duke University Press, 1997), 192–97.

15. Barbara Grizzuti Harrison, "Psyching Out Ayn Rand," in *Feminist Interpretations of Ayn Rand*, ed. Mimi Reisel Gladstein and Chris Matthew Sciabarra (University Park: Pennsylvania State University Press, 1999), 67–76. In his memoir of the early days of objectivism, Jerome Tuccille addresses Rand directly as "Ayn, you sweet, loveable, crazy bitch." Tuccille, *It Usually Begins with Ayn Rand. Twenty-fifth Anniversary Edition* (San Francisco: Fox and Wilkes, 1997), 179.

16. Jennifer Burns, *Goddess of the Market: Ayn Rand and the American Right* (Oxford: Oxford University Press, 2009), 4.

17. BB&T, a banking company headquartered in North Carolina, has donated millions of dollars to American institutions of higher education to endow chairs in the study of Rand and objectivism and with the stipulation either that particular books, such as *Atlas Shrugged*, will be taught or that professors will integrate Rand's work and perspectives into programs and courses. Recipients who have agreed to BB&T's terms in order to receive the funds include the University of Texas at Austin (BB&T Chair for the Study of Objectivism and the Anthem Fellowship for the Study of Objectivism), Johnson C. Smith University (Ayn Rand essay scholarships that link students directly to the Ayn Rand Institute), Marshall University (the BB&T Center for the Advancement of American Capitalism at the Lewis College of Business), and the University of North Carolina, Charlotte (Ayn Rand Reading Room). See Matthew, Keenan, "CEOs Pushing Ayn Rand Studies Use Money to Overcome Resistance" (Boomburg.com, April 11, 2008) http://www.bloomberg.com/apps/news?pid=20601109&sid=as6BR0QV4KE8&refer=home (accessed April 7, 2009); Office of Public Affairs, "Symposium Celebrates Ayn Rand's *Atlas Shrugged* (University of Texas at Austin, February 9, 2009) http://www.utexas.edu/news/2009/02/09/atlas-shrugged/ (accessed April 6, 2009).

18. Roy Edroso, "Rightbloggers Say: Go Galt! We'll Catch Up with You Later!" (*Village Voice*, March 9, 2009) http://blogs.villagevoice.com/runninscared/archives/2009/03/rightbloggers_s_1.php (accessed April 6, 2009).

19. For an example of the latter, see "Going Galt Is New Code Word For 'Laid Off'" (*Wonkette*, March 18, 2009) http://wonkette.com/407074/going-galt-is-new-code-word-for-laid-off (accessed April 6, 2009).

20. Gary Weiss, *Ayn Rand Nation* (New York: St. Martin's, 2012), 157–58.

21. Burns, *Goddess of the Market*, 247–78.

22. *Atlas Shrugged* was in production when Rand was asked by a Random House book representative if she could recite the essential tenets of her philosophy while standing on one foot. She did so. I have added "psychology" to the list she offered because psychology has played a large role in the theory and practice

of objectivism. See Ayn Rand Institute, "Essentials of Objectivism" (*Ayn Rand Institute*, 2009) http://www.aynrand.org/site/PageServer?pagename=objectivism_essentials (accessed July 3, 2009).

23. Kristeva, *Melanie Klein*, 11.

24. Phyllis Grosskurth, *Melanie Klein: Her World and Her Work* (New York: Alfred A. Knopf, 1986), 196.

25. Hannah Arendt, *The Life of the Mind: Thinking* (New York: Harcourt Brace Jovanovich, 1978). See especially part 3, "What Makes Us Think?" Arendt completed the first two parts of what was to be a three-part volume; she had only begun to write the final part, *Judging*, at the time of her death in 1975.

26. Elisabeth Young-Bruehl, *Mind and the Body Politic* (New York: Routledge, 1989), 24, 43.

27. C. Fred Alford, *Psychology and the Natural Law of Reparation* (Cambridge: Cambridge University Press, 2006), 96.

28. Robert M. Young, "Bion and Experiences in Groups" (*Robert M. Young*, 2005) http://www.human-nature.com/rmyoung/papers/pap148h.html (accessed August, 23, 2009).

29. Jonathan Haidt and Jesse Graham, "When Morality Opposes Justice: Conservatives Have Moral Intuitions That Liberals May Not Recognize, *Social Justice Research* 20 (2007): 113, 101.

30. Yoel Inbar, David A. Pizarro, and Paul Bloom, "Conservatives Are More Easily Disgusted Than Liberals," *Cognition and Emotion* 23, no. 4 (2008).

31. In research conducted by Erik G. Helzer and David A. Pizarro, the mere suggestion to research subjects that the environment in which they were responding to questions might be dirty prompted more conservative responses in those subjects, especially regarding issues related to sexuality. See Helzer and Pizarro, "Dirty Liberals! Reminders of Physical Cleanliness Influence Moral and Political Attitudes" 22, no. 4 (2011): 517–22.

32. Susan B. Miller, *Disgust: The Gatekeeper Emotion* (Hillsdale, NJ: Analytic, 2004), 114.

33. Martha C. Nussbaum, *Hiding from Humanity: Disgust, Shame, and the Law* (Princeton, NJ: Princeton University Press, 2006); *From Disgust to Humanity: Sexual Orientation and Constitutional Law* (Oxford: Oxford University Press, 2010).

34. Mary Anne Case, "A Lot to Ask: Review Essay of Martha Nussbaum's *From Disgust to Humanity: Sexual Orientation and Constitutional Law*," *Columbia Journal of Gender and Law* 19, no. 1 (2010).

35. Nussbaum, *From Disgust to Humanity*, xviii.

36. Ibid., 205–06. For Elisabeth Young-Bruehl's psychoanalytic taxonomy of prejudices see *The Anatomy of Prejudices* (Cambridge, MA: Harvard University Press, 1998).

37. In a poll conducted for the University of Washington Institute for the Study of Ethnicity, Race, and Sexuality (WISER), political scientists Matt A. Barreto and Christopher Parker found not only antigay but also racist beliefs to be common among those who approved of the tea party movement. For example,

of those who strongly approved of the tea party, 46 percent agreed that "if blacks would only try harder they would be just as well off as whites" (versus 26 percent for all voters). See "May 2010 Washington Poll" (*WISER*, May 2010) http://www.washingtonpoll.org/results/June1_teaparty.pdf (accessed September 22, 2010).

38. These and other experimental conditions are tested and the results reported in Simone Schnall, Jonathan Haidt, Gerald L. Clore, and Alexander H. Jordan, "Disgust as Embodied Moral Judgment," *Personality and Social Psychology Bulletin* 34, no. 8 (2008): 1096–1109. See also Helzer and Pizarro, "Dirty Liberals! Reminders of Physical Cleanliness Influence Moral and Political Attitudes."

39. John Alan Lee and Sheldon Ungar, "A Coding Method for the Analysis of Moral Discourse," *Human Relations* 42, no. 8 (1989): 693.

40. There is a large literature on uses of fetal imagery, but see: Nick Hopkins, Suzanne Zeedyk, and Fiona Raitt, "Visualizing Abortion: Emotion Discourse and Fetal Imagery in a Contemporary Abortion Debate," *Social Science and Medicine* 61 (2005): 393–403. For the tactical use of—and advocacy for—fetal images intended to encourage pregnant women to bear children, see Carol Stabile, "Shooting the Mother: Fetal Photography and the Politics of Disappearance," *Camera Obscura* 28 (1992): 178–205.

41. See, for example, Jasper A. J. Smits, Michael Joseph Telch, and Patrick K. Randall, "An Examination of the Decline in Fear and Disgust during Exposure-Based Treatment," *Behaviour Research and Therapy* 40, no. 11 (2002): 1243–53; William Ian Miller, *The Anatomy of Disgust* (Cambridge, MA: Harvard University Press, 1998).

42. Paul Cameron, "Homosexuals Disruptive from the 'Get-Go'" (*Family Research Institute*, September, 2011) http://www.familyresearchinst.org/2011/09/frr-sep-2011-%E2%80%94-homosexuals-disruptive-from-the-get-go/ (accessed March, 11, 2012).

43. Paul Cameron, "The Psychology of Homosexuality" (*Family Research Institute*, February 3, 2009) http://www.familyresearchinst.org/2009/02/the-psychology-of-homosexuality/ (accessed March 11, 2012).

44. Cameron founded the Institute for the Scientific Investigation of Sexuality in 1982, and in 1987 he renamed the organization the Family Research Institute.

45. National Organization for Marriage, "Marriage Talking Points" (*National Organization for Marriage*, 2011) http://www.nationformarriage.org/site/c.omL2KeN0LzH/b.4475595/k.566A/Marriage_Talking_Points.htm (accessed March 30, 2011). Emphasis in the original.

46. Gary D. Sherman and Jonathan Haidt, "Cuteness and Disgust: The Humanizing and Dehumanizing Effects of Emotion," *Emotion Review* 3, no. 3 (2011): 246; Jennifer L. Goetz, Dacher Keltner, and Emiliana Simon-Thomas, "Compassion: An Evolutionary Analysis and Empirical Review," *Psychological Bulletin* 136, no. 3 (2010): 351–74.

47. In a classic essay, Max Weber argued for the incompatibility of politics and Christian compassion in a way that frequently has been echoed by champions of church-state separation as well as by many fundamentalists: "[A]nyone seeking

to save his own soul and the souls of others does not take the path of politics in order to reach his goal, for politics has quite different tasks, namely those which can only be achieved by force. The genius—or demon—of politics lives in a state of inner tension with the god of love, and even with the Christian God as manifested in the institution of the church, a tension that may erupt at any moment into irresolvable conflict." Max Weber, "The Profession and Vocation of Politics," in *Identity: A Reader, ed.* Paul du Gay, Jessica Evans, and Peter Redman (London: Sage, 2000), 356. The essay has also been translated and published under the title "Politics as a Vocation."

Index

abstinence-only sex education, 48, 70
accountability partner(s), 10, 46
African American(s), 77–78, 128, 135, 151, 172, 187
   see also race, racism
agape, 98–99
Alcorn, Randy, 200n35
Alford, C. Fred, 160, 163, 185, 216n95, 224n14, 229n96
Allen, Peter L., 206n20
Altemeyer, Bob, 215n71
ambivalence, 143, 160, 184
American Association of Christian Counselors, 31
   see also Christian therapy
American Life League, 108
American Psychiatric Association, 30
American Psychological Association, 31, 65–66, 68–69
American Revolution, 88, 90, 93–95
American University, 19
Anderson, Benedict, 226n52
Anglicans for Life, 71, 108
anti-Semitism, 151; *see also* Jewish identity
Apartheid, *see* Truth and Reconciliation Commission
Arendt, Hannah, 111–13, 150–51, 160, 184–85, 191
   and compassion, 25, 85–99, 176, 178–80
   and Christianity, 109–10

and plurality, 99–106
Arias, Rhonda, 67
Aristotle, 5, 90, 92
Arkansas, University of, 20–21
Atlas Shrugged, 117–19, 122, 129–30, 133–34, 140, 182–83
Augustine, 109–10, 154, 164
Ayn Rand Institute, 216n96

Bachmann, Marcus, 34
Bachmann, Michele, 33–34, 40, 125
Bader, Eleanor J., 195n33, 205n14
Bailey, J. Michael, 51
Baird-Windle, Patricia, 195n33, 205n14
Baker, Christopher R., 214n52
Balmer, Randall, 58
Barclay, Scott, 214n64
Barkun, Michael, 199n10
Barker, James, 3
Barreto, Matt A., 232n37
Barton, David, 141
Bauer, Gary, 108–09, 195n28
Bazelon, Emily, 67
BB&T, 182
Bechdel, Alison, 200n32
Becker, Davida, 207n37
Beck, Glenn, 115
Beckstead, A. Lee, 210n74
Beckwith, Francis, 64
Beiner, Ronald, 212n33
Beliles, Mark A., 222n90

Benham, Philip "Flip," 59–60, 209n61
Benjamin, Jessica, 224n11
Bennett, William J., 8
Bereit, David, 108, 155
Berlant, Lauren, 5, 197n54
Berlet, Chip, 2
Bertonneau, Thomas F., 133–34
Besen, Wayne, 198n3, 200n25
Bessett, Danielle, 207n37
Bickford, Susan, 214n57
Bieber, Irving, 32
Big Five model of personality, 3
Bion, Wilfred, 157, 159, 185, 227n65
Biran, Hanna, 227n65
birth control, *see* contraception
Black Church, 43
Black, Stephen, 52
Blankenhorn, David, 223n2
Bloom, Paul, 197n61, 232n30
Bob Jones University, 58
Bohman, James, 214n54
Bowlby, John, 223n2
Boynes, Janet, 40–43
Bradley, Tamsin, 180
Branden, Barbara, 122, 125
Branden, Nathaniel, 121–22, 124, 127, 142, 181, 218n20
Brent, Linda, *see* Jacobs, Harriet
British School, *see* psychoanalysis
Brownback, Sam, 109
Brown, Susan Love, 126
Brown v. Board of Education, 42, 86, 187
Bryant, Anita, 135
bullying, 83
Burlein, Ann, 193n4
Burns, Jennifer, 182, 217n5, 217n14
Bush, George W., 6, 9, 70, 96
Bush, Jeb, 208n45
Buss, Doris, 7

Cadge, Wendy, 102
Cahill, Sean, 216n81
Cameron, Paul, 188–89, 213n40

Campbell, Cordy, 49
Campbell, Nancy, 8
Campolo, Peggy, 164–67
Campolo, Tony, 164–67
Canada, 74
Canino-Hussung, Mishara, 213n50
Canovan, Margaret, 89
Caper, Robert, 227n67
capitalism, 113, 136–37, 116–18, 135–37
caritas, 109–10
Carney, Dana Rose, 194n9
Case, Mary Anne, 187
Casey, Mark, 177
Cash, John D., 226n43, 226n51
Catholic(ism), 13, 33, 58, 78, 132
Catholic University School of Law, 51
Center for Urban Renewal and Education (CURE), 6
Centre for Social Justice, 18
Chait, Jonathan, 175
Chambers, Alan, 16, 36, 51–53, 80, 202n60
Chiba, Shin, 98–99
Chick tracts, 13, 222n95
Childs, Harwood L., 230n8
Chodorow, Nancy J., 224n11
Christian Coalition, 1
Christian therapy, 38–39
ChristianNewsWire, 33
Christians for Biblical Equality (CBE), 18
CitizenLink, 33
  see also Focus on the Family
citizenship, 99, 106, 110, 112, 186
Civil Rights Acts, 42, 135
climate change, 1
Clore, Gerald L., 233n38
co-belligerence, 9
Comiskey, Andrew, 52
compassionate conservatism, *see* conservatism, compassionate
Concerned Women for America (CWA), 21, 62, 77, 106

congruence, 51, 54
Connolly, William, 117
Conrad, Sheree D., 172, 227n67
conservatism, compassionate, 2, 6–8, 18, 85
ConservativeHome, 8–9
Conservative Political Action Conference (CPAC), 2007, 15
contraception, 10, 78
  opposition to, 24, 72, 99, 136, 186, 213n51
conversion therapy(ies), *see* reparative therapy
Cooperman, Alan, 193n1
Corbett, Christopher, 199n12
Coulter, Ann, 9, 15, 108
Courage, 132
CovenantEyes, 46
Craig, Barbara Hinkson, 205n6
Cress, Donald A., 194n13
Crisis Pregnancy Center(s), 6, 11, 69–72, 78
Curro, Ellen, 70–72
CyberPatrol, 45

Dailard, Cynthia, 208n45
Dailey, Timothy J., 197n63
Dallas, Joe, 16, 52, 163
d'Anconia, Francisco, 122
Davies, Bob, 200n27
Dean, Tim, 196n50
Declaration of Independence, 107
defenses, *see* denial, idealization, identification, projection, splitting
Degeneres, Ellen, 43
Desert Stream Ministries, 52
democracy, 27, 103, 105, 186, 189
  see also citizenship
Democratic National Convention, 2008, 1
denial, 26, 146, 159, 164, 168, 185
depressive position, 148–49, 152–53, 162–64, 168
  see also Klein, Melanie

de Magalhães, Theresa Calvet, 216n90
De Maré, Patrick B., 228n74
DeYoung, Colin G., 194n10
De Zordo, Silvia, 207n37
Diagnostic and Statistical Manual of Mental Disorders (DSM), 30
Diamond, Sara, 206n24, 209n70
Dillard, Angela, 42, 195n24, 210n3
Dinnerstein, Dorothy, 224n11
Dionne, E. J., 217n10
Disch, Lisa Jane, 212n30, 215n66
disgust, 19–23, 131, 153, 155, 186–88, 190
  and democracy, 27
  as God-given, 39, 81, 121, 139, 162, 188
Doan, Alesha E., 205n16, 215n80
Dobson, James, 33, 224n12
Dolphin, Lambert, 49
Dollimore, Jonathan, 196n50
Dominici, Thomas, 198n5, 224n10
Dossa, Shiraz, 211n20, 216n93
Dostoyevsky, Fyodor, 89
Drescher, Jack, 31, 198n2, 212n29
D'Souza, Dinesh, 135
du Gay, Paul, 234n47

Eckholm, Erik, 203n77
Edroso, Roy, 182–83
Edwards, John, 16
Ehrenreich, Barbara, 46–47
Eichmann, Adolf, 175, 179, 184
Eichmann in Jerusalem, 87, 91
Elliot, Elisabeth, 224n12
Elliot Institute, 62, 76–77
  see also Reardon, David C.
Ellison, Christopher G., 220n45
Ellison, Ralph, 151, 210n5
empathy, 92, 102, 150–51, 176, 179, 180
enlarged mentality, *see* representative thinking
Ertelt, Steven, 207n38
Erzen, Tanya, 36, 45, 131, 200n23, 212n38, 219n36

eschatology, 133–34, 221n64
ethnography, 15
Evangelical and Ecumenical Women's Caucus, 18
Evans, Jessica, 234n47
ex-gay testimony(ies), 39–40, 44, 81, 132
Exhale, 68–69
Exodus Church Network, 47
Exodus International, 33, 36, 47, 50, 107
   changes to, 52–53, 164, 214n63
   founding of, 35
   Freedom Conference, 31, 37, 45, 49, 51, 200n33
   Member Ministries, 47
   Student Ministries, 40
   see also Chambers, Alan

Faces of Abortion, 107–08
Falwell, Jerry, 132–33
Family Research Council (FRC), 22, 41, 66, 108, 216n81
Family Research Institute, 189
family, the, 3; natural, 14
feminism, 7, 98, 125–26, 134–35, 147, 150
Fergusson, David M., 66–67
Firehammer, Reginald, 120
First Stone Ministries, 52
Flax, Jane, 223n4
Focus on the Family, 33, 36–37, 106–07
Forney, Georgette, 108
40 Days for Life, 108, 155, 213n51
Foucault, Michel, 45
Foulkes, S. H., 227n59
Fountainhead, The, 117, 122, 129–30, 140, 182
Francon, Dominique, 123, 131
   see also *The Fountainhead*
Fraser, Mary, 220n53
Friedman, Richard C., 223n1
French Revolution, 88, 90, 92, 94–95

Freud, Anna, 223n2
Freud, Sigmund, 143, 146–48, 184
Friberg, Urban, 203n76
Fryrear, Melissa, 37, 49, 200n29

Gagnon, Robert, 52
Galt, John, 119
   see also *Atlas Shrugged*
Garrett, Scott, 75
Gaus, Günter, 179
Gavrilets, Sergey, 203n76
Gay and Lesbian Alliance against Defamation (GLAAD), 21–22
Geller, Pamela, 115
gender
   complementarity, 32, 38, 121, 123–25, 143, 198n6
   identity, 10, 17, 33, 36, 148, 170
   role(s), 31–32, 38, 101
Genesis Counseling, 52
genocide, 14, 99
Genocide Awareness Project (GAP), 59
Gerson, Michael, 9
Gibson, James L., 171
Gibson, John, 228n70
Gilgoff, Dan, 204n85
Ginsburg, Faye, 75
Gladstein, Mimi Reisel, 220n47
Glamour (magazine), 68
Goeke, Mike, 163
Goetz, Jennifer L., 233n46
Goffman, Erving, 80
Goldwater, Barry, 118
Gonzales v. Carhart, 76
Gordon, Linda, 220n53
Gosling, Samuel, 194n9
Good Samaritan, 154–56, 161, 164, 216n84
Graham, Elaine L., 214n52
Graham, Jesse, 186
Gramzow, Richard H., 207n37
Green, John C., 194n12
Green v. Connally, 58

Greta, Andrew, 217n18
Grief (novel), 19
Grimshaw, Jean, 223n3
Griswold v. Connecticut, 10, 135
Grosskurth, Phyllis, 225n25, 232n24
guilt, 69, 133
    attempt to avoid, 143, 159
    for Christian conservatives, 38–39, 72, 109, 168–69
    related to doing harm, 146, 152, 162–63, 166–67, 171, 185
Gutterman, David, 103, 202n64, 212n30

Haidt, Jonathan, 186, 190, 233n38
Hallman, Janelle, 33
Hamburger, Joseph, 212–13n39
Hancock, Ange-Marie, 21, 103
Hardesty, Jean, 199n15
Harding, Sandra, 223n4
Harrison, Barbara Grizzuti, 182
Harrison, Kristin, 207n42
hate crimes, 83
Hazen, Don, 217n2
Headlam, Bruce, 230n12
Healing the Effects of Abortion Related Trauma (HEART), 72
Heche, Anne, 43
Heche, Nancy, 43–44
Hedgebuilders, 46
Heller, Anne C., 119, 218n28, 230n7
Helzer, Erik G., 232n31
Hendershot, Heather, 223n95
Herman, Didi, 7, 34
Herrnstein, Richard J., 194n18
Hessini, Leila, 68
Heteronormative(ity), 20
Hickman, William, 116
Highly, Joanna, 213n50
Hinshelwood, R. D., 152, 225n25
Hintikka, Merrill B., 223n4
Hirsch, Fred, 222n81
Hirsch, Jacob B., 194n10
Hispanic women, 78

HIV/AIDS, 62
Hofstadter, Richard, 141
Holleran, Andrew, 19
Holocaust, *see* Nazi
homophile movement, 10
homophobia, 19–21
Honig, Bonnie, 214n55
Hook, Sidney, 140
Hopkins, Nick, 233n40
Horwood, L. John, 66
Hull, Margaret Betz, 101
Human Condition, The, 100, 110, 211n26
Hume, David, 173
Hunter, Joel, 1–2, 164
Hussung, Bill, 213n50

Ianora, Terry, 70
idealization, 149, 173
    and groups, 27, 157–58, 161, 168–69, 185
identification, 102, 104, 156, 180
    in groups, 152, 157–58, 162, 168–69
    resistance to, 143
immutability (of sexual identity), 33, 42, 50–54, 167
Inbar, Yoel, 22, 232n30
incest, 57, 63
Ingersoll, Julie, 18
Inhofe, James, 108
Iowa Caucuses (2012), 9
Islam, 13

Jackson, Harry R., 40
Jacobs, Harriet, 5
Jaques, Elliott, 157–58
Janet Boynes Ministries, *see* Boynes, Janet
Jefferson, Thomas, 88
Jenkins, Jerry B. 134
Jewish Agency, 100
Jewish identity, x, 86–87, 91, 100–01, 161, 179

Joffe, Carole, 77–78, 208n46
John, book of, 216n82
Jones, Kathleen, 88–89
Jones, Patricia, 201n38
Jordan, Alexander H., 233n38
Josephson, Jyl J., 36, 45, 50, 195n34, 202n64, 201n75
Jost, John, 194n9
Justice Foundation, 76, 107, 215n76

Kalmar, Roberta, 205–06n18
Kant, Immanuel, 92, 103
Kaplan, Morris, 86
Kateb, George, 87–88, 97
Kavanaugh, Megan L., 207n37
Keltner, Dacher, 233n46
Kennedy, Anthony, 76
Kennedy, D. James, 133
Khan, Surina, 196n42
Kintz, Linda, 8, 213n41, 231n14
Kitzinger, Celia, 225n34
Klein, Melanie, 26–27, 143, 176, 178, 183–85, 191
  model of development, 146–54
  and application to groups, 156–74
Kline, Phill, 108
Knights of Columbus, 73
Knobe, Joshua, 197n61
Kohn, Jerome, 214n54
Koop, C. Everett, 61–62, 67, 206n27
Kramer, Larry, 210n4
Kreeger, Lionel, 228n72
Kristeva, Julia, 184, 223n6
Kumar, Anuradha, 68

Lacan, Jacques, 148
LaHaye, Beverly, 124
LaHaye, Tim, 134, 199n11
Land, Richard, 94
Lane, Christopher, 196n50
Lane, Timothy S., 201n37
Lakoff, George, 2–3, 225n27
Leary, Warren E., 206n21
Left Behind, 134

Lemma, Alessandra, 227n67
Lerman, Hannah, 198n3
lesbian, 35, 98, 135, 146–47
Lesser, Ronnie, 198n5, 224n10
Leviticus, book of, 154, 169
Lewis, Helen B., 200n33
libertarianism, 117
  see also capitalism
LifeSite, 33
Lilling, Arthur H., 223n1
Limbaugh, David, 228n70
Lindsay, Michael, 219n43
Lindström, Per, 203n74
Lin, Vitoria, 208n45
Lipgar, Robert, 227n65
Lipstadt, Deborah E., 230n4
Lithwick, Dahlia, 178
Little Rock (Arkansas), 86, 151
Living Hope Ministries, 53
Locke, John, 128
Love and Saint Augustine, 87, 109–10
Love in Action, 35
Love Won Out, 16, 33, 107
  2004, 36–37, 45
  2012, 50–53, 163
Luke, book of, 154
Luker, Kristin, 208n46
Luskin, Donald L., 217n18

Maddoux, Marlin, 199n12
Maddux, Kristy, 222n95
Major, Brenda, 67–68, 207n37
Malkin, Michelle, 115
Maloney, Steven, 86
Mammen, Neil, 215n69
March for Life, 73–76
Marcus, Ruth, 219n44
marriage, same-sex, 41, 80, 86, 96, 141, 175, 186
Mason, Carol, 60
masturbation, 48–49
Maxwell, Carol J. C., 15, 71
May, Larry, 214n54
McAlister, Melani, 2

Index

McCorvey, Norma, 59, 77
McDowell, Stephen K., 222n90
McElroy, Wendy, 123
McGirr, Lisa, 117
McLaughlin, Janice, 177
Meckler, Mark, 183
Meltzer, Donald, 228n81
Melville, Herman, 89
Mercer, Ilana, 123
Merrill, Ronald E., 222n94
Milburn, Michael A. 172, 227n67
Mill John Stuart, 212n39
Miller, Susan B., 19-20, 187
Miller, William Ian, 196n50, 233n41
Mills, Charles W., 159
Mink, Gwendolyn, 220n53
Mitchell, Ellen M. H., 68
Moberly, Elizabeth R., 198n6, 223n1
Mollenkott, Virginia Ramey, 226n50
Montgomerie, Tim, 18
Moon, Dawne, 138, 170-71
Mooney, Christopher, 204n1
Moral Majority, 58
Mormon Church, 52
Moruzzi, Norma Claire, 211n21
Moynihan, Daniel Patrick, 7
Murphy, Andrew R., 202n64
Murray, Charles, 6

Narayan, Uma, 220n53
National Association for Research and Therapy of Homosexuality (NARTH), 30-34, 35, 79
National Association of Social Workers, 30
National Election Study (2000), 3
National Abortion Federation, 70
National Abortion Rights Action League (NARAL), 68
National Organization for Marriage (NOM), 189
National Organization of Episcopalians for Life (NOEL), see Anglicans for Life

National Right to Life (NRL) Educational Trust Fund, 67
Nazi, 59, 91, 100, 230n8
Nietzsche, Friedrich, 116, 142
Nelson, Deborah, 96-97, 210n77
NetNanny, 45
New Hope Ministry, 36, 45, 52, 131
New Republic, The, 175
New York Times, 67
Nicolosi, Joseph, 32-33, 36, 198n6, 219n35
Nicolosi, Linda Ames, 198n6, 219n35
normalization, 105-06
Norris, Alison, 207n37
Norris, Terry, 200-01n36
North Heights Lutheran Church, 36, 45
  see also Love Won Out
Nussbaum, Martha, 21, 92, 187, 194n14

Obama, Barack, 1, 75, 178, 183
Obamacare, *see* Patient Protection and Affordable Care Act
objectivism, 117-18, 120, 122, 133, 135, 181
  in contemporary politics, 116, 120, 183
Objectivist Newsletter, 134-35
objectivist therapy, 118, 181
O'Brien, David M., 205n6
O'Connor, Frank, 119, 122
O'Connor, Noreen, 147
Ogden, Thomas H., 224n18
Olasky, Marvin, 6, 8
Olson, Laura, 102
On Revolution, 87-88, 90, 94-95, 97
Operation Outcry, 107-08
Operation Rescue (film), 59
Operation Rescue (National), 58-59
Origins of Totalitarianism, The, 105
Osofsky, Howard J., 61
Osofsky, Joy D., 61
Ovesey, Lionel, 32

Pacific Justice Institute, 31
paranoid-schizoid position, 148–49, 152–53, 157–58, 163, 168
  see also Klein, Melanie
Parents and Friends of Ex-Gays and Gays (PFOX), 40, 208n56
Parker, Christopher, 232n37
Parker, Star, 6
Partial-Birth Abortion Ban Act, 76
Patient Protection and Affordable Care Act, 136
Paul (Apostle), 43, 138
Paul, Rand, 135
Paulk, Anne, 52, 198n6
Paulk, John, 36, 200n25
Pavone, Frank, 71, 155
Pawlowski, Lisa M. 202n63
Peikoff, Leonard, 120
Perkins, Rachel, 225n34
Perkins, Tony, 41
Peterson, Jordan B., 194n10
Pevy, Carolyn, 220n45
Pew Research Forum, 57, 215n70, 217n3
Phelan, Shane, 229n91
Philpott, Kent, 39
phobia(s), see homophobia
Pilbeam, Bruce, 2, 6
Pines, Malcolm, 227n65
Piper, Robin, 228n74
Pitkin, Hanna Fenichel, 101, 105
Pizarro, David A., 232n30, 232n31
pity, 88–90
Pizarro, David A., 197n61
Planned Parenthood, 77–78, 108
Playboy, 127
plurality, 100–01, 104–05, 112
positions, see paranoid-schizoid position, depressive position
Posner, Sarah, 193n3
Posnock, Ralph, 210n5
postabortion syndrome (PAS), 64–69, 72, 76
postabortion testimonies, 75–76, 81, 108

posttraumatic stress disorder (PTSD), 65
  see also postabortion syndrome
Potter, Jeff, 194n9
Pratto, Felicia, 48
presidential campaign, 2000, 6
Priests for Life, 71, 155
Project Rachel, 76
projection, 26, 146, 162
  in groups, 139, 158–59, 160, 162, 168
  projective identification, 149–51
Promise Keepers, 103, 219n43
Pruden, David, 199n14
psychoanalysis, 32–33, 35, 38;
  relational: 145–74

race, 41–43
racism, 20, 77–79, 86–87, 103, 137–38, 151, 187
racial reconciliation, 78
Rado, Sandor, 32
Raitt, Fiona, 233n40
Rand, Ayn, 26, 112–13, 115–43, 176, 178, 180–83
Rand studies, 231
Randall, Patrick K., 233n41
rape, 57, 63, 123
Reagan, Ronald, 61, 65
Rearden, Hank, 122, 130–31, 140
  see also *Atlas Shrugged*
Reardon, David C., 62–64, 66, 75–76
Reconciling congregation(s), 47, 169
Redman, Peter, 234n47
Register, Bryan, 220n46
reparation, 147, 152–53, 164–67, 176, 181, 185
  in groups, 161–62
  mock, 147, 153, 163–64, 167–69
reparative therapy, 30–31, 40, 51, 154
repentance, 101, 104, 108, 139, 156
  as prerequisite for compassion, 95, 132, 143, 161–63, 168, 170–71, 173
representative thinking, 92–93, 102–04, 112, 150–51, 178–79, 185

reproductive justice, *see* rights, reproductive
Republican Party, 8
Ress, Connie
Restored Hope Network, 52–54
Rice, William R., 203n76
Richardson, Diane, 177, 213n52
Ridder, Elizabeth M., 66
Ridgecrest Christian Conference Center (NC), 37
Riggle, Ellen, 229n89
Rimmerman, Craig A., 194n12
Ring, Jennifer, 86–87, 214n56
rights, 85–86, 101–02, 135, 151, 189
  Christian conservative opposition to, 80, 111
  reproductive, 25, 83, 97, 119, 135, 186, 190
  special, 126, 134, 136
Roark, Howard, 119, 129–31
  see also *Fountainhead, The*
Roberts, Dorothy, 78, 220n53
Robertson, Pat, 77, 132–33
Robespierre, 112
  see also French Revolution
Rockwell, W. Teed, 127
Roe v. Wade, 10, 58–60, 62, 73, 108, 135
Rogers, Julie, 53
Romans, book of, 165, 169, 222n85
Romer v. Evans, 96
Rose, Lila, 209n63, 209n68
Ross, Loretta, 209n68
Roth, Priscilla, 227n67
Rothbard, Murray, 118, 122
Rubin, Harriet, 217n6
Rostosky, Sharon S., 229n89
Rousseau, Jean Jacques, 5
Russo, Nancy, 68
Ryan, Joanna, 147

Saddleback Church, 75
Saia, Michael, 199n11, 199n19
Salmon, Jacqueline L., 222n79
same-sex marriage, *see* marriage, same-sex

Sanger, Margaret, 77
Santorum, Rick, 9
Satinover, Jeffrey, 33, 198n3
Save Our Children, 135
Savic, Ivanka, 203n74
Sayers, Janet, 223n6
Scalia, Antonin, 96
Scanzoni, Letha Dawson, 226n50
Scarborough, Rick, 108
Schaeffer, Francis, 195n32
Schaeffer, Roy, 225n23
Schapiro, Jeff, 203n78
Scharff, Jill Savege, 225n28
Schnall, Simone, 233n38
Scholem, Gershom, 91, 100, 179
Schroeder, Michael, 198n5
Sciabarra, Chris Matthew, 120
Scott, Daryl Michael, 211n23
Scott, James C., 217n2
Scott, Joanna Vecchiarelli, 110
Scott, Peter Manley, 214n52
Segal, Hanna, 153
segregation, 86
  see also race; racism
September 11, 2001, 133
700 Club, 132–33
Shanley, Mary Lyndon, 220n53
Shapiro, Roger L., 225n28
Sheldon, Ben, 213n51
Sherman, Gary D., 190
Shidlo, Ariel, 198n5
Sidanius, Jim, 48
Silent No More Awareness Campaign, 71, 74, 76, 108
Simon, Stephanie, 200n24
Simon-Thomas, Emiliana, 233n46
shame, 38–39, 102
Skocpol, Theda, 128
slaves(ery), 88, 91, 94–95
Smid, John J., 199n22
Smith, Andrea, 197n65
Smith, Anna Marie, 195n24
Smith, John David, 220n56
Smith, Susan, 59
Smits, Jasper A. J., 233n41

Sneeringer, Christine, 49, 198n7
Snyder, R. Claire, 210n72
Socarides, Charles W., 32, 223n1
Sodom, 133
Solinger, Rickie, 209n70
Sontag, Susan, 5
Soto-Crespo, Ramón, 224n9
Southern Baptist Convention, 62, 94
Sojourners, see Wallis, Jim
Spillius, Elizabeth Bott, 224n18, 225n21
Spitz, David, 210n5
Spelman, Elizabeth, 5
Spitzer, Robert L., 198n2
splitting, 26, 146, 168, 185
Stabile, Carol, 233n40
Stan, Adele M., 217n2, 217n3
Stanlake, Laura Leigh, 213n47
Staub, Ervin, 196n43
Stein, Arlene, 222n78, 223n96
Stein, Howard F., 227n56, 228n78
Steinberg, Julia R., 207n37
Steiner, Mark Allen, 58–59
Stein, Rob, 196n48
Steuerman, Emili, 164, 226n39
stigma, 68, 85–86, 171, 185, 187
  as a natural consequence, 81, 92, 96, 104, 138, 168, 170, 188–89
Stoker, Bram, 218n19
Stow, Simon, 211n22, 230n11
Stozier, Charles B., 221n73
submission, women's, 121–25, 148
Sullivan, Andrew, 210n6
Supreme Court, 74
Surfwatch, 45
Swope, Paul, 64
Szasz, Thomas, 200n31

Taggart, Dagney, 119, 122, 125, 130
  see also Atlas Shrugged
Tan, Erica S. N., 202n63
Tavistock Model of Group Relations, 157
  see also Bion, Wilfred

Tea Party Express, 115
tea party (movement), 9, 115–16, 128
Telch, Michael Joseph, 233n41
Terry, Jennifer, 197n57
Terry, Randall, 58
testimonies, see ex-gay testimonies; postabortion testimonies
Thatcher, Margaret, 226n50
therapy, see Christian therapy; objectivist therapy
Thomas, Gary, 209n62
Thomas, Jerry D., 229n89
Thompson, Sheila, 228n74
Throckmorton, Warren, 51, 54, 66
Tiller, George, 60
Tinnick, James D. III, 3
Toohey, Ellsworth, 129, 140
  see also Fountainhead, The
Transforming congregation(s), 47, 170
Truth and Reconciliation Commission, South Africa, 171
Tucille, Jerome, 118, 231n15
Tumin, Melvin, 210n5
Turquet, Pierre, 227n62

United Kingdom, 74
Urla, Jacqueline, 197n57

Values Voter Summit, 94, 108, 195n28
  see also Family Research Council
van den Aardweg, Gerard J. M., 32
Varnell, Paul, 218n22
Varnhagen, Rahel, 85–86, 100, 106, 111
Vatican, 7
Vidal, Gore, 117
Village Voice, 182
Vision America, 108
Volkan, Vamik, 158

Wadsworth, Nancy, 209n69
Wald, Kenneth D., 194n12
WallBuilders, 141
Wallis, Jim, 94, 212n36
Wanzo, Rebecca, 172

Warner, Michael, 197n54
Warren, Rick, 75
Washington Blade, 21
Washington, DC, 19
Waxman, Henry, 70, 194n21
Weddington, Sarah, 77
Weinberg, George, 20
Weiss, Gary, 116, 183
Welch, Liz, 207n38
Welcoming congregation(s), 47, 169
West Shore Evangelical Free Church, 50
see also Love Won Out
Weyrich, Paul, 58
Wilcox, Clyde, 194n12
Wieseltier, Leon, 212n27
Williams, Brian Keith, 23, 226n48
Williams, Christine L., 220n45
Williamson, Vanessa, 128
Wilson, Angelia R., 37, 59–60, 203n69, 209n61, 213n52, 219n37
Winnicott, Donald, 38, 223n2, 224n16
Woliver, Laura R., 205n7
Wolkomir, Michelle, 98, 124

Women Exploited by Abortion (WEBA), 63
Women's Movement, *see* feminism
Wood, Douglas S., 209n62
World War II, 10
Worthen, Anita, 36
Worthen, Frank, 36, 52
Worthy Creation, 49
Wright, Frank Lloyd, 129
Wuthnow, Robert, 16–17

Xu, Xiaowen, 194n10

Yarhouse, Mark A., 202n63
Yoshino, Kenji, 197n1
Young-Bruehl, Elisabeth, 184–85, 210n1, 232n36
Young, Iris, 103
Young, Robert M., 185
Yuan, Angela, 163

Zeedyk, Suzanne, 233n40
Zinner, John, 225n28
Zucker, Kenneth J., 198n2